Business English in a Global Context

Best Practice
Intermediate

Sara Helm and Rebecca Utteridge

Teachers' Resource Book

THOMSON
HEINLE

United Kingdom • United States • Australia • Canada • Mexico • Singapore • Spain

THOMSON
HEINLE

Best Practice Intermediate Teachers' Resource Book
Sara Helm / Rebecca Utteridge

Publisher: *Christopher Wenger*
Director of Content Development: *Anita Raducanu*
Director of Product Marketing: *Amy Mabley*
ELT Editorial Manager: *Bryan Fletcher*
Development Editor: *Sarah O'Driscoll*
Production Editor: *Maeve Healy*
Manufacturing Buyer: *Maeve Healy*

Cover Image: © *Getty Images*

Copyright © 2007 Thomson Heinle, a part of The Thomson Corporation. Thomson, and the Star logo, are trademarks used herein under license.

All rights reserved. No part of this work covered by the copyright hereon may be reproduced or used in any form or by any means—graphic, electronic, or mechanical, including photocopying, recording, taping, Web distribution or information storage and retrieval systems—without the written permission of the publisher.

Printed in Italy.
1 2 3 4 5 6 7 8 9 10 11 10 09 08 07

For more information contact Thomson Learning, High Holborn House, 50/51 Bedford Row, London WC1R 4LR United Kingdom or Thomson Heinle, 25 Thomson Place, Boston, Massachusetts 02210 USA. You can visit our website at elt.thomson.com

Compositor: *Process ELT (www.process-elt.com)*
Project Manager: *Howard Middle/HM ELT Services*
Text Designer: *Studio Image & Photographic Art (www.studio-image.com)*
Cover Designer: *Thomas Manss & Company*
Printer: *Canale*

For permission to use material from this text or product, submit a request online at www.thomsonrights.com

Any additional questions about permissions can be submitted by email to thomsonrights@thomson.com

ISBN 10: 1-4130-2858-6
ISBN 13: 978-1-4130-2858-4

Contents

TEACHERS' RESOURCE BOOK

	Coursebook contents	4
	Introduction	6
MODULE 1	PERFORMANCE	9
MODULE 2	INNOVATION	35
MODULE 3	PROMOTION	58
MODULE 4	INVESTMENT	81
MODULE 5	WRITING RESOURCE	102
	PHOTOCOPIABLE RESOURCE	108

Coursebook contents

Best Practice is a business English series designed for both pre-work and in-work students. Its topic-based modules train students in the skills needed to communicate in the professional and personal sides of modern business life.

MODULE 1   PERFORMANCE
pages 4–25

This module looks at some of the factors that affect performance at work – job satisfaction, what motivates people, the incentives they receive, and how to get a balance between work and home life.

	Business Inputs	Language Work	Communication	Business across Cultures
1 Happiness at work	**Listening**: The happiest workers	**Grammar**: Comparisons	Talking about yourself	Understanding your own culture
2 Motivation	**Reading**: Theory X and Theory Y **Listening**: Employers' views on Theory X and Theory Y	**Expressions** to describe Theory X and Y work environments	Finding out about people	Understanding different types of culture
3 Incentives	**Reading**: SAS Institutes **Listening**: Discussing incentives and benefits	**Grammar**: First conditional	Building transparency in communication	Individuals and groups
4 Work and leisure	**Listening**: An interview with a 'work–life' balance expert	**Grammar**: Past simple and present perfect	Responding and developing communication	Women at work

Business Scenario 1   Improving morale

Review and Development 1–4

MODULE 2   INNOVATION
pages 26–47

This module deals with how companies and individuals create innovative products and try to enter new markets. It focuses on both the creative side of invention, and on the business challenges.

	Business Inputs	Language Work	Communication	Business across Cultures
5 Entrepreneurs	**Reading**: An article about entrepreneur Simon Woodroffe **Listening**: An interview about what makes a successful entrepreneur	**Expressions** to describe entrepreneurs	Socialising 1: Small Talk	Public and private space
6 Creativity	**Listening**: An interview with a trade consultant	**Grammar**: The future	Socialising 2: Positive Responses	The culture of organisations
7 Start-ups	**Listening**: A conversation about how to set up a business	**Grammar**: passives	Meetings 1: Running a meeting	Attitudes towards time
8 Inventions	**Listening**: An interview with the inventor, Mandy Haberman	**Grammar**: Past perfect and past simple	Meetings 2: Participating in meetings	Developing a culture of innovation

Business Scenario 2   Pitching for finance

Review and Development 5–8

Student B material *pages 102–113*   Audio script *pages 114–127*   Answer key *pages 128–149*   Communication *pages 150–152*

MODULE 3 PROMOTION
pages 48–69

Here we look at the different aspects of promotion – global marketing, advertising to people of different ages, promoting yourself confidently, and the global importance of promotion.

		Business Inputs	**Language Work**	**Communication**	**Business across Cultures**
9	Kids as consumers	**Reading**: Using "pester-power" is no way to build a brand	**Grammar**: Count and uncount nouns	**Telephoning 1**: Opening and responding	Understanding corporate culture
10	Selling yourself	**Listening**: An interview with a human resources specialist	**Adjectives and nouns** for self-promotion	**Telephoning 2**: Leaving and taking messages	Customer service culture
11	Think global, act local	**Listening**: An interview with an expert on global advertising	**Grammar**: Infinitives and -ing forms	**Telephoning 3**: Structuring a call	Work and play
12	The grey market	**Reading**: Advertising for the over-50s.	**Grammar**: Present perfect simple and continuous	**Telephoning 4**: Closing a call	Working in cross-functional teams

Business Scenario 3 Bolton Bikes

Review and Development 9–12

MODULE 4 INVESTMENT
pages 70–91

This module looks at global investment and some of the challenges facing a range of industries – cars, newspapers, supermarkets and the Indian film industry.

		Business Inputs	**Language Work**	**Communication**	**Business across Cultures**
13	The industry of industries	**Reading**: Reasons for choosing a car	**Expressions** to describe manufacturing	**Presentations 1**: Opening	Body language
14	Something for nothing?	**Reading**: Pelle the conqueror **Listening**: Different types of media	**Expressions**: Compounds	**Presentations 2**: Developing the message	Communication style
15	In search of new markets	**Listening**: Carrefour's experiences in the Japanese market	**Grammar**: speculating about the past: should / shouldn't have, could have	**Presentations 3**: Using visuals	Leadership
16	Bollywood goes global	**Listening**: An interview about Bollywood	**Grammar**: Second conditional	**Presentations 4**: Closing	Decision-making

Business Scenario 4 Seniorservices

Review and Development 13–16

MODULE 5 WRITING RESOURCE
pages 92–101

17	Nice job	Job advertisements, CVs, Job applications
18	Getting the go ahead	Emails
19	Unhappy customers	Letters of complaint
20	Local partners	Faxes

Review and Development 17–20

Business across Cultures *pages 153–155*   Grammar overview *pages 156–170*   Glossary *pages 171–174*

5

Introduction

Best Practice Intermediate, is a four-level course designed for those learning English for international communication in business contexts.

It is suitable for:

- people working in companies and other organisations who use English for international communication
- pre-work students in business schools or further/higher education where business English is taught

Course components

- Coursebook
- This Teacher's Resource Book
- Workbook
- Audio cassette / CD
- Testing and evaluation

Learning approach

The Coursebook consists of four main modules each comprising four units, with an additional range of built-in reference and resource sections. Both the Communication pages and the Business across Cultures pages stand alone and have their own clearly defined syllabus. Together, and combined with the other course components, such as the Workbook, these elements provide great flexibility in course planning for varying periods of study and for learners with different needs.

Emphasis is on developing spoken **communication**, with mini role-plays, information gap activities and listening activities.

Writing is also well covered, with a module of four units that further develop writing skills in business contexts.

Intercultural issues are an important feature of each unit and these are dealt with through the use of case studies, discussion activities, and listening tasks.

Unit structure

The Coursebook is designed to develop the four skills of **listening, speaking, reading** and **writing** as well as **intercultural awareness**. Each unit provides material for approximately two hours of classroom activity and combines a variety of these elements.

The **language syllabus** is based around:

Grammar. All the key structures for the level are covered, and learners are often asked to complete grammar explanations using inference and their own prior knowledge as part of a discovery process. Grammatical structures are consolidated through communication activities.

Communication. The course covers key functional language for meeting people, developing conversation, telephoning, presenting, etc. There is also emphasis on the 'social' English in business contexts, which is often requested by learners and teachers.

Vocabulary. A range of general and business areas is included. Key vocabulary areas for the level are presented. Emphasis is also put on word combinations.

These inputs are often contained in **short reading texts**, **simulated web pages** or **listening extracts**.

Other important elements of the Coursebook units are:

Fact features. At the start of each unit, there is a fact feature, giving key snippets of information relating to the business area of the unit. These can be used to initiate discussion and prepare students for the theme of each unit.

Key language boxes. Each Communication section features a Key language box which introduces useful phrases for social situations, telephoning, discussions, presentations, etc.

Business across Cultures. Each unit includes a section on an intercultural issue commonly faced by international business people. The aim of this section is to provide students with an awareness of intercultural terms and concepts in a clear and simple way.

Role-plays. A key element of *Best Practice Intermediate* is the role-play sections. These sections give learners systematic opportunities to apply and use the language that they have seen in the Communication section. The situations where they do this have been chosen to mirror the ones they are likely to encounter in their own work situations.

Business Scenarios. After the four main units of each module, there is a Business Scenario unit, the aim of which is to consolidate language and skills that are introduced in the module. It consists of a variety of activities all relating to one business situation, and its main feature is a communication exercise such as a meeting or presentation. Finally, there is a writing task which relates to the content or outcome of the communication task.

Review and Development. Each module ends with a Review and Development unit which provides students with further practice of the grammar points, vocabulary and communication skills presented in the module.

Course outcomes

At the end of the course, learners will:

- be able to perform **practical business tasks** such as discussing their ideas and expressing their opinions, speaking on the telephone, presenting information and so on

- be used to hearing a **range of accents**, both native and non-native
- be able to use **business vocabulary** to speak and write about a range of business topics: incentives, personal qualities and characteristics, production, etc.
- be able to **apply their grammatical knowledge** to different professional and personal contexts, rather than treating grammar as an end in itself
- **have learned how to learn** – this is actively developed in the course, for example in learning grammar by discovery, and in developing vocabulary through typical word combinations to build larger blocks of language
- be aware of different values, behaviour, and styles of communication in other cultures and, therefore, **operate more effectively in an international environment**

Overall organisation of the Coursebook

The subject matter has been designed to appeal to **adult learners in a business context**.

The core units are grouped into **four main modules**.

Module 1: Performance

This module looks at job satisfaction, motivation, incentives, and work–life balance – areas that both experienced and pre-work students can easily relate to.

Module 2: Innovation

Here we look at the characteristics of successful entrepreneurs, creativity in business, start-ups, and inventions.

Module 3: Promotion

The themes in this module include promotion of products and services, to a range of target audiences. It also covers global advertising with local awareness and *selling yourself*.

Module 4: Investment

Learners look at a range of areas relating to investment, including the car industry, free newspapers, entering new markets, and the global film industry.

Writing resource

In this module, students practise writing a number of realistic texts such as CVs and job applications. It also concentrates on written communication relating to projects and making arrangements. In addition, we look at writing and responding to a letter of complaint and writing a letter of enquiry. This module also provides reading practice and some model examples of letters, CVs, faxes and emails.

Further resources section

The final pages of the Coursebook contain:

Photocopiable resource. This section contains information and photocopiable material for the role-plays.

Audio script. All listening material is included.

Answer key. Answers to all exercises are included.

Communication. This section corresponds to the Communication sections in the main units. It provides additional information on the language, as well as other issues such as body language, intercultural awareness, intonation, etc.

Business across Cultures. This section provides further information on the issues that feature in each Business across cultures section.

Grammar overview. This reference section includes all the main grammar points covered in the book. It allows learners to check that they have grasped all the grammar they need to know at this level. It reviews and expands on the key information presented in the book and also gives students the opportunity to practise it again through a variety of exercises.

Glossary. This section provides students with a detailed glossary of key terms presented in the book.

For a full overview of the contents of the Coursebook, please see the contents list of the book. If short of time and unable to cover all the material, you can use it to select areas and activities of particular relevance to your learners.

The Workbook

The Workbook of *Best Practice Intermediate* has been designed to fulfil several functions, and can be used as a logical and dynamic framework in which Coursebook materials can be reinforced.

The Workbook themes follow those of the Coursebook, unit by unit. Many Workbook units include **writing** exercises, most of which are ideal for homework.

There are basically two ways to exploit the Workbook: either at the end of each unit (the 'classic' method) or during the teaching of each unit as different grammatical/functional points arise. Use of the Workbook will vary depending on the unit.

The Workbook has been designed and written to be more than a 'homework depository'. It is down to the teacher to provide an impetus for its use, and through dynamic classroom practices, to show how the Coursebook and Workbook can form a 'learning synergy' for the benefit of students.

The audio materials

Listening materials are available on CD and audio cassette. These feature the **listening** exercises in the Coursebook and present a range of accents, not only of people from different parts of the English-speaking world, but also a number of non-native accents.

This Teacher's Resource Book

A 'maximalist' approach has been adopted in this Teacher's Resource Book, which has been written with two potential

INTRODUCTION

'teacher audiences' in mind: teachers who are relatively inexperienced in teaching professional English and require step-by-step guidelines, and more experienced teachers who might welcome some of the suggestions but ignore others.

This approach is clear from the layout of the Teacher's Resource Book:

Module overview. At the beginning of each module there is an overview which gives all necessary background information, including business and cultural notes.

Preview. At the beginning of each unit there is a short description of the grammar, functions and vocabulary to be encountered, pointing out grammar meanings and suggesting potential student difficulties.

Introductory activities. These are suggested at the beginning of each unit.

Step-by-step notes. The Teacher's Resource Book follows the Coursebook contents step-by-step, suggesting presentational, brainstorming and discussion activities, as well as different ways of exploiting the audio component.

In many units, stress and intonation exercises are suggested, as well as grammar consolidation and vocabulary building tasks.

Answer keys follow each exercise where appropriate, and all audio scripts are presented in full as they occur throughout the units.

At the end of each unit, the **Checklist** usually suggests a final review activity of the main grammatical/functional elements of the unit.

Some general points

The exact number of audio plays is rarely indicated, as this depends on the listening level and motivation of the class – something best known to the teacher.

Normally, in the core units, it is not specified whether students do a particular exercise individually or in pairs, with pair checking or whole class feedback. Again, this is best left to the individual teacher.

During the role-play activities, it is important to go over the particular roles of Students A and B, checking that they understand the vocabulary and the requirements of the role. It may be necessary to help with question formation prior to beginning the activity.

Do not hesitate to skip exercises if the class seems not to need them. On the other hand, do review ill-assimilated elements (without repeating the exercises, if possible).

If you have a long (i.e. extensive) course, aim to vary the exploitation as much as possible, using the Workbook as review and the role-plays, information exchanges, and grammar overview to a maximum. You could also use simple or 'doctored' authentic materials as additional input; suggestions for such activities are included in the Teachers' Resource Book. If you have a short (i.e. intensive) course, concentrate on the main grammar points, the most important vocabulary and functional areas to link with the students' needs, and the maximum possible listening input.

Photocopiable resource. Each module includes two photocopiable activities, found on pages 110–120. These include communication exercises such as role-plays or information exchanges suitable for pair or small-group exploitation in class. These activities have been designed to review/practise the main grammatical/functional features of the different modules, adding a personal element where possible. Detailed exploitation suggestions for each activity are given (see pages 108 and 109).

Frameworks. There are eight frameworks, which can be found on pages 121–128, to be used before or after communication exercises. Some have been designed to help students prepare for communication tasks while others provide teachers with a clear structure for providing feedback. Appropriate stages at which to use specific frameworks are suggested in this Teacher's Resource Book.

Best Practice Intermediate corresponds to BEC Preliminary, leading to BEC Vantage by the end of the book, and CEF levels B1–B2.

We hope you and your students enjoy using *Best Practice Intermediate* and its companion books at *Elementary*, *Pre-intermediate* and *Upper Intermediate* levels.

Performance

MODULE OVERVIEW

AIMS AND OBJECTIVES

This module focuses on performance and the related themes of job satisfaction, motivation and work–life balance. A number of grammar patterns are reviewed: comparisons within the theme of happiness at work, the use of the first conditional in discussing and negotiating benefits, and the use of the past simple and present perfect tenses in describing trends.

It also covers communication skills in the context of meeting someone for the first time and achieving transparency. The Business across Cultures sections concentrate on understanding different cultures in terms of attitudes and behaviour.

At the end of the module, students should be able to:

- draw comparisons, using appropriate adjectival forms
- discuss and compare jobs
- use the past simple and present perfect tenses to describe trends and personal/professional experience
- use the first conditional to discuss future possibilities
- talk about personal strengths and weaknesses
- talk about themselves in a social context
- ask questions, respond to comments and develop communication when meeting people for the first time
- achieve effective communication through checking, clarifying and confirming understanding
- use a variety of nouns to talk about motivation and incentives
- understand the challenges faced by people working in a new culture
- understand the different layers of culture that have an impact on our behaviour
- understand cultural differences in terms of attitude and behaviour

THEMATIC OVERVIEW

The themes in this module are interlinked through their association with the word *performance*. In business, *performance* means reaching targets, achieving a certain level of output, or accomplishing efficiency in a process or procedure.

To achieve greater performance, companies strive to modify their employees' behaviour. Companies are constantly experimenting with new incentive schemes in the hope that it will increase motivation. However, the results are often unpredictable.

Companies, and indeed governments, are becoming increasingly aware of the importance of work–life balance. It has been found to reduce stress levels and increase job satisfaction while providing benefits for employers. Businesses with satisfied employees profit from higher performance and thus increased productivity.

Job satisfaction can stem from a range of factors including the level of pay and benefits, the quality of working conditions, relationships with colleagues, degree of responsibility, and the job itself.

These are areas that students often have strong feelings about, for good reason. They possess an intense human element; for example, the way in which incentives are used to reward (and punish if withheld), the dilemma of putting work before family, how happiness is achieved at work, and so on. Learners with little or no experience in the world of work easily relate to these themes which can often be translated into everyday scenarios.

MAIN AUDIO CONTENTS

Unit 1: interviews in which people describe what they like about their jobs; extracts in which people introduce themselves; extracts in which people talk about their strengths and weaknesses

Unit 2: extracts in which managers talk about their preferred ways of motivating employees; extracts in which employees describe the way they are managed and their feelings about it

Unit 3: a job interview in which a candidate discusses incentives and benefits with an interviewer; a telephone conversation in which information is checked and clarified; examples of project leaders in different cultures giving feedback to their teams

Unit 4: an interview with a work–life balance expert in which he describes the changing trend of working hours over the years; a dialogue between a businessman and his client

PHOTOCOPIABLE RESOURCES (PAGES 110–111)

1.1 can be used any time after Unit 1.
1.2 can be used any time after Unit 3.

BUSINESS AND CULTURAL NOTES

Finding out about people. The range of topics people are willing to discuss the first time they meet differs from culture to culture. In some cultures, it is acceptable to discuss personal details early in the relationship; in others, it is usual to maintain distance and choose more impersonal topics of conversation, such as your job.

Performance

Responding and showing interest. Responding and showing interest are key skills in building a good rapport. The ways in which people respond and develop communication vary dramatically in different cultures. Making positive responses is more appreciated in U.S. culture than European cultures. Indeed, in Finland, silence is actually a cultural value. Similarly, in Asian cultures silence is respected and it is a clear sign that a person is thinking and reflecting. In a multinational group, it would be valuable for the class to learn how people in other cultures develop communication.

Motivation. There are cultural differences in terms of what motivates people. Praise and public recognition may work in most western countries, but in some Asian cultures individuals are likely to feel embarrassed if picked out in such a way.

PERFORMANCE **UNIT 1**

1 Happiness at work

PREVIEW

Listening and speaking

The listening exercise consists of short extracts in which people describe their jobs and their feelings about their roles. This section also includes adjectives used to describe jobs such as *secure*, *stimulating*, and *rewarding*. In the speaking exercise, students discuss why certain workers are happier than others.

Grammar

comparisons

In this section, students identify and use the *comparative* and *superlative* forms of a range of adjectives used to describe the qualities and characteristics of different jobs.

Communication

talking about yourself

This section focuses on developing skills for introducing and talking about oneself. This is good preparation for interviews, appraisals, and team-building sessions. The key language feature introduces a variety of common questions and responses which students can use to give and ask about personal information.

Business across Cultures

understanding your own culture

This involves examining the students' culture (or cultures in a multinational class) and will help them to identify aspects of their cultures which can be easily observed, and others which are less obvious and therefore may create challenges for people from other cultures.

Introductory activity

Tell students to turn to page 4 of their coursebooks, and direct their attention to the title of the unit and the fact feature: *The King of Bhutan says that the overall happiness of his people is more important than how rich they are.* Ask the students if they agree with him, and then ask how this could relate to the world of work (i.e. being happy at work is more important than having a high salary). Ask what is important for happiness at work and write students' responses on the board. Possible responses may include:

a good relationship with colleagues / boss / clients

a pleasant environment

an interesting / stimulating / challenging job

autonomy and responsibility

success / recognition / praise

security / a good salary / good benefits

[N.B. If your students are pre-work, ask them what is important for happiness in their educational institutions.]

Start-up

A Ask students to work in subgroups and discuss the tips and add three more to the list. Set a time limit of five minutes. Note their tips on the board and invite comments from the other groups. Write up any useful language or new vocabulary on the board.

Listening and speaking

A AUDIO 1.1 Before listening to the interviews, direct students' attention to the information in the table and ask: *What do you know about these jobs? What do you think each person might like about their job?*

Possible answers may include:

lawyer – meeting different clients / a good salary

fitness instructor – working with a variety of people / not working in an office

Play AUDIO 1.1 once, asking students to complete the table as indicated. Students should then check their answers in pairs. As there is a lot of information to note down, students will probably need to hear the audio a second time. Pause after each speaker if necessary. Check answers in class.

KEY

Job	Speciality	What they like about the job
1 Lawyer	property law	meeting different clients
2 Fitness instructor	fitness classes / exercise programmes	organising own time seeing people being fit and healthy
3 Accountant	bankruptcy	flexibility well-paid
4 Civil servant	regional investment	teamwork security

AUDIO SCRIPT

1 I'm a lawyer. I work in property law – I do all the legal work connected with buying and selling buildings and land. My job is always interesting. I especially like meeting different clients – every day is different, in fact. I work 60 hours a week and sometimes I get very stressed, but most of the time I feel very positive about my job.

2 I'm a fitness instructor. I run fitness classes at gyms and leisure clubs but I have some private clients too. I plan exercise programmes for them and go to their homes to help them get fit. I like this job a lot because I can organise my own time. And it's very rewarding to see people get fit and healthy. It's more satisfying than my old job – I used to work in an office. I hated that!

3 I'm an accountant. I specialise in bankruptcy – so I spend all my time dealing with companies that have gone out of business. My job is pretty varied. I like the flexibility – in my company, you can start work when you want and leave when you want, as long as you're there during the core

11

PERFORMANCE UNIT 1

hours, from ten to three every day. That's a real bonus for a working mother. It's much more flexible than some of the larger accountancy firms. And it's well-paid so I'm very lucky, really.

4 I'm a civil servant. I work in regional government. I'm in a department with ten other people. Our job is to attract investment into the area. In the past five years, we've persuaded more than 20 overseas companies to set up operations here. I love the teamwork – I'm at my best working in a team. This is the most stimulating job I've ever had, and I'm happier in my work than most people I know. And, of course, as a civil servant, my job is very secure.

B AUDIO 1.1 Check understanding and pronunciation of the adjectives. Ask students to provide explanations or definitions. Play the audio again and do the exercise as indicated. Students should check their answers first in pairs, then in class.

KEY

varied – 3	stressed – 1
interesting – 1	stimulating – 4
secure – 4	rewarding – 2
well-paid – 3	satisfying – 2

C Ask students to work in pairs to ask and answer questions about their jobs, or a job they would to like to have. Encourage students to use adjectives from exercise B. You could round up this activity by asking each person to report briefly to the group what his/her partner said.

Speaking

A Before the activity, ask students to close their books, and write on the board:

<u>Happiness index</u>

The happiest ⟶ _____

In the middle ⟶ _____

The least happy ⟶ _____

Jobs: builders, hairdressers, clergy, health care professionals, civil servants, architects.

Ask students: *Where do you think these jobs go in the happiness index? Why?*

Ask students to open their books again. Focus students' attention on the City & Guilds index of the happiest workers. Check understanding of some of the jobs: *clergy, plumbers, florists, care assistants*. Ask students to provide explanations or definitions. Discuss the question in exercise A in class.

B Check students' understanding of certain jobs: *DJ, estate agent*. Get students to work in pairs and do the exercise orally. Make sure they give their reasons. Before checking answers on page 128, ask students to share their opinions with the rest of the class.

KEY

3 Chefs/Cooks	18 DJs
6 Mechanics	23 Accountants
10 Fitness instructors	27 Estate agents

C Ask students to do this exercise in pairs or subgroups. After the activity, get the pairs or groups to share their ideas with the rest of the class. Invite other students to add to their ideas or contradict them, explaining why they do so. Write their suggestions on the board.

Possible patterns:

Top five jobs are: vocational, all except clergy are manual and not based in an office.

Bottom five jobs are: generally based in offices, better-paid than the top five.

[N.B. During the above speaking activities, comparisons language is likely to emerge. If you identify errors or good examples of this language, make a note of them to use in the following grammar section on comparisons.]

▶ FOR FURTHER READING AND VOCABULARY PRACTICE ON THE TOPIC OF HAPPINESS AT WORK, REFER STUDENTS TO PAGE 4 OF THE WORKBOOK.

Grammar

Comparisons

Ask students to close their Coursebooks. To assess the students' use of *comparatives* and *superlatives*, if it didn't emerge in the speaking section, write on the board:

   Lawyers   Estate agents   Architects

Then add:

   long hours   happy   satisfied   creative

Ask students to compare the three jobs using these adjectives. Try to elicit superlative as well as comparative forms. Write the students' sentences on the board.

A Ask students to open their Coursebooks and draw their attention to the grammar explanation. Ask students which sentence features a comparative form and which features a superlative form. Check students understand the word *syllable* by writing some of their names on the board and asking them to identify the number of syllables in each. Complete the table as a class. You could ask students to suggest other adjectives that fit into the base form column. It is important to remind students that superlatives are always preceded by *the*. Depending on the ability of your class, it may also be necessary to review spelling rules.

KEY

Type of adjective	Base form	Rule	Comparative	Superlative
One syllable	long	Add -er/est	longer	the longest
Two syllables ending -y	happy	Change -y to -ier/iest	happier	the happiest
Two or more syllables	rewarding	Put more/the most before the adjective	more rewarding	the most rewarding
Ending in -ed*	stressed	Add more/ the most	more stressed	the most stressed
Irregular	good bad	– –	better worse	the best the worst

PERFORMANCE **UNIT 1**

B Tell students to refer to the table in A to help them decide on the correct comparative and superlative forms. Look at the first example together and ask: *Is it a comparative or superlative sentence? Why?* (Because it includes *-er* and the word *than*.) In a weaker group, before allowing students to do the exercises, check that they know how many syllables there are in each word in the box. Some students may think there are two syllables in *stressed*. This exercise should be done individually and checked in class.

KEY

2 *Lawyers are more stressed than fitness instructors.*
3 *I worked in IT for three years but I hated it. It was the worst job I've ever had!*
4 *Builders have noisier working conditions than bankers.*
5 *I'm in R&D. I love developing new products. It's the most fascinating work in the company.*

C Once again, students should do the exercise individually.

KEY

1 e 2 a 3 c 4 b 5 d

D This could be done as a pair activity and checked in class.

KEY

2 *Scientists are as happy as pharmacists.*
3 *Teachers are not as happy as mechanics.*
4 *IT specialists are slightly happier than estate agents.*
5 *Hairdressers are much happier than civil servants.*

E This could be done in subgroups or pairs. Beforehand, it may be a good idea to briefly elicit phrases for giving reasons: *because + verb phrase / because of + noun / due to + noun / so + verb phrase*. Write one or two examples on the board. Look at the examples and elicit the meaning of *downside*. Set a time limit of five minutes for this exercise. Students should compare and discuss their different reasons in class.

F This should be done orally as a pair activity as indicated in the Coursebook. Encourage students to give reasons for their statements. Circulate during the activity, noting the use of comparatives and the new adjectives, giving help where necessary.

▶ FOR FURTHER INFORMATION ON COMPARISONS, REFER STUDENTS TO GRAMMAR OVERVIEW ON PAGE 156.

▶ GRAMMAR REVIEW AND DEVELOPMENT, PAGE 32, CAN BE DONE AT THIS STAGE.

▶ FOR FURTHER PRACTICE OF COMPARISONS, SEE PAGE 5 OF THE WORKBOOK.

▶ FOR LESS CONTROLLED PRACTICE OF COMPARISONS, SEE PHOTOCOPIABLE MATERIALS 1 ON PAGES 110–111.

Communication
Talking about yourself

With Coursebooks closed, ask students to work in subgroups and briefly discuss the following questions you can write on the board:

What do you talk about when you meet someone for the first time?

What do you avoid talking about?

Write students' responses on the board. For example:

Common topics	Avoid
Job	Politics
Origins	Religion
Family	Personal problems
Interests	
Weather	

With a multinational class, you are likely to identify differences in what is perceived as an acceptable topic of discussion for a first meeting. For example, in some cultures talking about family is considered extremely personal. In terms of cross-cultural awareness, students may benefit from time spent discussing these differences and the reasoning behind them.

▶ REFER TO THE COMMUNICATION NOTES ON PAGE 150.

A AUDIO **1.2** Keeping coursebooks closed, write on the board:

Job   Origins   Family   Interests

Tell students that they will hear six people introducing themselves and they should match each speaker to the topics on the board. Play the audio once and ask students to check their answers in pairs.

KEY

1 c 2 b 3 a 4 d 5 b 6 a

AUDIO SCRIPT

1 Françoise: My name's Françoise. I'm 38 and I live in Paris. I have three children under the age of ten. When I'm not at work, I spend all my time with them.

2 Harvey: Let me say a few words about myself. My name's Harvey. I'm from Wisconsin. I was born in Milwaukee, on Lake Michigan. Now I work on the East Coast, but I love going back to my hometown whenever I can.

3 Lyn: My name's Lyn. I work in sales and I love my job! I work for Digicom – it's a big IT distributor. It's a great company to work for.

4 Michael: Hi, my name's Michael but everybody calls me Mick. My passion is bridges. I always spend my holidays visiting them. Last year we went to the south of France to see the new bridge at Millau. It's absolutely fantastic.

5 Lucy: Hello, my name's Lucy. I was brought up in the north of England. My family moved south when I was a teenager and I've lived near London ever since.

6 Ludwig: My name's Ludwig. I'm in retail. I work for a large chain of furniture stores. We're based in Frankfurt but I travel all over the world for my job.

B Ask students to open their books and look at the Key language box. You could play AUDIO **1.2** again, pausing after each speaker, and ask students to tick the phrases they hear. Play it again and ask students to identify the intonation for closed questions (rising) and *wh-* type questions (falling). Drill some of these questions.

Exercise B should be done as indicated in pairs. If you have a culturally diverse class, ask people of different nationalities to work together. Prior to the exercise, they

13

PERFORMANCE UNIT 1

should find out what topics are acceptable when meeting someone for the first time in their partner's culture. Encourage students to use the key language, particularly phrases that are new to them. Circulate during the exercise, making a note of errors as well as good use of the target language. After the exercise, if the students are unfamiliar with each other, you could ask each person to present his/her partner to the group using the information learned during the exercise. Provide feedback and corrections.

For more individual feedback, use a Social English Framework Sheet (see Frameworks, page 122). Go through the Framework with students before exercise B so that they are aware of areas upon which their performance will be assessed. Do not get into a discussion about the different question forms that appear on the sheet at this stage, but tell students that questions will be dealt with in the next unit. Draw students' attention to the fact that, according to the Framework, showing interest and listening actively are important skills when socialising.

C AUDIO 1.3 Ask students to close their Coursebooks again. Explain that you are going to focus on describing strengths and weaknesses in relation to professional skills. Brainstorm different types of professional skills (and study skills if a pre-work class), and put them on the board. For example:

Interpersonal / People
Organisational
Communication
IT / Technical
Administrative
Management / Leadership
Problem-solving

Ask students to open their Coursebooks and read the instructions. Find out what students understand by *appraisal*. In the case of pre-work learners, ask if there is a similar procedure at university/college. Ask students to do exercise C individually as indicated in the Coursebook. Play AUDIO 1.3 once and ask students to check their answers in pairs.

You could play the audio again and ask students to identify the language used to describe strengths and weaknesses.

KEY

1 organisational skills
2 communication skills
3 people skills

AUDIO SCRIPT

1 I'm not so good at structuring my day. I take time to sort things out and sometimes I find it difficult to decide on my priorities.
2 People tell me that I'm a good listener. Some of my colleagues talk to me when they have problems. I'm happy to help if I can.
3 I get on well with my colleagues and I really enjoy working with my team. We go out together a lot – for a meal or a drink after work.

D Focus students' attention on the Key language box at the bottom of the page. Do the exercise as indicated in subgroups. Before starting, elicit typical interview/appraisal questions.

For example:
  What are your strengths / weaknesses?
  What areas do you think you need to improve?
  What do you find difficult?
  What are you good at?

Rather than simply finding out about each others' strengths and weaknesses, students could role-play an interview or appraisal. Depending on the dynamics of the group, you could make this activity fun by asking the interviewee to take on an imaginary persona (write adjectives on the board, e.g. *big-headed, modest*). Circulate and make a note of good use of the target language and any common errors within the group. Provide feedback after the exercise.

▶ FOR SELF-STUDY EXERCISES RELATING TO THE SUBJECT OF TALKING ABOUT YOURSELF, SEE PAGE 6 OF THE WORKBOOK.

▶ REFER STUDENTS TO PAGE 150 OF THE COURSEBOOK FOR A SUMMARY OF THE POINTS COVERED IN THIS COMMUNICATION SECTION.

Business across Cultures
Understanding your own culture

If you have a multinational class, as preparation for this topic, ask students to bring in objects that represent their culture to present to the group. This could be art, craft, an instrument, clothing, an image, music, food and so on. Ask students to explain briefly what the objects represent and why they are important to their cultures. Set a time limit of two minutes per person, particularly if you have a large group.

Ask students to open their Coursebooks and read the introduction.

A Ask students to work in subgroups to agree on a definition of the word *culture*. Students should then compare their definitions in class.

Draw an iceberg on the board, and ask students to brainstorm different elements of culture and tell you where to put them on the iceberg. If the class lacks ideas, write a few of the elements on the board and ask where they should be placed. For example:

  Above the surface: greetings, language, gestures, dress, music, food, climate, geography, festivals.
  Just below the surface: gender roles, humour, friendship, relationships with colleagues, industry, work, politics.
  Deep below: beliefs, class, social organisation, emotions.

B The exercise should be done individually as indicated. Answers should be checked in pairs.

KEY

geography, climate, politics, work, festivals

C This exercise could be done individually or in groups, particularly if there are students of the same nationality who could brainstorm their ideas together. Students should present a summary to the group and be prepared to answer any questions. Meanwhile, the other students should be encouraged to ask questions or make comments.

D This exercise could be set as a writing exercise for homework.

Extension activity. This exercise is quite stimulating but requires lateral thinking and imagination. Divide the class into groups of three or four and provide them with about five different images of people engaged in everyday activities around the world (*dances, business situations,* *eating, gesturing, driving,* etc.) and a blank iceberg. Ask them to identify cultural elements in the photos that are above the surface and below the surface and label their icebergs. Explain that elements above the surface are often the result of what is beneath. For example, modest dress could be the result of religious beliefs; the fabric of the clothing may be the result of industry in that country, and so on. Before allowing groups to embark on the exercise, do an example with one image, as a class. Set a time limit for students to study their images, and then ask them to present their icebergs and give an overview of what they identified. Ask other students to add their ideas. Some interesting language and vocabulary may well emerge; make a note of it on the board.

▶ FOR READING PRACTICE ON THE SUBJECT OF HAPPINESS AROUND THE WORLD, SEE PAGE 7 OF THE WORKBOOK.

▶ REFER STUDENTS TO PAGE 153 OF THE COURSEBOOK FOR A SUMMARY OF THE POINTS COVERED IN UNDERSTANDING YOUR OWN CULTURE.

Checklist

As a review activity, ask students to refer to the checklist in their Coursebooks and go over the items with them.

For further practice of the vocabulary seen in this unit, divide students into groups, and ask each group to write definitions of five different vocabulary items (e.g. *stimulating, rewarding, well-paid, estate agent, DJ*). Students should then give their definitions to other subgroups, with each having to work out what the vocabulary items are.

PERFORMANCE **UNIT 2**

2 Motivation

PREVIEW

Reading and vocabulary
The vocabulary in this section relates to motivation, for example *encouragement, supervision* and *responsibility*. As many of the words have the same suffixes and therefore share the same stress patterns, this is a good stage at which to focus on word stress. The reading exercise gives an overview of two conflicting motivation theories and the related exercises provide controlled practice at using the target vocabulary.

Listening and speaking
In the listening exercise, students hear managers describing their own management styles and employees expressing their attitudes towards these styles.

Communication **finding out about people**
This section focuses on the different question forms and response patterns used when meeting people for the first time. Extension activities for introducing intonation patterns are suggested.

Business across Cultures **understanding different types of culture**
This section provides students working in an international environment with an awareness of the different aspects of culture that have an impact on our behaviour. A lack of understanding of this area often leads to a breakdown in communication.

Introductory activity

With Coursebooks closed, ask students to define *motivation*. Write their definitions on the board. Ask students to open their Coursebooks and direct their attention to the fact feature. Ask students: *What do you think companies spend millions on in order to improve motivation?* They are likely to suggest *benefits, bonuses, performance related pay, prizes*. Tell students that Unit 3 focuses on these areas. Then ask: *Do companies need to spend millions on motivation? How can companies improve motivation without spending so much money?* List students' ideas on the board (*giving employees responsibility, encouragement, praise*, etc.) but don't spend too much time on this – this is simply to prepare students for the theme of the unit. Finally, ask students: *What motivates you?*

You may identify cultural differences in terms of what motivates individuals. Praise and public recognition may work in most western countries, but in parts of Asia individuals may feel embarrassed if singled out in such a way.

[N.B. Pre-work students could focus on what motivates them in their studies and what methods their tutors use to increase motivation.]

Start-up

A Treat this as an open-class discussion. Ask students to give reasons for their opinions. This not only gets students thinking about the topic of motivation but also provides the opportunity for students to use some of the vocabulary that appears in this unit (*initiative, supervision, responsibility*, etc.) Do not try to elicit this vocabulary, but make a note of it on the board if it arises naturally.

Reading and vocabulary

A Ask students to read the nouns out loud before starting the activity to check their pronunciation. Ask students to identify the main stress on the words. Write the words on the board and show students how to mark the stress (i.e. add a dot above the appropriate syllable or underline it). If students have difficulty with this, an extension activity focusing on word stress is suggested below. The matching exercise should be done individually, then answers checked in pairs.

KEY

1g 2d 3f 4a 5c 6h 7b 8e

B First, ask students to look at the photo behind the text. Ask: *What kind of office is this?* (Open plan with cubicles.) *Do you think the employees feel motivated in this environment?*

Tell students that they are going to read about two theories on employee motivation. Read the instructions together and ask students to work individually and check their answers in pairs. Correct answers in class.

KEY

1 supervision   2 satisfaction   3 responsibility
4 initiative   5 commitment

C Tell students to look at the example, and identify the noun (*commitment*) and verbs (*to be committed to, to commit to*). Then write the following sentences on the board and ask students for the appropriate noun and verb forms:

He _____ this job.

_____ is essential for this job.

Instruct students to do exercise C in pairs. Provide dictionaries and encourage them to use them.

[N.B. Some students are quite attached to translation dictionaries, but at this level they should be able to use English-English dictionaries for simple exercises like this. If they are unfamiliar with such dictionaries, show them how to find verb forms of nouns and vice versa.]

When the students have finished the exercise, draw a table on the board:

Noun	Verb(s)

16

PERFORMANCE UNIT 2

Elicit the verb forms in class and complete the table on the board. Then ask each student to write five questions using the verb forms. The questions will be used to interview another person about his/her job or studies. Do one or two examples with a strong student:

What motivates you, Joanna? – I feel motivated when I'm given a challenging exercise.

Are you supervised all of the time? – No, I'm not. I have to use my initiative.

Encourage the interviewees to offer more information than simply *Yes* or *No* (in some cultures such short responses are considered rude). To remind students of this during the activity, write on the board:

Yes, I am. / I do.

+ more information

No, I'm not. / I don't.

Set a time limit of five minutes for them to write the questions. While students are interviewing each other, circulate and make a note of any vocabulary errors and any interesting or useful phrases that could be shared with the group during feedback.

KEY

commitment – to be committed to, to commit to
satisfaction – to be satisfied, to satisfy
responsibility – to be responsible for, to take responsibility for
initiative – to take the initiative, to initiate
supervision – to be supervised by, to supervise
motivation – to be motivated, to motivate
imagination – to be imaginative, to imagine
encouragement – to encourage, to give encouragement, to be encouraged by

---

D This could be done briefly in class.

Extension activity. Introducing word stress. Some nationalities have great difficulty with English word stress. This is a good place to introduce some simple rules on word stress as many of the words in this unit have the same suffixes and therefore the same stress patterns. There are many irregularities in English word stress patterns which can be very discouraging for learners, but in suffixes we can find some reliable and easy rules.

[N.B. In weaker groups, review syllables prior to looking at word stress. Write some of the students' names on the board and ask how many syllables are in each and where the main stress is. Mark the syllables and stress above each name. For example:

● o o
Adrian

Mention Adrian and demonstrate that volume and tone rise a little where there is stress.]

On page 8 of the Coursebook, there are words that have the same suffixes:

- ion	*- ity*
satisfaction	responsibility
supervision	creativity
motivation	opportunity
imagination	ability
decision	

Write *-ion* and *-ity* at the top of the board and ask students to scan page 8 for words which have these suffixes. Write the words under the suffix headings on the board and ask where the main stress is on each word. If they have difficulty, read the words out loud and see if they can identify the stress. Ask them to mark the stress on the words. Ask: *What is the rule?* (The stress is on the syllable before the suffix.) Drill the words.

Next tell them that this rule applies to many suffixes. Write on the board:

-ial   -ian   -ual(ly)   -ic (al/ally)   -ogy   -ious

Put the class into teams and ask them to brainstorm as many words as possible that have those suffixes. Give them a time limit of five minutes. The team that has the most correct words at the end, is the winning team.

Put each team's words under the appropriate heading on the board. Elicit the correct pronunciation of the words and drill where necessary.

[N.B. Try not to get sidetracked by the fact that some words have a secondary stress. Concentrate on the main stress at this stage.]

[N.B. Tell students that word stress can be checked in dictionaries. Show them how to do it. Also mention that some dictionaries come in the form of a CD-ROM and provide audio demonstrations of American and British English pronunciation.]

Word stress game. For extensive practice of these stress patterns, you could create a 'happy families' game. You will need to make seven 'suffix families' of cards (e.g. one family would be: *politician, electrician, mathematician, technician*) – four cards in each family. The game is for three to five players. Provide each player with a list of all the cards in the 'pack' so that they know what the 'families' consist of. At the start of the game, all of the cards are dealt face down. The players look at their hands and decide which 'families' they are going to collect. The idea of the game is to collect whole families. This is done by asking another player whether they have a specific card. If they do, they have to pass it to the asker, who can ask any of the other players again. If a player doesn't have the requested card, the asker's turn is over. Each time a player creates a family, he or she should place it on the table where everyone can see. The game continues until a player has matched all of his/her cards into family groups.

[N.B. As the aim of the game is to practise word stress, it should be made clear that players can only receive a card if they pronounce the word correctly. Be very strict about this.]

▶ VOCABULARY REVIEW AND DEVELOPMENT, PAGE 23, CAN BE DONE AT THIS STAGE.

Listening and speaking

A Read the instructions and look at the table together. Play AUDIO **2.1** once and allow students to compare answers with a partner's.

Ask: *What do you think the employees would say about their bosses and organisations?*

KEY

	Organisation	**Industry**	**Theory X or Theory Y?**
1	Call centre	Financial services	Y
2	Insurance company	Insurance	X
3	Oil company	Oil	Y
4	Department store	Retail	X

17

PERFORMANCE UNIT 2

AUDIO SCRIPT

1 I'm a call centre manager in the financial services industry. I believe it's important to let people work without constant supervision – you have to let them use their initiative. Otherwise they feel they're being treated like children. Of course, there are procedures to follow, but we like to give employees as much flexibility as possible within those procedures.

2 I'm a section manager in an insurance company. We do the paperwork relating to insurance claims. The employees must be here by 8 a.m. and they can't leave before 5 p.m. I want to see what they're doing the whole time. That way I can be sure they're doing the work we're paying them to do.

3 I'm a senior manager in an oil company. I encourage younger managers in my department to use their initiative. They respond to this well – it motivates them and you can see their work improving. It's also a good way to identify potential future managers among them – the ones who are going to reach the top of the organisation in the future.

4 I work in the retail industry for a large chain of department stores. I'm in charge of 20 sales assistants. All they're interested in is getting to the weekend, and doing as little as possible. I have to keep an eye on them the whole time. We don't allow any sort of initiative – it just leads to problems when people start ignoring the established procedures.

B Read the instructions together. Play AUDIO 2.2 and ask students to check their answers with a partner.

KEY

1 oil company   2 department store
3 insurance company   4 call centre

AUDIO SCRIPT

1 I've worked in the oil industry since I graduated. I like the way they do things in this company. We're encouraged to use our initiative – to think for ourselves and solve problems. We get our own projects to look after – I think they realise that people with MBAs need that kind of independence. And we're judged on results, not by the amount of time we spend on the job.

2 The manager's breathing down my neck all the time! He walks around the different departments, checking on the sales people – you never know when he's going to appear. The only thing he's interested in is reaching his sales targets. We can't do anything without asking him first!

3 In this organisation, like in all insurance companies, you just follow established procedures. Decisions are imposed from above – there's no consultation. And don't ever dream about working from home, not even one day a week! That would never be allowed – they want to see what you're doing the whole time.

4 I've worked in other places where they measure your work very precisely – they don't want you to spend more than three minutes on each call. But here there's more flexibility, and you can spend as much time as you want with each customer, within reason, of course. As a team leader, I get a lot of responsibility, which I like, and I get a lot of satisfaction from my work. I think that motivates people. And valued employees make for valued customers!

C Read the expressions in class and check understanding. Ask: *Which expressions seem positive? Which seem negative?* Play AUDIO 2.2 again. Students check their answers in pairs, then in class.

KEY

Speaker 1:   Expressions 2 9
Speaker 2:   Expression 4
Speaker 3:   Expressions 3 6 7
Speaker 4:   Expressions 1 5 8

D Discuss this question in class.

KEY

Theory X organisations: 3 4 6 7
Theory Y organisations: 1 2 5 8 9

E Ask students to work in pairs and to do the exercise as indicated. Elicit an exchange and put it on the board. For example:

Theory Y: *We can work from home. How about in your organisation?*

Theory X: *We can't. We are supervised all of the time.*

[N.B. Encourage students to provide supplementary information rather than simply responding with *Yes* or *No*.]

Circulate during the activity to check and make a note of vocabulary, pronunciation, and general interaction. Give feedback after the exercise.

▶ FOR FURTHER READING ON THE SUBJECT OF MOTIVATION, DIRECT STUDENTS TO PAGE 8 OF THE WORKBOOK.

Communication

Finding out about people

With Coursebooks closed, ask: *What do you discuss when you meet someone for the first time?*

Put all suggestions on the board:

place of birth

education

family / home

first job / previous job / experience

interests

Write on the board:

closed questions   wh- questions

Ask students for an example of each type of question. Then ask: *Why do we sometimes use closed questions when we meet someone for the first time?* Students may work out that it is because a closed question allows the person to respond with as little information as they please – simply *Yes* or *No*, particularly if the topic is considered personal. There are cultural differences in terms of what is viewed as personal; for example, in some cultures, asking 'How much do you earn?' is acceptable, whereas in other cultures this would be frowned upon. However, remind students that in some cultures offering very little information is considered impolite.

Invite students to suggest further examples of closed questions and *wh-* questions for the discussion topics listed on the board. Write their questions on the board. Ask whether they are appropriate for a first meeting. Should some of their *wh-* questions be changed to closed questions?

18

PERFORMANCE **UNIT 2**

Read the questions yourself and ask the students to identify the intonation patterns. You could ask students to come up to the board and draw the intonation pattern (with an arrow) above the question. (Closed questions ▶ rising intonation / wh- questions ▶ falling intonation.) Drill class and ask students to practise asking the questions in pairs.

A With books still closed, write on the board:
  place of birth   education   family   first job

Read the instructions in A out to the class. Ask students to make notes while listening. Play AUDIO 2.3 and tell students to compare their answers to a partner's. It is likely that you will need to play the audio again.

KEY

place of birth	– Freiburg, south Germany
education	– studied in London
family	– father worked in the States, parents still in the States, sister in England
first job	– trainee buyer for fashion house in London, travelled a lot with this job, very competitive

AUDIO SCRIPT

Michael: Would you like coffee or tea?
Susanne: Coffee, please.
Michael: It's over here. Just help yourself. Where do you come from, Susanne?
Susanne: I was born in Germany, in Freiburg, in the south of Germany.
Michael: Really? I thought you were American.
Susanne: Well, I was brought up in the States. My father worked there.
Michael: Oh, that explains the accent! Where did you live?
Susanne: We moved around, but mostly we lived on the East coast.
Michael: Did you go to university there?
Susanne: No, I studied in London. And I've been in England since I graduated.
Michael: Do you miss your family?
Susanne: Well, my sister is in England, too, and my parents come over to visit sometimes.
Michael: Do you get back to the States much?
Susanne: Once or twice a year. In my first job after graduation, I used to travel a lot so I saw my parents more often.
Michael: What were you doing?
Susanne: I was a trainee buyer for a fashion house in London.
Michael: That sounds fun!
Susanne: It was, but after a couple of years, I decided the fashion business wasn't for me.
Michael: Why was that?
Susanne: Oh, I don't know. The fashion business is very …
Michael: I guess it's very competitive? Lots of beautiful people?
Susanne: That's right. It's all about image, as you would expect.
Michael: So how exactly did you end up in this line of business?
Susanne: Well, that's a long story …

B Ask students if they can recall any of Michael's questions, but keep this brief. Ask them to turn to page 10 and focus on the key language. Check understanding of *probing questions, reflecting comments* and so on. Ask students why we use such questions or comments (refer to the Communication notes on page 150). Ask students to listen to AUDIO 2.3 again and tick the questions and comments as indicated in the Coursebook. Students should check their answers in pairs.

Extension activity. For further intonation practice, ask students to turn to page 115 of their Coursebooks for the audio script. Tell them to listen to the dialogue again and mark the intonation of the speakers on the script. Ask half of the class to focus on Michael and the other half to focus on Susanne. You will need to play the recording at least twice. Compare answers in class and drill some of Michael's questions. You could play parts of the audio and ask students to listen and repeat. Finally, ask students to practise the dialogue in pairs using the identified intonation. Circulate and help where necessary. Listen out for sentences or questions that students seem to find particularly difficult and correct or drill during feedback.

C Ask students to complete the dialogue in pairs. Then ask them to identify the different question forms (e.g. *open, closed, probing*) and how Susanne shows interest. Draw their attention to how Petra doesn't simply respond with *Yes*, but offers more information.

KEY
1 do   2 mean   3 Could … tell   4 do
5 sounds   6 exactly

D Ask students to work in pairs and imagine that they have just met. Tell them that the aim of the activity is to find out about each other using the different question forms. After five minutes, ask students to work with someone new. Circulate and check question forms, responses and intonation. Give feedback and make corrections after the exercise.

To provide individual feedback, use a Social English Framework Sheet (see Frameworks, page 122). Go through the Framework with students before exercise D so that they are aware of areas upon which their performance will be assessed. Draw students' attention to the fact that, according to the Framework, showing interest and listening actively are important skills when socialising.

▶ FOR SELF-STUDY EXERCISES RELATING TO FINDING OUT ABOUT PEOPLE, SEE PAGE 10 OF THE WORKBOOK.

▶ REFER STUDENTS TO PAGE 150 OF THE COURSEBOOK FOR A SUMMARY OF THE POINTS COVERED IN THIS COMMUNICATION SECTION.

Business across Cultures
Understanding different types of culture

With Coursebooks closed, draw a diagram (as seen on page 11 of the Coursebook) on the board. Write *You* in the centre of the diagram. Explain that the layers of the onion represent the different types of culture that have an impact on our behaviour. Elicit different types of culture (*company/university/college culture, department culture, sector culture, functional culture, team culture, country culture, regional culture,* etc.)

19

PERFORMANCE UNIT 2

A AUDIO 2.4 Ask students to open their Coursebooks and read the introduction to the exercise. Focusing on the first diagram, ask: *What types of culture do the three labelled layers represent?* (Asian Finance ▶ Company culture / Investment banking ▶ Sector culture / Singapore ▶ Country culture)

Ask students to listen to the audio again and label the Finvest diagram. Compare answers in pairs and then with the whole class.

KEY

Centre ring:	Lin Ho
Next ring:	Finvest
Third ring:	International finance
Outer ring:	France

AUDIO SCRIPT

For us, the family is the most important element in our lives. I used to work for a local investment banking company, Asian Finance. It was a Singaporean company, run by a local family – the father and two sons. At Asian Finance, family ties were very important. Many of the people who worked there were related to each other. Now I work for Finvest, an international finance company. The head office is in France and some of the managers are from there, but there are also some Americans, one or two other Europeans, and some from other parts of Asia as well. So family doesn't count for much here. The Americans tell me that the company is very French, but I can't really tell. I have some friends who work for American multinationals and they are very different, that's true. Finvest is quite a traditional company, maybe that's a European thing, I don't know. It certainly has its own culture – people dress very formally and there's a lot of handshaking!

B You could demonstrate the activity by explaining the types of culture that surround you at work (prepare an onion diagram like the one on page 11 of the Coursebook before class). Give students a maximum of five minutes to prepare their diagrams. Students should present their diagram to a partner as suggested in the Coursebook.

C Ask students to do the exercise individually. Play AUDIO 2.5 and get students to check their answers in pairs.

KEY

dress, body language, organisation, communication, history

AUDIO SCRIPT

As I was saying, everybody dresses very formally – that's true for the men and the women. And I notice that the French managers tend to shake hands or even kiss when they meet each other. It's a well-established business – it's been going for generations. There are pictures on the walls of some of the founders and key people over the years. I notice the formality in letters and reports – the expressions they use are much more formal than I'm used to and generally when you write, even emails, you need to be careful what you say.

D Ask students to turn back to page 7 and refer to the iceberg. Get pre-work students to draw an iceberg for their college or university. This exercise could be done for homework, and the icebergs presented in class or subgroups in the next session. To provide individual feedback after the presentations, you could use an Accuracy Feedback Sheet (see Frameworks, page 121).

▶ FOR READING AND WRITING EXERCISES ON THE SUBJECT OF CULTURE SHOCK, SEE PAGE 11 OF THE WORKBOOK.

▶ REFER STUDENTS TO PAGE 153 OF THE COURSEBOOK.

Checklist

As a review activity, ask students to refer to the checklist in their Coursebooks and go over the items with them.

To review the language for finding out about people, ask each student to imagine that they are a well-known person, one that everyone in the class will know, and that they are all at a party. Ask them to circulate, meet and find out about the other *personalities*. Tell them to ask appropriate questions (they cannot ask for names) using the right intonation, and to respond with interest. Set a time limit for students to mingle and meet as many people as possible. During the activity make a note of common errors, particularly in question forms and intonation. When they have finished, ask if they can guess who they have met.

PERFORMANCE **UNIT 3**

3 Incentives

PREVIEW

Reading and speaking
The article in this unit describes the unusual and generous benefits system at the US software company, SAS.

Vocabulary and listening
The vocabulary in this unit deals with different types of benefits, ranging from maternity leave to company pensions to performance bonuses. This vocabulary features in a listening exercise in which a job candidate discusses benefits with an interviewer.

Grammar **first conditional**
Students are likely to be familiar with the first conditional, but may use it incorrectly or be unsure of when to use it. In this unit, the first conditional is used for negotiating work benefits.

Communication **building transparency**
The skills of checking, clarifying and confirming understanding are presented and practised. This is an essential, yet often ignored, area.

Business across Cultures **individuals and groups**
Different cultural attitudes, expectations and behaviour relating to individuals and groups are explored in this unit. This will help students to understand the potential difficulties experienced when faced with different attitudes towards groups and individuals.

Introductory activity

With Coursebooks closed, write *Incentives* on the board and ask students what they understand by this word and get them to suggest examples (*performance bonuses, free trips, prizes*, etc.) Write their suggestions on the board, then ask: *Why do companies offer incentives?*

[N.B. Some pre-work learners will not be familiar with benefits and incentives so you may need to throw in a few suggestions to help them build up a picture of this area. There may also be cultural/organisational differences in terms of the nature and number of incentives offered to employees.]

Ask students: *On average, how much do mid-size American companies spend on benefits per employee per year?* Allow students to guess and then give them the exact amount. Ask: *Are you surprised? Why? Why not? Why do you think they spend so much money?*

Vocabulary from the previous units may arise, e.g. *motivate, encourage*. Make a note of it on the board.

Ask students to open their Coursebooks and read the fact feature.

Start-up

A Read the instructions and check understanding of the vocabulary. Ask students to work in pairs and do the exercise as indicated. Responses should then be compared in class. Do not spend too much time on this activity.

Reading and speaking

A Direct students' attention to the three photos. Ask them what kinds of benefits they show (gym facilities, spa, day-care centre). Ask two students to divide the text and read it out loud to the class. Students should be able to decipher the meaning of any new vocabulary from the context. If not, ask others to provide explanations. To check that they have got the gist of the text, ask two or three students to summarise the main points very briefly.

B To focus students', attention, write on the board:
   The article mentions ...
   The company already provides ...
Do one example together in class, then ask students to work in pairs. Check their answers in class.

KEY
The article mentions: a c d e f g
The company already provides: c d f g

C Ask students to work in pairs and then check their answers in class.
Ask students: *Would you like to work for SAS? What are the disadvantages of working for this type of company?* (Work–life balance perhaps – if this is mentioned, tell students that Unit 4 deals with this topic.)

KEY
1 True
2 False, employees can stay at home to care for sick family members.
3 False, the company has adopted a seven-hour workday.
4 True
5 False, they are analysed according to three criteria.

Vocabulary and listening

A Check pronunciation of the vocabulary. To build on the word stress activity suggested on page 17 of this book, write the following various stress patterns on the board:

o o   o o o   o o o   o o o o

Ask students to identify words in 1–7 which fit into the word stress patterns on the board. For example:

21

PERFORMANCE UNIT 3

○ ○ ○ ○ ○ ○ ○ ○ ○ ○ ○ ○
package benefits incentives maternity
bonus company performance paternity
pension

Drill pronunciation in class.

Ask students to do the exercise in pairs, and check answers in class.

KEY

1 b   2 a   3 g   4 c   5 d   6 e   7 f

B If your students have professional experience, this could be done as a subgroup activity and reported back to the group. With an inexperienced group who may be unaware of other benefits, brainstorm for benefits in class and provide a little prompting if necessary. Ask students to give reasons for their preferences.

C Ask students to close their Coursebooks and ask them to list the benefits mentioned during the discussion between a job candidate and interviewer. Play AUDIO **3.1**. Students should compare their answers in pairs, then check them in class.

KEY

health insurance
gym membership
sick leave
company pension scheme
financial planning advice
paternity leave

AUDIO SCRIPT

A: ... So what exactly are the incentives if I exceed my performance target?

B: If you reach 110 per cent of your target for the year, you'll get a performance bonus of €1000. But you won't get a bonus unless you reach the target.

A: What will the benefits package contain if I join the company?

B: Well, let's see ... health insurance, gym membership ... We have an excellent new gym on-site with all the latest equipment ...

A: I see. Could you tell me more about the health insurance?

B: The company will pay all hospital bills, unless you do something that's not covered by the policy, such as participating in dangerous sports.

A: What happens if I'm ill?

B: If you're ill, you'll be able to take sick leave. But unless you phone your manager, you won't be able to take more than three days off.

A: How much does the company contribute to the company pension scheme?

B: The company pays 80 per cent of the contributions, and the employee is responsible for 20 per cent. Our financial advisor will advise you if you need help with financial planning.

A: How much paternity leave will I get if we have children?

B: Fathers can take three months' paid leave, unless they decide to work instead, of course!

▶ FOR FURTHER READING AND VOCABULARY PRACTICE AND A WRITING EXERCISE RELATING TO THE TOPIC OF INCENTIVES, DIRECT STUDENTS TO PAGE 13 OF THE WORKBOOK.

▶ VOCABULARY REVIEW AND DEVELOPMENT, PAGE 23, CAN BE DONE AT THIS STAGE.

Grammar

First conditional

Ask students to keep their Coursebooks closed. To introduce the first conditional, AUDIO **3.1** can be exploited further. First, write on the board:

Performance bonus   Health insurance   Sick leave

Divide the class into three groups and assign each group the exercise of listening for the conditions attached to one of the benefits. Play AUDIO **3.1**, then allow the groups to compare their answers before reporting back. Students may not produce the first conditional automatically, but you can elicit it by writing half sentences on the board:

_____, you'll get a
performance bonus of €1000.
The company pays all hospital bills _____.
_____, you'll be able to take sick leave.

Finally, ask: *When do we use the first conditional?* (To talk about a possible future situation.)

Ask students to open their Coursebooks and look at the grammar section.

A Read through the grammar rules together and check that students understand how to use *unless* correctly (with *unless*, the main clause is always negative). It is important to point out a common mistake: *If I will ...* Also, to remind students how punctuation changes when the clauses change position, write two sentences on the board and ask one student to come to the board and punctuate the sentences where necessary. For example:

If I see him, I'll tell him. (Comma.)

I'll tell him if I see him. (No comma.)

Drill pronunciation of the contraction of *will* (I'll / You'll / He'll, etc.) Many students find this difficult to reproduce, and, quite often, they don't hear it when listening to a native speaker.

Ask students to do exercise A in pairs. Tell them that some gaps feature more than one word. Check their answers in class.

KEY

1 What will the benefits package contain if I join the company?

2 We'll pay all the bills, if you need hospital treatment.

3 If you become seriously ill, the company will give you up to four months' sick leave on full pay.

4 If you need to have your clothes cleaned, our on-site laundry service will take care of it.

5 You'll get fired if you call in sick six Mondays in a row!

B Go over the example together in class. Ask students to do the exercise in pairs and remind them to punctuate the sentences correctly. Check their answers in class.

22

PERFORMANCE **UNIT 3**

KEY

2 You can't go to dance classes unless you finish your work first.
3 Employees will not get the end-of-year bonus unless they arrive on time in the mornings.
4 You can't take more than three days off sick unless you phone your manager.
5 Unless you tell your boss about your summer holiday dates by 31 January, you will not get the dates you want.

▶ FOR FURTHER INFORMATION ON THE FIRST CONDITIONAL, REFER STUDENTS TO GRAMMAR OVERVIEW, PAGE 157.
▶ FOR FIRST CONDITIONAL SELF-STUDY EXERCISES, SEE PAGE 12 OF THE WORKBOOK.
▶ GRAMMAR REVIEW AND DEVELOPMENT, PAGE 33, CAN BE DONE AT THIS STAGE.
▶ FOR LESS CONTROLLED PRACTICE OF THE FIRST CONDITIONAL, SEE PHOTOCOPIABLE MATERIALS 2.

Communication
Building transparency

Checking, clarifying and confirming understanding, are essential skills for all learners of English. Much emphasis is placed on speaking, when understanding is key to successful communication. Students should always be encouraged to listen actively and control the speaker, using phrases like: *Slowly, please. / Could you rephrase that, please? / Could you repeat that, please?* They should use these phrases particularly when faced with native English speakers who are often unaware of the difficulties involved in communicating in a foreign language.

To highlight the importance of checking and clarifying, you could do a fun activity that requires the use of active listening: a short quiz (about 15–20 questions) on a topic such as culture or international business, or simply general knowledge. Quizzes are easy to find in magazines and on the Internet. It should include difficult language and vocabulary that will force students to clarify meaning. Before starting, briefly review phrases and techniques for clarifying and checking information. Divide the class into teams and ask them to make a note of their answers after each question. Mention that answers will not be given until after the quiz. Read the questions quickly so that the students have to ask you to slow down. Praise checking and clarifying throughout activity, and make a note of any useful active listening language on the board.

A Read the exercise and notes together. Make sure it is clear what kind of information is missing (e.g. gap (4) is a date). For this listening exercise, mention that the answers do not always appear in order. Play AUDIO **3.2** and ask students to check their answers in pairs, then compare in class.

KEY

1 15th of each month   2 250 units   3 $15 per unit
4 28th 5 20   6 10   7 20

AUDIO SCRIPT

Nikos: Could we go through the details again, please?
Phil: Of course. We will supply the circuit boards on an annual contract, delivering once a month, unless you request extra deliveries or you want to postpone.
Nikos: Could you clarify that? We need to be sure that we can change the order, if necessary.
Phil: Yes, that's OK. We will deliver on the fifteenth of each month, according to the agreed schedule. If you contact us by the 28th of the previous month, we will accept a change of order.
Nikos: So, this means that we can increase or decrease the quantity?
Phil: Yes, that's correct. But, of course, there will be a knock-on effect on price.
Nikos: What do you mean by 'knock-on'?
Phil: I mean that we have agreed a unit price based on the schedule of monthly orders. If you decrease the quantity, we can't offer you the same price.
Nikos: Yes, I understand. So will you charge us at list price if we decrease our monthly order by more than 20 per cent?
Phil: That's right. On the other hand, at the end of the year, you may qualify for a further discount if you have exceeded the planned quantity significantly.
Nikos: Sorry, I'm not with you. What do you mean by 'significantly'?
Phil: You will qualify for a further 10 per cent discount if orders exceed the planned quantity by more than 20 per cent.
Nikos: Right. And we would expect to receive this as a credit note at the end of the year.
Phil: That's fine.
Nikos: So, let me just confirm that. We will contract you to deliver 250 circuit boards per month, on the 15th of each month. This will be invoiced at the end of each month at a rate of $15 per unit.

B Ask students to look at the key language and check that students understand phrases and expressions such as *go through* and *go over*. Tell them that *so* is used a lot during active listening. Students should do the exercise as indicated then compare their answers with a partner's. Use the audio script to check.

C Ask students to work in pairs and do the exercise as indicated. Circulate during the activity and note down errors and good use of checking and clarifying language. Provide feedback and corrections after the exercise. To provide individual feedback, you could use an Accuracy Feedback Sheet (See Frameworks, page 121).

Extension activity. Ask students to work in pairs. They will describe a process or procedure to their partners (system they use at work, the rules to a game, a scientific process, a native dance, etc.) To demonstrate, describe a process yourself (the stages of this activity would be ideal as it is a little complicated). Tell students to listen carefully and take notes because you will ask them to summarise the process afterwards.

Give students a few minutes to work out how to describe their process. Explain that they will describe it to their partners, who will take notes and check and clarify details. Once they have grasped their partner's process, they themselves will describe it to a new partner, who in turn will eventually present the process to the person who described it in the first place. Set a strict time limit for each stage of the activity.

▶ FOR SELF-STUDY PRACTICE OF THE LANGUAGE USED FOR BUILDING TRANSPARENCY, DIRECT STUDENTS TO PAGE 14 OF THE WORKBOOK.
▶ REFER STUDENTS TO PAGE 150 OF THE COURSEBOOK FOR A SUMMARY OF THE POINTS COVERED IN THIS COMMUNICATION SECTION.

PERFORMANCE UNIT 3

Business across Cultures
Individuals and groups

Read the introduction and explain that they will hear two project leaders giving feedback to their teams. Tell them that one is from a culture in which individuals are encouraged to stand out and the other is from a culture in which people are expected to work in groups. Ask: *What differences do you expect in their style of feedback?*

A AUDIO 3.3 Ask students to make notes on the feedback. Play the audio. Check students' responses in class.

KEY

They are on track but there are some difficulties.

The project leader doesn't give Peter any feedback. Marta is given negative feedback and Miguel is given very positive feedback.

AUDIO SCRIPT

Project leader A: Thanks for coming to the meeting today. We're at a critical stage of the project, as you know, and I'd like to give you all some feedback. I think we're on track but there are some difficulties. How do you think it's going? Peter?

Peter: Pretty well. As you say, there are a few problems but my side of things is going OK.

Project leader A: I am pleased to hear that, Peter. What about you, Marta?

Marta: Well, I've got some problems with my contractor in Spain.

Project leader A: That's what I've heard. I'm worried about this, Marta. The markets are not sure if you can deliver on time. I think you need to put pressure on your contractor. Otherwise we're going to miss the deadline. Miguel, what about you?

Miguel: I've been getting good feedback.

Project leader A: That's good. You've been doing a great job, Miguel. OK, let's move on and look at the ...

B AUDIO 3.4 As in the previous activity, ask students to make notes on the feedback. Play the audio. Check students' responses in class.

KEY

The project leader thanks all the team for their hard work, but says that they are starting to run into some problems.

It is different from the feedback given by project leader A because it focuses on the team and how the team can solve the problems together. Project leader A focused on the individuals not the team.

AUDIO SCRIPT

Project leader B: Thanks for coming to the meeting today and thanks for all your hard work on this project. We're at a critical stage of the project, as you know, and we're starting to run into some problems. We have some tight deadlines to meet and I'm sure we all want to stay on track. So I want to use this meeting to look at the problems and try to work out some solutions. OK, let's start with ...

C Students should discuss the question briefly in pairs and report back to the class.

D If the students are from the same culture or company this could be done in subgroups. However, if they are from a variety of cultures, it is best if this is done in pairs where they can discuss and compare their cultures. After the discussion, ask students to share their opinions with the rest of the class.

E Before reading, write on the board:

An individualist in a collectivist culture.   *A collectivist in an individualistic culture.*

Divide the class into two groups. Assign one of the above situations to each group and instruct them to list the problems that may be encountered (i.e. if a business person from an individualistic culture goes to work for a company in a collectivist culture or vice versa). To check understanding, elicit one or two problems. Compare the two groups' responses in class.

Before reading the text in E, ask students to look at the photo. Ask: *What are they doing?   What kind of culture do you think they are from?*

Ask students to read the text individually. They should then discuss their attitudes in subgroups (if you have a culturally diverse class, create subgroups consisting of a variety of nationalities). During feedback, ask students if they shared each others' views or if they had contrasting attitudes. Allow some time for class discussion.

[N.B. If your class is multinational, remind students to avoid being judgemental, and rather to value the opportunity they have to observe one another's cultures. It is important to mention that the differences we notice in other cultures' attitudes often reveal more about particular attitudes of our own culture, which we might previously have accepted as the norm.]

▶ FOR A QUIZ ON INDIVIDUALISM VERSUS COLLECTIVISM, SEE PAGE 15 OF THE WORKBOOK.

▶ REFER STUDENTS TO PAGE 153 OF THE COURSEBOOK FOR A SUMMARY OF THE POINTS COVERED IN THIS BUSINESS ACROSS CULTURES SECTION.

Checklist

As a review activity, ask students to refer to the checklist in their Coursebooks and go over the items with them.

To review checking and clarifying, ask students to write down a topic on a piece of paper. Tell them it must be something that everyone can relate to and talk about (*sport, TV, study skills,* etc.) Collect the pieces of paper, shuffle them and redistribute them. Now ask students to form groups of four. Each person will talk about their topic for two minutes, and another person in the group will listen, take notes, and reformulate what was said. The listener must, of course, check and clarify information. The other two students in the group should make a note of all active listening phrases so as to increase their own awareness and encourage the speaker to use the phrases. They should also provide feedback to the listener after the end of the exercise. Students should rotate roles within their groups.

PERFORMANCE **UNIT 4**

4 Work and leisure

PREVIEW

Listening and speaking	The listening and speaking exercises in this unit deal with the issue of work–life balance.
Grammar	**past simple and present perfect** Most students will be familiar with the present perfect tense but will benefit from a review of its use. In this section students identify and practise using the past simple and present perfect tenses when talking about trends.
Communication	**responding and developing communication** This section highlights the skills and language used in responding to and showing interest in what someone is saying. In many cultures, these are essential skills in building a good rapport with acquaintances, colleagues and business associates. In other cultures, an attentive silence is considered more appropriate.
Business across Cultures	**women at work** This section explores attitudes and behaviour towards women. The activities involve students in building up a profile of their own culture's view on gender roles. In a multicultural class, some of the exercises need to be set up with care to avoid the expression of judgemental views.

Introductory activity

Create a mind map relating to leisure activities on the board: Write 'leisure activities' on the board in a circle and ask students to suggest as many activities as possible. Record their suggestions on the board.

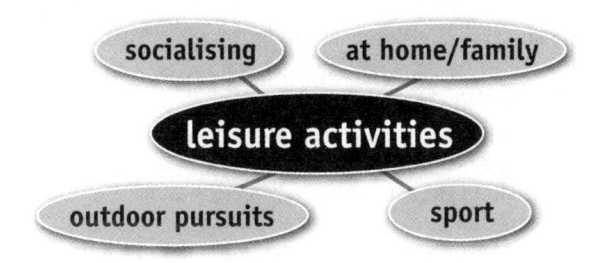

```
    socialising        at home/family
            leisure activities
    outdoor pursuits        sport
```

Next, ask: *Which leisure activities are common in your country? Which ones do you do?*

And finally: *Do you have enough free time for these activities? Do your work or studies prevent you from doing any of these activities?*

Keep the discussion general at this stage as ways of achieving a good work–life balance will be discussed later.

You could then write the phrase 'Work to live. Don't live to work.' on the board. Ask students if people hold this attitude in their culture. Do they know of any similar or contrasting phrases?

Ask students to open their Coursebooks and direct their attention to the fact feature on the right. Ask: *Were those experts right?* Ask students to give reasons for their opinions.

Start-up

As a group, brainstorm for definitions of work–life balance. Then ask: *Why is it important to have a good work–life balance?* Responses may include words such *as health, well-being, illness, and life expectancy*, which feature in the audio below. Write these words on the board. Ask: *Are there any laws in your country that limit the number of hours people can work?*

Listening and speaking

A AUDIO **4.1** Read through the questions together. Play the audio. Students should check their answers in pairs, and then discuss them in class.

KEY

1 A balance between work and life outside work.
2 48 hours per week.
3 Serious negative effects on health and well-being.
4 France, 35 hours a week.
5 The 19th century, 18 or 20 hours a day.

AUDIO SCRIPT

Interviewer: What do people mean by work–life balance?

Jack Stevens: Well, many people these days feel that work takes up too much of their time and energy, so it's the idea that people want a balance between work and life outside the office – family, friends, leisure activities, and so on.

Interviewer: Aha ...

Jack Stevens: Of course, there are laws in many countries to limit the number of hours that people can work. In the EU, for example, there is a law that prevents people working more than 48 hours per week. It's widely known that working long hours can have serious negative effects on people's health and well-being – working long hours can cause illness and reduce life expectancy.

Interviewer: Right ...

Jack Stevens: And in some countries, the weekly limit is much lower. For example, France has a 35-hour week.

Interviewer: But aren't people spending more on leisure activities? Businesses like gyms and travel companies have benefited enormously ...

25

PERFORMANCE UNIT 4

Jack Stevens: That's true. Of course things have improved since the 19th century ...

Interviewer: Aha ...

Jack Stevens: In those days people often worked 18 or 20 hours a day, and sometimes slept in the factory next to their machines – no gyms or weekends away for them! So we've come a long way since then.

B Read the instructions for the exercise and focus students' attention on the graph. Before playing the audio, ask: *What do the horizontal and vertical axes represent?* Then ask: *Do you expect the average number of working hours to increase or decrease in the future? Why?*

Play AUDIO 4.2. Instruct students to compare their graphs with a partner's. You may need to play the audio again. Compare graphs in class.

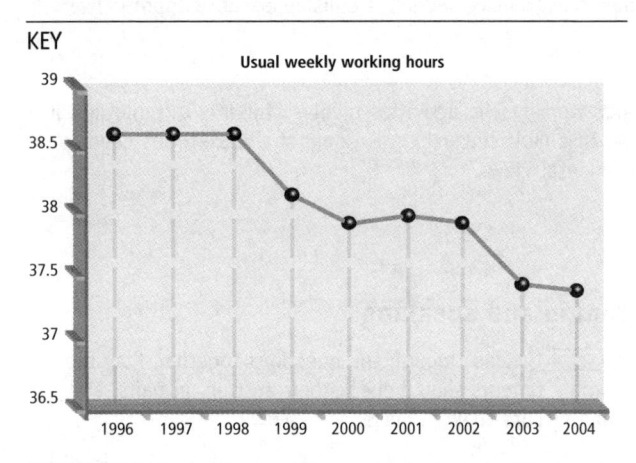

KEY

Usual weekly working hours

(Graph showing values from 1996 to 2004, declining from approximately 38.6 to 37.3)

AUDIO SCRIPT

Interviewer: So, have working hours gone down all over Europe?

Jack Stevens: Yes. If you look at the figures from 1996 onwards, they remained steady at about 38.7 hours per week and then they fell quite quickly, to 38.3 in 1999 and 37.9 in 2000.

Interviewer: Aha ...

Jack Stevens: The number of hours worked rose slightly in 2001 – that year people worked 38 hours a week on average ...

Interviewer: OK.

Jack Stevens: ... but then the figures started falling again: they fell to 37.9 in 2002, then they decreased to 37.4 in 2003 and went down again slightly to 37.3 in 2004.

Interviewer: So, since 1996, the number of working hours has decreased from 38.7 to 37.3 per week?

Jack Stevens: That's right. Now some people may find this ...

C Ask students to study the photos. Ask: *What do you see?* (A stressed father working from home. An employee working in an office when everyone else has gone home.)
The questions in C could be discussed in pairs or subgroups. Set a time limit and ask for a brief summary of views from each group at the end of the exercise.

▶ FOR FURTHER READING AND VOCABULARY PRACTICE RELATING TO THE TOPIC OF WORK–LIFE BALANCE, DIRECT STUDENTS TO PAGE 16 OF THE WORKBOOK.

▶ VOCABULARY REVIEW AND DEVELOPMENT, PAGE 24, CAN BE DONE AT THIS STAGE.

Grammar
Past simple and present perfect

Ask students to close their books. To introduce the past simple and the present perfect, you can use AUDIO 4.2 again. First, write on the board:

In 2001,   Since 1996,

Tell students to listen for information relating to these time references. Play the audio and ask students to tell you what they heard (The number of hours worked rose slightly in 2001. / Since 1996, the number of working hours has decreased.) Ask: *Which tense is used in each sentence? Why?*

There is no need to write the rules on the board at this stage because they will be dealt with below.

Erase the board and write:

1 I've worked in London _____.		*Time references*
_____.		in 2000
_____.		for three years
		this year
2 I worked in London _____.		since 2000
_____.		last year
_____.		

Ask students which time references can be used in each sentence. Tell them that one can be used with both (for three years).

Elicit the rules and write them on the board. For example:

present perfect ▶ *not used with past time references*
past simple ▶ *not used with present time references*
since ▶ *only used with the present perfect*
for ▶ *used with the present perfect and the past simple*

[N.B. Be prepared for some students to be surprised that the present perfect can be used with present time references. Point out that it is a *present* tense.]

To check students' understanding, get them to write sentences about themselves which include: *for, since, this year, last year, in 2003*. Circulate while the students are writing and make a note of any errors that should be highlighted during feedback. Ask each student to read one of two of their sentences out loud.

If you find that students have difficulty using *for* and *since* correctly, write on the board:

For   *Since*

Call out time references such as: *last month, 1999, my birthday, two weeks, a long time, January, Saturday, one hour,* etc. and ask students whether they are used with *for* or *since*. Write the time references in the appropriate column. Elicit the rules and write them on the board:

for ▶ *used to describe the length of an activity or state*
since ▶ *used to indicate the point when an activity or state began*

Ask students to open their Coursebooks.

A Go through this in class.

KEY

In 2001, people <u>worked</u> 38 hours a week on average.
past simple

Since 1996 the number of working hours <u>has decreased</u> from 38.7 per cent to 37.3 per cent.
present perfect

PERFORMANCE UNIT 4

B Also do this exercise in class. Check and drill pronunciation of the contracted form of *have* (I've/You've, etc.)

KEY

We use the past simple tense to talk about actions and events that happened at a specific time in the past.

We use the present perfect tense to talk about actions and events that happened in the past and continue in the present.

C Before doing the exercise in the Coursebook, draw three arrows on the board:

↑ ↓ →

Ask students which verbs in exercise C describe the different arrows, then elicit more verbs (*grow, improve, drop, slump, remain stable, stay the same*, etc.)

Ask students to complete the exercise in pairs, as indicated. Check the answers in class. You may need to drill pronunciation of *rise / rose / risen*.

[N.B. Students may ask what the difference between *raise* and *rise* is. *Raise* is transitive, it needs a direct object, e.g. *We raised prices. Rise* is intransitive, so there's no direct object, e.g. *Prices rose*. Elicit some examples to highlight the difference. Drill the pronunciation of the two verbs as students often confuse them in both meaning and sound.]

KEY

rise – rose – risen	fall – fell – fallen
go up – went up – gone up	go down – went down – gone down
increase – increased – increased	decrease – decreased – decreased
remain steady – remained steady – remained steady	

D Elicit the meaning of words that appear in the text, such as *survey* and *disposable income*. Ask students to do the exercise as indicated in the Coursebook, then check answers in class.

KEY

1 has fallen	4 has risen
2 went up	5 has gone down
3 has increased	6 remained

Extension activity. Find authentic graphs in newspapers or on the Internet that illustrate work–life balance, leisure activities or any of the topics covered in previous units, such as job satisfaction, perks and benefits. Try to find ones that show trends leading up to the current date as this would require students to use the present perfect (e.g. *Since 2003, job satisfaction has decreased*.) Put students in pairs and give one student in each pair a graph and a sheet of blank graph paper to the other one. Explain that while one describes the graph, the other, without looking, has to listen (checking and clarifying where necessary) and draw it. Briefly demonstrate the activity by describing a graph for the students to draw. It would be helpful to pre-teach phrases such as *The horizontal / vertical axis represents ... '* and *'In 2000, ... stood at ... '*.

For homework, you could ask students to prepare a graph depicting a trend in their line of work or specialisation, and to present it to the class or to a subgroup in the next session.

Speaking

A Discuss this question in class. In monocultural groups ask students to form subgroups and ask them to prepare a graph showing the trend of a particular activity in their country to present to the class. In a multinational class, ask students to prepare a graph individually to present to a subgroup. Encourage other students to ask questions and make comments.

▶ FOR FURTHER INFORMATION ON THE PAST SIMPLE AND PRESENT PERFECT, REFER STUDENTS TO GRAMMAR OVERVIEW, PAGE 158.

▶ FOR SELF-STUDY EXERCISES ON THE PAST SIMPLE AND PRESENT PERFECT, SEE PAGE 17 OF THE WORKBOOK.

▶ GRAMMAR REVIEW AND DEVELOPMENT, PAGE 24, CAN BE DONE AT THIS STAGE.

Communication

Responding and developing communication

Like the language of checking and clarifying, this is a much neglected area but in many cultures it is vital in building up a rapport. However, in some cultures, an attentive silence is preferred when listening. Students from such cultures are likely to find *interrupting* a speaker with interjections quite a challenge. This is a good stage at which to focus on further intonation practice.

Ask students to describe how they show interest when someone is speaking. Ask: *What kind of body language do you use? What phrases or expressions do you use?* This could be particularly interesting if you have a multinational class as an awareness of how other cultures listen is extremely valuable in international business. Read the introduction together.

A AUDIO 4.3 Read the instructions and check that students know what kind of information to expect. Play the audio. Students should compare their answers in pairs, and then check in class.

KEY

SOUTHERN SECURITY SYSTEMS

Founded: 20 years ago

First big client: Ministry of Health

Ratio of private to public sector business: 6:10

New target markets: South-East Asia

Key to breaking into these markets: good local partners

AUDIO SCRIPT

Frank: We started nearly 20 years ago. It was very tough at the beginning to establish the business and build our client base. We worked night and day.

Dieter: That must have been hard.

Frank: It was. It took us nearly three years to get established. Our first big breakthrough was when we won a contract to supply the Ministry of Health.

Dieter: Really?

Frank: Yeah. To begin with, we supplied a couple of hospitals with alarm systems but now this has grown, and we now cover the whole country. And we also supply hospitals abroad.

27

PERFORMANCE UNIT 4

Dieter: I didn't know that. So, is the Ministry of Health your biggest customer?

Frank: Yes, it is. But we've worked hard to find other customers, especially in the private sector. In fact, almost 60 per cent of our work is in the private sector now.

Dieter: Is that where you see your business developing?

Frank: Yes, I think so. At the moment, we're trying to break into new markets in South-East Asia.

Dieter: Oh that can't be easy.

Frank: No, it isn't. You need to have good local partners. Luckily, we've found an excellent partner in Malaysia.

Dieter: That's interesting. I wonder if it's the same people we work with.

Frank: I've got their card here somewhere ... here it is ... Sunset Trading Company.

Dieter: I don't believe it! I was just talking to them yesterday ...

B Go through the key language together and do the exercise as indicated.

Check answers in pairs.

Pronunciation extension activity. Read some of the sentences in the Key language box aloud and ask students to listen and mark the intonation. Warn students that the wrong intonation in phrases like *That's interesting*, can sound insincere. Drill class and ask them to practise the intonation briefly in pairs. Then, in class, invite students to respond to various spoken statements and write their responses on the board (correct intonation as you go along):

I failed my driving test. ▶ *What a shame.*

I went diving in the Caribbean. ▶ ...

I saw Bill Gates yesterday.

I passed my exam.

I've lost my wallet.

Ask students to practise the statements and responses in pairs. Make sure they respond using the correct intonation.

For further focused pronunciation practice, you could elicit a dialogue from a framework such as the one below. Write the framework on the board and invite students to suggest sentences for Person A and Person B. Write the sentences, replacing the framework prompts, as you elicit them. If your group isn't particularly imaginative, be prepared to throw in a few suggestions here and there. Once the dialogue is complete, elicit intonation patterns and pronunciation of difficult words.

PERSON A	PERSON B
Wh- question about B's last business trip	⟶ Respond
Make an encouraging comment	⟶ Mention interesting fact about trip
Express surprise	⟶ Mention bad experience on trip
Express sympathy and draw conclusions	⟶ Respond Talk about successful deal
Congratulate	⟶ Respond
Express enthusiasm	⟶ Give further information about deal

There are two options for continuing this activity:

1. If your class is very large or some students are quite inhibited, you could ask students to act out the dialogue in pairs.
2. If your class is not very large and the students are confident, you could use the dialogue for a disappearing dialogue activity.

First, ask students to copy the dialogue into their notebooks, then ask them to close their books so they cannot see it. Next, ask two students to act out the dialogue. Correct pronunciation immediately after the exercise. Then, erase the final sentence, and ask two more students to act out the complete dialogue (including the erased part). Once again, correct any pronunciation errors. Erase another sentence, and ask another pair to act it out, and so on. Continue until the dialogue has completely disappeared and students are acting it out from memory.

C Emphasise that the aim of this exercise is to practise responding and showing interest. Given that some students may find this exercise difficult, you could put students in groups of three for this activity. Ask them to work with students they do not know very well so that you have two speakers and one observer. The observer's role is to make a note of the language used to respond and show interest, and give feedback at the end. This should remind or encourage students to use the target language. You can rotate roles within the groups so that everyone has a chance to practise responding and developing conversation.

To provide individual feedback, use a Social English Framework Sheet (see Frameworks, page 122). Go through the Framework with students before exercise C so that they are aware of areas upon which their performance will be assessed. Draw students' attention to the fact that, according to the Framework, showing interest and listening actively are important skills when socialising.

▶ FOR DEVELOPMENT AND CONSOLIDATION OF THE LANGUAGE ABOVE, SEE PAGE 18 OF THE WORKBOOK.

▶ REFER STUDENTS TO PAGE 150 OF THE COURSEBOOK FOR A SUMMARY OF THE POINTS COVERED IN THIS COMMUNICATION SECTION.

▶ COMMUNICATION REVIEW AND DEVELOPMENT EXERCISES, PAGE 25, CAN BE DONE AT THIS STAGE.

Business across Cultures
Women at work

To introduce the theme of this section, divide the class into two groups (or four if a very large class). Write two headings on the board:

Masculine characteristics   *Feminine characteristics*

Ask each group to brainstorm a list of adjectives for one of the above. Ask: *What characteristics are traditionally viewed as masculine/feminine?* Allow the groups up to five minutes to do the exercise. Ask the groups for their lists, write them up on the board, and compare them. Are there any adjectives in one list that have opposite adjectives (antonyms) in the other list? If you form opposites of adjectives in one list, will they fit into the other? Get students to discuss opposites and decide whether or not they can be used as specific gender characteristics. For example:

Masculine	*Feminine*
direct	indirect
tough	kind
uncooperative	cooperative

PERFORMANCE **UNIT 4**

[N.B. Throughout this activity, remind students that these are characteristics traditionally viewed as masculine or feminine. These are gender stereotypes.]

Divide the class into two groups again and assign each group the exercise of listing jobs/roles that are associated with either masculine or feminine characteristics, e.g. *kind* ▶ *nurse/care assistant*. Students can refer to the list of jobs on page 4 in Unit 1. Do two examples in class and write them on the board. Allow a few minutes, and then ask students to share their ideas. Finally, ask students if there are clearly defined gender roles in their culture(s). For example, referring to the list of jobs associated with feminine characteristics, ask: *In your culture, do men do these jobs?* This is simply to identify whether the students' culture(s) have clearly defined gender roles and should not lead to any judgements being made.

Read the introduction on page 19 and refer to the photos: *What kind of work are the people doing? Which part of the world are they from? Do you think they have clearly defined gender roles in their cultures?*

A Read the topic headings in class. Divide the class into four subgroups (or pairs, if a large class) and assign a different text to each subgroup. Ask them to read their paragraph and find out which of the topics are mentioned. Ask all students to close their Coursebooks and ask each subgroup to summarise its text.

Ask students to open their Coursebooks and read all four texts in class.

KEY

Norway: a c   Netherlands: d f
Japan: j b g   India: g i

B Depending on your class, two approaches are suggested here:

For a monolingual class ▶ divide the class into two groups and assign five topics from C to each group. Ask students to consider the topics while building up a profile of their culture's attitude and behaviour towards men and women. Give each group a flipchart and ask them to note key points to present to the other students.

For a multinational group ▶ ask pairs or subgroups (consisting of different nationalities) to create their cultures' profiles based on the topics mentioned in A. Then, ask them to note the key differences and similarities, which they will present to the group on a flipchart.

During the presentations, invite comments and questions from other students.

[N.B. The subject of women and work may be a sensitive issue in some cultures, and students may be offended by each others' views. Throughout the whole of this section, remind them to be non-judgemental. If you feel that views are likely to clash, you may prefer to set exercise B as a writing exercise for homework.]

C It may be necessary to elicit the meaning of certain words and phrases in the text e.g. *to compliment someone*. Ask one student to read the text out loud. Check understanding by asking one or two students to summarise Patrick's situation and problem. In subgroups, students discuss what is happening and the kind of advice they would give. Students should then share their ideas in class.

Extension activity. In pairs, students can roleplay a situation where Patrick is being given advice by a friend. Beforehand, go briefly through the language used for giving advice and making suggestions.

KEY

Most of Patrick's experience is in more masculine cultures (see page 153). In these cultures, he will have been encouraged to be assertive and directive in his management style. He also comes from a sales and marketing background where the working culture tends to be fast-paced and results-oriented. He is now working with mainly women from an HR background. They will favour a more mutually supportive way of working and will not appreciate his directive approach. They will also see the value of giving time to people and making sure that everybody is involved in decisions. There is also a strong feminist dimension to life in the UK which means that many women will find compliments about their appearance inappropriate in the work environment, maybe even outside work.

Patrick needs to adapt his management style. He should try to involve everybody in decision making and make sure he does not push his own personality too much. He should avoid making comments about women's appearances when he is at work.

▶ FOR READING PRACTICE ON THE SUBJECT OF THE DIFFERENT COMMUNICATION STYLES OF MEN AND WOMEN, REFER STUDENTS TO PAGE 19 OF THE WORKBOOK.

▶ REFER STUDENTS TO PAGE 153 OF THE COURSEBOOK FOR A SUMMARY OF THE POINTS COVERED IN THIS BUSINESS ACROSS CULTURES SECTION.

Checklist

As a review activity, ask students to refer to the checklist in their Coursebooks and go over the items with them.

To review *for* and *since*, put on the board:

How long ... ?

live in

work for

study

be a (profession)

have your own car

Ask students to work in pairs and ask each other 'How long ... ?' questions using the prompts on the board. This is a brief activity, so make sure students change partners after every two or three questions.

BUSINESS SCENARIO 1

IMPROVING MORALE

> The information exchange activity in this section requires the use of checking and clarifying language, which appears in the Communication section of Unit 3. The information is from a faxed report on staff morale, which provides students with information for the meeting activity in the role-play section of this unit. The grammar section concentrates on describing percentages, and introduces phrases such as *just over*, *more than half*, and *the vast majority*. This language is used to describe figures from another part of the report. For the role-play activity, you may need to review and pre-teach the language of meetings. The meeting is on the topic of low morale and will require students to use vocabulary that has featured in this first module. The writing section involves writing a short report on a meeting and its outcomes.

INTRODUCTORY ACTIVITY

Ask students to open their books and look at the title. Ask them what they understand by the word *morale*. If they are unsure, direct their attention to the photo at the bottom of the page and ask: *Do you think there is low or high morale in this business? How do these employees look?* (Unmotivated and bored.) When students have guessed the meaning of *morale*, write on the board:

    Causes   *Results*

Ask: *What causes low morale? What is the result of low morale?* Elicit one or two examples and put them on the board then ask students to discuss this briefly in subgroups. Students should compare their ideas in class.

BACKGROUND

Read the background information in class.

SPEAKING

This is a classic information exchange activity. This allows students to practise checking and clarifying information which was dealt with in the Communication section in Unit 3. Before embarking on this activity, ask students to turn to page 14 and study the Key language box just to remind them of the target language. Tell them that they should try to use some of this language during the speaking activity.

This should be done as indicated in the Coursebook in pairs. Ask Student B to turn to page 103 of the Coursebook. To model the exercise and demonstrate checking and clarifying, do one or two examples with a strong student. Circulate and make a note of the use of not only checking and clarifying, but also the way students describe the percentages, as this is the main focus of the grammar section on page 21.

GRAMMAR: TALKING ABOUT FIGURES

With Coursebooks closed, write on the board:

    1/2   1/3   2/3   1/4   3/4

Elicit *half, one third, two thirds* and so on. Then write the following on the board:

50%	▶	exactly 50 per cent / exactly half
51.2%	▶	_____
		_____
49%	▶	_____
		_____

Ask students to describe the numbers on the board using phrases such as: *just over, more than, nearly, just under*.

Tell students to open their Coursebooks and look at the language in the report. Check understanding of *vast majority*. Ask: *Is this a small majority or a large majority?*

Students should look at James Murdo's report in pairs and do the exercise orally. Check answers and make corrections in class.

ROLE-PLAY

Before setting up the meeting activity, write the following headings on the board:

    Chair   *Participants*

Ask: *To have a successful meeting, what should the chair do?* (Be well organised. Involve all participants.) *How should the participants behave?* (Listen to each other.)

PERFORMANCE **BUSINESS SCENARIO 1**

Express opinions clearly and concisely. Etc.) Brainstorm ideas and write them below each heading.

You may need to review the language of meetings and discussions. Elicit phrases for expressing opinions, agreeing, disagreeing, and making suggestions. Write the more useful examples on the board. Identify phrases that are weak / neutral / strong, formal / informal and direct / indirect.

For brief practice of this language, ask students to hold five-minute mini discussions in pairs. Write a short list of discussion topics on the board:

Ideas

To introduce a flexitime system.

To work longer hours from Monday to Thursday and finish early on Fridays.

To allow telecommuting.

To introduce performance related pay, rather than increasing salaries.

Ask students to imagine that they are heads of a company. They will choose one of the ideas to discuss, and decide whether or not to introduce it in their company. To make the discussion slightly more interesting, ask students to assume roles of *for* and *against*. After five minutes, students should change partners and repeat the activity. Circulate and provide class feedback on the use of discussion language as well as other important skills such as active listening, body language, and intonation.

To set up the role-play activity, divide the class into groups of three and assign roles. If this is impractical for the size of your group, one or two roles can be shared by students or you could invent additional roles for more imaginative students. (Trade union representative, director of finance, etc.) In this activity, Student A is the chair of the meeting so give this role to a confident and well-organised student. Tell Students B and C to turn to page 108 and page 110 respectively. Allow time for students to read their roles and prepare their arguments; circulate while they are doing so and help if necessary. Make sure they take notes about their decisions and any new facts learnt during the meeting (they will need this information to do the writing exercise below). During the activity, check language, positive exchanges, grammar and pronunciation errors. If you have a small group and therefore only one meeting taking place, record it on video or audio to use during feedback. Students often find it useful to observe their own strengths and weaknesses, as well as body language. However, do not spend too much time listening to or watching the recording as students may lose interest. Try to use it selectively to highlight positive interaction and to help students identify areas that could be improved. It is important to ask students for their opinions about the meeting: *Did you achieve the aim of the meeting? Is everyone satisfied with the results? Did everyone have a chance to speak? Did you understand each other?* To provide more individual feedback, you could use an Accuracy Feedback Form (see Frameworks, page 121).

WRITING

This could be set for homework. Ask students to decide who the report is for before they begin writing. Brainstorm possibilities (their department, share holders, the board of directors, all company employees, etc.) Ask them what could be mentioned in the report. For example:

Background and reason for the meeting

Facts (findings of the questionnaire)

Participants and their opinions

Options discussed

Decisions (and reasons)

Review and development 1–4

Grammar: Comparisons

A Go through the rules and examples on page 5 in class. Alternatively, elicit the rules and examples, then check them on page 5. Write the following sentences on the board:

The car is slower as a train.
That job is much more interesting than mine.
Paul is more lazier than John.
Paris is as expensive than London.
This is best option.

Ask students whether each sentence is correct. If they think it is incorrect, ask a volunteer to come to the board and correct it.

Ask students to do exercise A individually or set it for homework. Check answers in class.

KEY
b efficient – two syllables or more – more efficient
c pretty – two syllables ending in -y – prettier
d powerful – two syllables or more – more powerful
e relaxed – ends in -ed – more relaxed

B Like the previous activity, this should be done individually or set for homework.

KEY
1 thicker 2 prettier 3 more powerful 4 more efficient
5 more relaxed

C Again, ask them to do this individually or set it for homework.

KEY
1b 2a 3c 4c 5b 6a

D Divide the class into three subgroups and ask them to compare two products of the same kind. You could provide images of products taken from magazines. Circulate and provide brief feedback at the end.

Extension activity. Divide the class into subgroups and give each one a graph illustrating a trend relating to any of the topics covered in Module 1. Ask students to compare and explain statistics shown by the graph. They will present their summary to the rest of the class. Remind them to use the language of comparisons. To focus their attention, elicit some examples and write them on the board:

much (-er / more) than

slightly (-er / more) than

almost

nearly as ... as ...

not

To demonstrate how the graphs can be described, show a graph on an OHP or handout and invite students to compare different aspects of it. For example:

The number of women on maternity leave in 2004 was slightly higher than in 2003.
Maternity leave in 2000 was as low as in 1998.

Ask students to try to give reasons or explanations for trends. For example:

This is probably due to improved legislation.

While the subgroups are presenting their summary, encourage the other students to listen actively and make comments (particularly if they disagree with the reasons given for certain trends).

Vocabulary: Motivation

A Write on the board:

VERB	NOUN
motivate	?
?	consultation
promote	?
?	satisfaction
supervise	?
commit	?
?	discussion
encourage	?
produce	?
decide	?
?	initiative

Ask for the verb/noun equivalents. Then elicit the pronunciation of the words ending in -ion and briefly review the word stress rules relating to suffixes.

Ask students to do the exercise as indicated in pairs.

KEY
1 motivation 2 consulted 3 supervision 4 committed
5 encouragement 6 Discussion, decision 7 initiated

B Briefly elicit the main points of Theory X and Theory Y to refresh students' memories. Ask students to do the exercise as indicated in pairs. Encourage them to respond and show interest in their partners' comments. Elicit some useful phrases from the Communication section of Unit 4 beforehand. For example:

Expressing interest	Drawing conclusions
That's interesting.	That must be (+adjective)
Really?	That can't be (+adjective)

That sounds (+ adjective)

Extension activity. This is a writing exercise that could be set for homework. Tell students to imagine that they are business consultants who believe in Theory Y. They have been asked to give advice to a manager who believes in Theory X and has been experiencing problems motivating his team. Beforehand, you could briefly elicit the language used to give formal advice:

It is recommended ...
We would strongly advise ...
One solution would be to ...
Alternatively, you could ...

Grammar: First conditional

A Look at the examples and rules on page 13 together in class. To check students', understanding of the use and structure of the *first conditional*, write the following sentences on the board:

1) ... if it rains this weekend ...

2) ... I will look for another job ...

Ask students to complete the sentences. Circulate very quickly while they are writing, to check for errors. Ask students to compare their responses in pairs, then ask for a few example sentences in class. Write one or two on the board and elicit the correct punctuation.

Ask students to do exercise A in pairs, then check answers in class.

KEY

3 We'll promote you quickly if you have management potential.

4 If you improve your communication skills, we'll put you in charge of a team of engineers.

5 We'll increase your budget if you win the contract.

6 If you exceed your sales targets, we'll give you a top-of-the-range BMW.

7 You'll go far if you produce results.

B To check students', use of *unless*, write the following sentences on the board:

... unless you work harder ...

Ask students to work in pairs and write a sentence including the phrase which is on the board. Ask the pairs to share their sentences with the rest of the class. Write two or three of the example sentences on the board and elicit the rules (unless = if not). Again, check students' punctuation of the sentences.

Exercise B is best done individually or in pairs. Compare answers in class.

KEY

2 Unless you complete the first year successfully, we won't send you to our Paris office.

3 We won't promote you quickly unless you have management potential.

4 Unless you improve your communication skills, we won't put you in charge of a team of engineers.

5 We won't increase your budget unless you win the contract.

6 Unless you exceed your sales targets, we won't give you a top-of-the-range BMW.

7 You won't go far unless you produce results.

C Ask students to read the instructions and the example. Ask them to work in pairs and tell them that they will present their conditions to their employees (i.e. the rest of the class). Give them five minutes to prepare their ideas, then ask each pair to stand at the front of the class to present their various conditions. Encourage the 'employees' to ask questions. At the end, ask students which employer they would prefer to work for and why. Provide feedback and corrections.

Vocabulary: Company incentives

A Before embarking on the exercise, review simple article rules. Write the following words taken from Module 1 on the board:

Maternity leave (U)   Skill (C)   Satisfaction   Commitment   Advice   Restaurant   Balance   Accountant   Responsibility   Food   Geography   Supervision   Brand   Perk   Body language

Elicit which words are countable and which are uncountable. As you come to each word, mark *U* or *C* next it.

Then write on the board:

Accountant who I met yesterday was very nice. (Incorrect)

He's accountant. (Incorrect)

He gave me an advice. (Incorrect)

He didn't appreciate advice I gave him. (Incorrect)

Ask students to correct the sentences in pairs. Check their corrections together. Do not get into discussion about why they are incorrect at this stage.

Finally, ask subgroups to refer to the sentences above in working out the rules for putting articles with countable and uncountable nouns. Give them a time limit of five minutes and then as a class create a simple set of rules. You may need to guide the students a little in organising the rules. For example:

	General ▶ No article
Uncountable	(never use a/an with uncountable nouns)
	Specific ▶ the
	Specific (singular/plural) ▶ the
Countable	General (singular) ▶ a/an
	General (plural) ▶ no article

As instructed in the Coursebook, ask students to look at the vocabulary on page 13 and do the exercise in pairs. Check answers in class.

KEY

2 c   the benefits package

3 f   the company pension

4 e   the perks

5 a   a performance bonus

6 b   maternity leave

Grammar: Past simple and present perfect

A Look at the examples and rules on page 17 together in class. Draw students' attention to the sentences in exercise A and elicit the rules for positioning the adjectives in *past simple* and *present perfect* sentences. You could cut up *past simple* and *present perfect* sentences which include the adjectives and ask students to put them in the correct order.

B Ask students to do the exercise as indicated in pairs. Check answers in class.

KEY

1 first became	5 has raised	9 have now reached
2 was	6 invested	10 has made
3 did not finish	7 lent	11 has she ever had
4 left	8 has needed	12 has always shown

C Ask students to do the exercise as indicated in pairs. Before allowing them to embark on the exercise, remind the 'business journalists' to show interest and respond appropriately, and the interviewees to avoid responding with simply *Yes* or *No*. During the activity, make a note, in particular, of the use of *past simple* and *present perfect* language. Provide feedback after the exercise.

Communication

To review the language which features in the Communication skills pages in Units 1–4, do the following activities:

1 Go through the language on pages 6 and 10. Then ask students to work with a partner whom they do not know very well and role-play meeting someone for the first time at a conference. They should try to use the key language to talk about themselves and find out about the other person.

2 Go through the key language on pages 14 and 18 in class. Also elicit ways in which people pay attention and show interest when listening. Ask students to work in groups of three or four. Tell them that they are going to practise checking, clarifying and confirming understanding, as well as responding and developing communication. Write the following topics on the board:

a decision

a difficulty at work / university

a meeting / presentation / conference / interview / lecture that I have attended

One person will talk about one of the topics for a maximum of two minutes and another will listen actively using the key language and will summarise/reformulate the information at the end. The other student(s) will observe and make a note of active listening skills. Roles should be rotated within the groups. Circulate during the activity and make a note of good active listening language and behaviour. Provide feedback after the exercise.

A Ask the students to do the exercise as indicated in the Coursebook in pairs. Check answers in class.

KEY			
1 i	4 k	7 f	10 j
2 c	5 h	8 a	11 b
3 e	6 l	9 g	12 d

Extension activity. Put all of the phrases in A onto strips of paper. Divide the class into four groups and allow each group to pick three strips (without seeing them). The groups then have ten minutes to write a dialogue that includes all three phrases. As the phrases don't logically relate to one another, the dialogues could be quite amusing. After writing, get two students from each group to perform their dialogue. This activity works well with creative groups.

B Ask the students to do the exercise in pairs. Check answers in class, then elicit and drill the intonation patterns of the various questions and interjections in the dialogue. Ask students to act it out using the correct intonation in pairs.

KEY	
1 born	5 sounds
2 brought up	6 tell
3 worked	7 move
4 based	8 mean

C This could be approached in different ways. Do the exercise as indicated in the Coursebook. Alternatively, students could write their notes in the form of a CV. First, elicit the components of a CV and put them on the board. Step 2 is then acted out as a job interview. You may need to review typical interview questions beforehand.

Ask students to imagine that they are a famous person. They can invent a personality, such as a sportstar, an entrepreneur, or a politician. In step 1, they will write information about their invented selves. In step 2, the personality is interviewed by a journalist. As a follow-up activity, reports of the interview could be written, highlighting the main points of the interview. Generally, the success of this activity depends on an imaginative and motivated class.

Whichever way you decide to set up the activity, set a strict time limit for each stage and provide feedback on the language used to respond, show interest, check information and ask questions.

Innovation

MODULE OVERVIEW

AIMS AND OBJECTIVES

Module 2 deals with the area of innovation, exploring the personal qualities essential to entrepreneurship, the business impact of creativity, the process of starting up new business ventures and getting new inventions recognised, financially backed and into mass production. The grammar and functions reflect elements of these themes. The Communication sections focus on building business relationships, developing meetings and communication skills. The Business across Cultures section develops students' awareness of cultural differences, started in the first module, looking at differing attitudes to public and private space, organisational culture, time, and finally, innovation. At the end of this module, students should be able to:

- use adjective and noun forms to describe the personal characteristics of entrepreneurs
- make predictions about the future using several future forms
- describe future plans and intentions
- make promises
- use passives in a variety of tenses to describe procedures and processes
- be comfortable interlinking both past simple and past perfect tenses to explain past events
- make social small talk, particularly for business socialising
- lead and participate in different types of meetings effectively
- have a greater awareness of and be able to discuss and describe differences in cultural attitudes which affect social interactions in the global business environment, both in and out of work
- have an understanding of some basic cross-cultural differences in attitudes to organisational hierarchy and the concept of time
- be able to make, discuss and judge a competent business capital seeking pitch
- write an email of rejection

THEMATIC OVERVIEW

In an increasingly technological and competitive age, innovation is vital. Companies need to maintain a competitive edge. At the same time, industry is all too often dominated by global giants, whose complex management structures stifle creativity and innovation. Some of the best ideas are the simplest. What does it take to be an entrepreneur or inventor of a revolutionary new product or service? How do you get your idea off the ground? How do you persuade potential backers to finance your idea? Will your innovation shape the future in ways even you had never imagined?

MAIN AUDIO CONTENTS

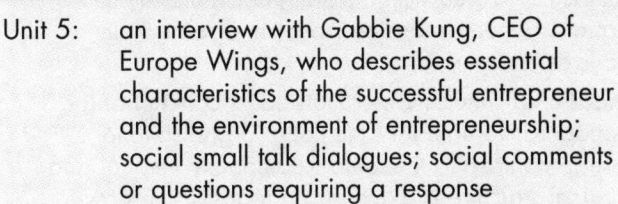

Unit 5: an interview with Gabbie Kung, CEO of Europe Wings, who describes essential characteristics of the successful entrepreneur and the environment of entrepreneurship; social small talk dialogues; social comments or questions requiring a response

Unit 6: an interview with Jackie Lang on the subject of unforeseen impacts of creativity, such as the simple idea of containerisation; social English comments requiring an appropriate response; extracts describing company structure and management style

Unit 7: a discussion between a new business advisor and a customer; vocabulary for meetings in short dialogues

Unit 8: an interview with an inventor describing the process of getting your inventions onto the market; short opening meetings, extracts – managing the process; an extract from a brainstorming meeting – exchanging ideas and opinions

PHOTOCOPIABLE RESOURCES (PAGES 113-116)
2.1 can be used any time after Unit 7.
2.2 can be used any time after Unit 8.

BUSINESS AND CULTURAL NOTES

Communication notes. The communication skills in this section tie in with the Business across Cultures section for this unit as well as that of Unit 11. Students explore their assumptions about which topics of conversation they consider to be suitable, particularly for business relationship building. In a given culture certain facial expressions and gestures, may aid this process, along with specific intonation patterns. The examples in this unit, of rising and falling tones to indicate mood are specifically Anglo-Saxon in order to reflect the culture of the language being practised. In Units 7–8, supporting tips for leading and participating in meetings are given. The focus is on the '3 Ps' (purpose, process, and people). Notes on the concepts of individualist and collectivist cultures, and their impact on the degree of employee participation expected or desired in meetings, particularly in brainstorming activities, are given.

Peach versus coconut. Students develop a deeper understanding of differences in acceptability of certain topics of conversation between cultures, and it's

Innovation

potentially positive or negative impact on business relationship building, particularly with business partners from other cultures. Notes are given on the peach and coconut concept, the degree to which different cultures reveal their private self. The open peach-like culture of the USA is contrasted with the more coconut-like culture of Germany, where in business people discuss their private lives less at work.

Organisational culture. Geert Hofstede's concept of the more cooperative nature of the flatter organisational structure in contrast to the more traditionally vertical and hierarchical structure is explored, in terms of the power distance between people in those organisations and the effect that has on communication.

Time. The subject of differing attitudes to time are explored through the concept of polychronic and monochronic cultures. Issues such as time keeping, punctuality and a structured approach to task performance can vary greatly from culture to culture and cause confusion and misunderstanding in multinational companies.

Innovation. In the same way that organisational power distances can vary greatly from culture to culture, as explored in Unit 6, in this unit students explore how freely organisations allow their employees to innovate, relating to the degree to which they are willing to accept a level of uncertainty.

INNOVATION **UNIT 5**

5 Entrepreneurs

PREVIEW

Reading and speaking
This article introduces the vocabulary used to talk about entrepreneurs and the qualities needed to set up and run successful business ventures.

Vocabulary and listening
word formation
This unit concentrates on adjectives used to describe entrepreneurs, and the nouns derived from them. It is useful to explore patterns in the adjective/noun shift as this can present difficulties for students.

Communication
socialising 1: small talk
This unit focuses on developing small talk in social situations, to help build business relationships.

Business across Cultures
public and private space
Cultural differences in building relationships and discussing one's private life with colleagues are explored through the peach/coconut concept. It is useful for students to develop an awareness of how this can have a positive or negative impact on building professional relationships in an international environment.

Introductory activity
Ask students to turn to pages 26 and 27 of their Coursebooks. Direct students' attention to the definition of an entrepreneur at the top of the page.

Ask students to brainstorm the names of successful entrepreneurs, along with the type of product/service/brand they became famous for. Alternatively, you could use magazine photos of well-known entrepreneurs as prompts.

Start-up
In subgroups, ask students to consider which personal qualities the entrepreneurs listed must have, in order to have become successful. You probably won't need to spend too long on this. Write them up on the board. Instruct the groups to briefly discuss and present their answer to question 2.

Reading and speaking

A Ask one or two students to read the text to the class. By the end, students will probably have solved one or two of their vocabulary difficulties through context but you might allow them time to read the text again, checking vocabulary. Other students could be asked to provide vocabulary definitions wherever possible. Alternatively, put the following words up on the board while they are reading and elicit explanations from the class:

conveyor belt   PVC   chain   branch   majority stake
proceeds   basement   mood lighting   affordable
creed   preaching

B Ask students to answer the questions individually, and then do a class answer check. You might ask the class supplementary questions such as: *Would you be happy to stay in one of these small underground hotel rooms in the future? Do they represent value for money? Do you think this hotel concept will be as successful as that of Yo! Sushi?* Encourage them to give detailed explanations. Depending on your class, this might develop into a class discussion about the hotel industry.

KEY

1 He worked as a record producer with rock bands, in theatre stage design and in TV programme distribution.
2 He set up Yo! Sushi in 1997.
3 Selling sushi on conveyor belts like restaurants in Japan and staffing the café with girls in short PVC skirts. He introduced the conveyor belts.
4 There were 13 restaurants and three bars in Britain and a branch in Dubai.
5 He sold his stake for £10 million.
6 It means idea.
7 From flying first class on British Airways – he saw the way comfort can be created in a very small space.
8 They are small but the space is well used. They have mood lighting and wi-fi facilities.
9 Professionals who want to work, play and then sleep in luxury that is affordable.
10 Students' own answers.

Vocabulary and listening

A Ask students to match adjectives to their meanings in pairs. Group check the answers. Get each pair to decide and tell the class which single characteristic they consider to be the most important for entrepreneurship and why.

KEY

1 d   2 f   3 i   4 h   5 c   6 g   7 a   8 e   9 b

B Get pairs to re-read the text and decide which characteristics from the list in A they would use to describe Simon Woodroffe and why. Do a class check.

KEY

Possible answer: innovative, bold, self-confident

37

INNOVATION UNIT 5

C AUDIO 5.1 To introduce the topic of the next listening activity, ask the class to brainstorm names of any young and innovative airline companies they know or have used. Put the names on the board. You could elicit supplementary information such as: *Who owns them? What nationality are they? What is different about them? Which routes do they fly?*

Explain that students are going to listen to a text about the founder and CEO of an airline called 'Europe Wings'. Ask students to listen to the audio text for general understanding and specifically for any adjectives from A, which Gabbie Kung mentions as characteristics of entrepreneurs. Play AUDIO 5.1.

Check questions 2–4 for understanding, and then ask students to answer them individually during a second listening. Do a class answer check. Write up adjectives from answers 1 and 2 on the board.

KEY

1 self-confident, persistent, innovative

2 over-cautious, unrealistic, inflexible

3 She gives three reasons: the product or service may not offer anything new; people may not want it or need it; the general economic situation may not be right.

4 Because individuals have much more freedom to act. They do not have to wait for people on committees to make a decision.

AUDIO SCRIPT

Interviewer: Gabbie, you founded one of the most successful airlines on the continent. What, in your opinion, makes a good entrepreneur?

Gabbie Kung: Well, entrepreneurs have to be excellent communicators. You need to persuade investors to invest in your idea. Then, when you start your business you have to communicate your vision to the people who work for you. And then, of course, you have to communicate your product or service to potential customers.

Interviewer: What other characteristics do successful entrepreneurs need?

Gabbie Kung: Entrepreneurs have to be self-confident individuals. They have to have confidence in themselves and their idea. They also have to be persistent as they'll need to overcome all sorts of obstacles to achieve success.

Interviewer: And what about vision, which you mentioned earlier?

Gabbie Kung: Yes, it's vital to be innovative and creative. You need to offer something new, something that isn't already on the market. You need to be able to grasp ideas and opportunities that other people may miss.

Interviewer: Why do you think so many entrepreneurs fail?

Gabbie Kung: There are all sorts of reasons. If we look at personal characteristics, some entrepreneurs are over-cautious – they just aren't prepared to take risks. Or they're unrealistic – their goals and plans for the business and themselves just won't work in practice. Or they might be inflexible – sometimes you have to be prepared to change your plans and strategies to make sure the business succeeds.

Interviewer: And what about the businesses themselves – why do so many new businesses fail?

Gabbie Kung: There are all sorts of reasons: perhaps the product or service doesn't really offer anything new, or people don't need or want it, or the general economic situation may not be right.

Interviewer: And why do you think a lot of successful business ideas start with individual entrepreneurs, and not in large companies?

Gabbie Kung: Well, many large companies are very bureaucratic, and new ideas have to go through lots of committees before a decision is taken. There may even be active resistance to doing something new and unfamiliar. Individual entrepreneurs have a lot more freedom to act.

D Go through the example sentences with the class then ask students to do this exercise individually. Check in class. Ask students to spell out the nouns and write them up on the board. Depending on the needs of your class you could get students to identify any patterns they notice between noun and adjective endings.

KEY

Adjective	Noun
independent	independence
innovative	innovation
self-confident	self-confidence
inquisitive	inquisitiveness
persistent	persistence
bold	boldness
reliable	reliability
strong	strength
competitive	competitiveness

E Get students to complete this gap fill exercise individually, recycling adjectives from D. Ask students to read out their sentences in class.

KEY

1 inquisitive   2 independent   3 innovation
4 persistent   5 reliability

Extension activities. Distribute job advertisements from the national press, business magazines, or the Internet, containing desired personal characteristics for job applicants. Similarly, small articles about entrepreneurs and business people could be used. Get students in subgroups to read out the ads and articles to each other. They should then collate a list of personal characteristic adjectives and nouns and write definitions for them, with the help of a dictionary. Circulate, providing help where needed. Groups take it in turns to put their target language on the board and read out their definitions to the other groups who have to guess which word each definition relates to.

Word stress exercise. Distribute a table of all the adjectives (in one column) and nouns (in a second column) from exercise D and the previous extension activity. Mark the primary stress in the first word as an example. Ask students to follow suit with the others. Do a class activity. Go round the class, getting students to pronounce a few words, one after the other. Try to get them to remember and explain common word stress patterns.

INNOVATION **UNIT 5**

▶ REVIEW AND DEVELOPMENT PAGE 44 AND 45, EXERCISES A–C CAN BE DONE AT THIS STAGE.

Communication

Socialising 1: Small talk

Getting to know someone depends on finding topics of common interest to talk about. This section focuses on developing students' socialising skills. The Communication notes for this section can be reviewed on page 151 of the Coursebook.

Direct students to the photo at the top of page 28. Ask: *What kind of social event is this? Is it purely social?* Ask the class whether they have to socialise for business. If they do, you might ask questions such as: *How formal are these social events? Where do they take place? Who do you socialise with? What is the dress code?*

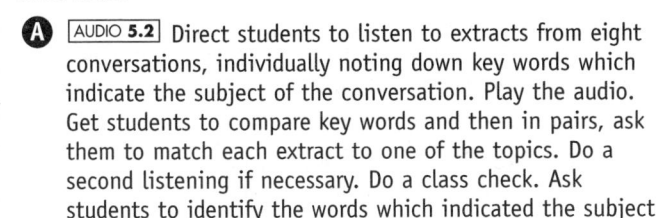

A AUDIO 5.2 Direct students to listen to extracts from eight conversations, individually noting down key words which indicate the subject of the conversation. Play the audio. Get students to compare key words and then in pairs, ask them to match each extract to one of the topics. Do a second listening if necessary. Do a class check. Ask students to identify the words which indicated the subject of each conversation.

KEY

1 c   2 e   3 f   4 b   5 h   6 d   7 g   8 a

AUDIO SCRIPT

1 A: We moved recently. We used to live in a small flat in London. Now we have a big house in the country.
   B: That's quite a change. Do you like the country?
   A: Yes, I do. We have so much space and it's really quiet. I love it.

2 A: Have you seen the latest Spielberg film?
   B: No, I haven't. Is it any good?
   A: It's had good reviews. We were thinking of going to see it this evening.
   B: I'm not keen on action films. I prefer a good horror film.

3 A: How's the business going?
   B: Very tough, at the moment. Sales are pretty flat.
   A: Same for us. There's not much growth and it looks like higher taxes again next year.
   B: I can't believe it. I thought this government was meant to be pro-business.

4 A: How's the family?
   B: Fine, thanks. Our daughter has just started at university. She's having a great time. How are things with you?
   A: Well, did you know that Jane and I separated a few months ago? I'm living in a flat on my own.

5 A: We went on a cruise for the first time this year.
   B: Wasn't it boring? Being on a ship all the time?
   A: No, there was plenty to do. And we stopped at a number of different places.

6 A: Did you see the match yesterday?
   B: No, I didn't. What was the score?
   A: Four three. It was a great match. City scored first and …

7 A: I really must give up. For one thing, it's costing me a fortune.
   B: You should. You'd feel much better.
   A: I know, but I'm worried that I'd just put on weight.
   B: I don't think you will. I didn't.

8 A: Have you always worked in the public sector?
   B: No, I used to work for an IT company. They made me redundant two years ago. It took me nearly a year to find this job.
   A: Yeah, it's not easy these days. How is the new job?
   B: It's OK, but sometimes I get a bit bored.

B Get pairs to brainstorm several other topics they might discuss in a social situation, and do a round the class check on topics. You might allow comment from students about the suitability of suggested subjects. Are there any subjects they should be careful not to talk about?

Extension activity. Replay the first dialogue, sentence by sentence, so that the class can write it down. Ask them to read it out and write it up on the board. Replay it once more and ask students to notice and mark the words which are stressed, (you can mention that volume and tone rise a little where there is stress). They can listen for falling and rising tones, marking the words in the dialogue. Do a check and mark them on the dialogue on the board. Ask them to suggest why tones go up and down in these places.

Replay some or all of the other dialogues, depending on your class, and get students to copy them down. Check for vocabulary and understanding. Get pairs to role-play the dialogues in front of the class, aiming for as authentic a rhythm as possible. Playing each dialogue on cassette just before it is performed can help weaker students. Record students and play the class set of dialogues back to them so they can hear their progress.

Get pairs to write their own short social dialogues. They can act them out to the class, following help and correction. Make a class audio or video recording and get the class to listen and write down other pairs' dialogues.

With a strong class, ask the class which topics of conversation were most difficult to identify. In which exchanges was the exact subject not actually mentioned? Highlight dialogue number 7. Ask students to identify which phrases made them decide that this dialogue was about smoking – unless they just got there by a process of elimination of course. The word 'smoking' is not actually mentioned. Explain that this is typical of many social interactions. In many exchanges, some prior knowledge of the subject is shared by the speakers, or the body language (such as lighting up a cigarette) indicates the subject and is therefore not necessarily referred to. Equally, dialogue number 6 does not actually mention the word 'football'. You would have to know that 'match' refers to a football match and that 'City' is part of the name of a football club, which both speakers know. In the same way, short social exchanges often involve a lot of incomplete sentences e.g. *You should* rather than *You should give up smoking*. This can make the conversation move on much more quickly and make the subject less easy to follow for the learner of English who spends much of their time trying to form grammatically complete sentences.

C Split the class into four groups and give each group one of the boxes to complete. When they have finished ask them

39

INNOVATION UNIT 5

to compare and revise their answers with the rest of their group. Then get students to pair up with a person from one of the other three groups to dictate their completed text to and then, in turn, to listen to and fill in that of their partner. When all the boxes have been completed, get individuals to read out each text and do a class check for vocabulary and pronunciation.

KEY

1 applied	8 work	15 move
2 joined	9 divorced	16 commute
3 redundant	10 partner	17 fit
4 look	11 see	18 shape
5 promoted	12 share	19 lose
6 married	13 buy	20 diet
7 had	14 build	21 exercise

D Ask your students to talk to someone they didn't talk to during the last activity, or perhaps don't know well, about a couple of the topics. Set a short time limit.

Extension activity. After pairs have talked about a couple of the topics for a few minutes, get them to change partners, to explain what their previous partners told them about themselves, and to find out what their current partner learned from their previous partner. Depending on the size of the class, this activity can be repeated several times. Students move on to a new partner, passing on any information they found out about their previous partner so that the conversations change each time. At the end of the exercise it can be fun to ask each student to relate to the class the last piece of information they heard. Ask the student concerned to confirm if their information is accurate. If students know each other well, they can assume a fictitious persona for this exercise to add an element of fun.

Business across Cultures
Public and private space

This section explores how relationships both at and out of work are built in different cultures. The *peach / coconut* concept is introduced. Suitable small talk subject matter may vary greatly from culture to culture and can have a very positive or negative effect on relationship building. With a mixed nationality/culture class there is obvious material for valuable information exchange and learning about different cultural values. However, many students will have travelled abroad so even a mono-cultural class will be able to supply interesting ideas.

▶ BUSINESS AND CULTURAL NOTES FOR THIS SECTION CAN BE REVIEWED ON PAGE 153 OF THE COURSEBOOK.

Ask the class whether they have travelled, either for business or pleasure. Ask them to talk about where they have been and what differences they noticed in terms of behaviour and customs, particularly in a social context. You could elicit any conversational taboos, or subjects which certain nationalities discuss more than others.

A AUDIO 5.3 Tell students they are going to listen to a few social remarks or questions. Instruct them to match each remark to its purpose. Give them time to read the purposes (a–f) they are about to hear. Play the audio.

KEY
1 c   2 e   3 f   4 b   5 d   6 a

AUDIO SCRIPT

1 I thought the meeting was a waste of time. What did you think?
2 You look really tired.
3 You've got some time. Join me for a drink.
4 You didn't mention it, but are you married?
5 I thought you were very good in that meeting – very well prepared and clear.
6 I'd like to invite you home. You could meet my wife and family.

B Ask students to listen again. Ask them to mention which remarks they would not expect to hear in their country or might make them feel uncomfortable, especially if socialising in a business environment.

C Ask the class to look at the photo of the peach and the coconut. Elicit peach and coconut. Ask: *How would you describe these fruit in appearance? What adjectives would you use?* Direct them to match the photos of the people in social situations with the peach and coconut. Ask them to explain what the body language in the photos says about the people's attitude to protecting or revealing their private lives. Note any interesting ideas on the board. Instruct them to read the text and do a class check for understanding.

D It might be useful to explain at this point that when dealing with different cultures it is interesting to observe differences in social attitudes but equally important to be as non-judgemental as possible. Peaches and coconuts can be equally good. Instruct students to interview each other about their approach to relationship building, using the questions provided. They can then report back to the group on their partner's self-analysis. Individuals could then decide whether they are more *peach* or *coconut* in their relationship building style. The class can report back on any differences in attitudes they have discovered within the group. This activity will need sensitive handling!

E Explain that students are going to brief a foreign work colleague on living and working in their country. Set them a short time limit to individually note down ideas under the headings given in the Coursebook. Then, divide the class into small groups so they can pool their ideas on how best to advise a visitor to their country on building successful relationships. After that, get each student to find someone from another group to advise. With multi-cultural classes, the idea pooling groups can be made up of students with similar or the same cultures. If there are many students from different cultures in the class, it would probably be better not to do any group pooling. Just go straight into the advising activity, pairing up people from different cultures.

Ask individual students to present the country and culture they were advised about to the class.

Checklist

As a review activity, ask students to go over the checklist at the end of the unit and go over each item with them. As a quick vocabulary review and discussion of entrepreneurship, you could ask them questions like: *What qualities does a successful entrepreneur need? How would you describe Simon Woodroffe? Why do some businesses fail? Why do a lot of the best business ideas come from entrepreneurs instead of large organisations?*

Extension activity. Draw a spidergram with the central word 'Entrepreneurship' on the board. Around it, write up verbs from the reading and listening texts. Divide the class into two. Direct one half to brainstorm verb phrases relating to entrepreneurship using the reading texts and the other half to do the same with the listening text. Then ask them to exchange their language chunks in pairs to complete their spidergram. For example:

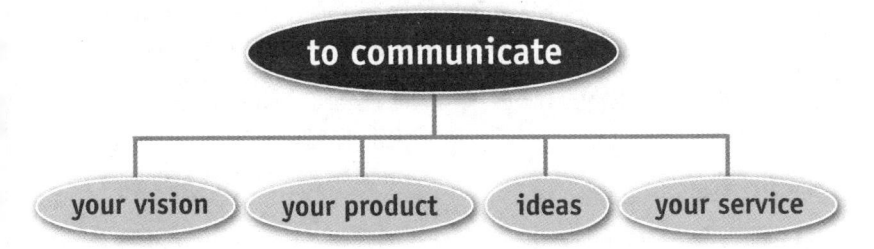

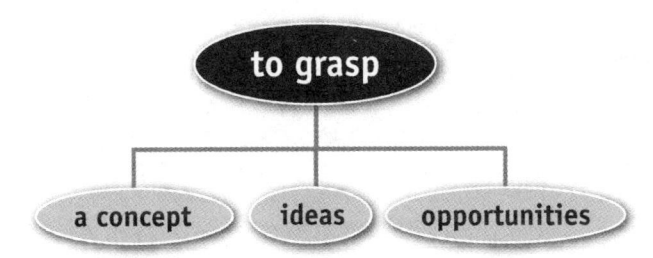

to communicate
- your vision
- your product
- ideas
- your service

to grasp
- a concept
- ideas
- opportunities

INNOVATION **UNIT 6**

6 Creativity

PREVIEW

Listening and speaking
This unit deals with vocabulary used in the areas of creativity, innovation and the foreseen and unforeseen consequences of innovation.

Grammar
the future
This unit tackles using *going to* and *will* in order to talk about the future in a variety of ways. Some difficulties can arise for students in the case of making predictions and talking about future certainties: the two forms are interchangeable, but when the future reference is based on concrete plans or decisions, only *going to* may be used. Many students erroneously try to use *will* here. The use of *will* to make requests, promises and to offer help is also introduced, so that by the end of the exercise, students should have a fairly comprehensive picture of the usage of these two forms. The use of *won't* instead of *will not* is also emphasised.

Communication
socialising 2: positive responses
The use of positive responses in social interaction is introduced.

Business across Cultures
the culture of organisations
Cultural differences in attitudes to *power distance* in organisations are explored through the concept *of high power distance* and *low power distance* cultures.

Start-up

A Write the word *Creativity* on the board. Ask subgroups to come up with a short definition of creativity and to present it to the class. Ask subgroups to brainstorm and present two or three areas of life which demand high levels of creativity. Get each group to very briefly explain their choices. Answers might include: car design, fashion design, architecture, interior design, art, sculpture, composing music, filmmaking, novel writing, etc.

Note any interesting lexical items on the board. Instruct students to turn to pages 30-31 of their Coursebooks. Direct students to the statement about creativity at the top of the page. Ask for opinions about this statement. Encourage students to give examples to justify their answers.

B Direct students' attention to the five company departments and ask subgroups to rank them in order of creative need. Ask students to give reasons for their choice. You might encourage students to personalise this by giving examples from their own industry where appropriate. This could lead to a class discussion on creativity in industry.

Listening and speaking

A AUDIO 6.1 Ask students to listen to the audio text for general understanding and for examples of creativity. At this point check any vocabulary difficulties. Get them to listen a second time and to answer questions 2–9. Do an answer check.

Refer back to answer 8. Ask students what everybody failed to do when containers were invented. Elicit the idea that they failed to predict the impact of containerisation on world trade. Ask students to note the *going to* form used to make predictions.

KEY

1 The Apple personal computer, the Internet, the cell phone.
2 Malcolm McLean.
3 In 1956.
4 They weren't mixed with other cargo, and they were of a standard size so they could be handled easily.
5 Five container ships would be enough for all the trade between Britain and the United States.
6 No.
7 Containers made it cheap enough to trade goods that weren't traded before.
8 Containers are going to change the world.
9 It's difficult to foresee how things are going to develop.

AUDIO SCRIPT

Interviewer: ... As we were saying earlier, creativity is very highly valued in business. Could you give us some examples?

Jackie Lang: When you think of creativity in business, you tend to think of brilliant new innovations like the Apple personal computer, the Internet or the cell phone.

Interviewer: Aha.

Jackie Lang: But creativity can come in much simpler forms, such as a metal box.

Interviewer: A metal box? How do you mean?

Jackie Lang: I'm thinking of the shipping container.

Interviewer: Oh ...

Jackie Lang: In 1956, Malcolm McLean, the boss of an American road transport company had the idea of putting goods into metal containers that could be transported by ship and offloaded onto trucks or railway wagons.

42

Interviewer: It's odd that no one had thought of containers before.

Jackie Lang: Well, they had, but the boxes were mixed with other cargo, and they weren't of a standard size so they couldn't be handled easily.

Interviewer: Right ...

Jackie Lang: No one realised how containers would change patterns of trade around the world. In 1968, there were consultants who confidently said: 'Five container ships will be enough for all the trade between Britain and the United States.'

Interviewer: That's incredible!

Jackie Lang: No one foresaw the expansion of trade that took place because containers made it cheap enough to trade goods that weren't traded before.

Interviewer: Right. So no one in the 1950s said 'Containers are going to change the world'?

Jackie Lang: Exactly. Creativity produces new products and services, but you can't always be sure of the impact.

B As a follow-up to this activity and in order to introduce the language used for describing consequences, ask one of the class to read out the example describing one of the affects supermarkets have had. Ask the class to think of further consequences supermarkets have had and to decide whether they were foreseen or unforeseen. Divide the class into four groups and ask each group to brainstorm and present a list of foreseen and unforeseen consequences of one of the innovations listed. Write up their sentences on the board and underline different ways to express cause and effect pointing out the need to pay particular attention to their position in the sentence: due to, because of, leading to, as a result, because, consequently, etc.

Grammar
The future

Instruct students to read the grammar section, presented on page 31. Get one of the students to read it out loud. The use of the future is often a source of confusion to students and teachers alike! In some cases, more than one form of the future can be used to express the same idea (e.g. *going to* and *will* for prediction). In other cases, the same form can be used to express different ideas (*will* for promises / requests / offers). Difficulties in expressing the future vary, often according to the mother tongue of the learner. A common problem, however, is the use of *will* instead of *going to* for making decisions or plans in the future. Another problem is the use of the full form of *will* in the negative, when only the contracted form sounds natural.

A Ask students, in pairs, to use the prompts to do the exercise as in the Coursebook. As a follow-up ask each pair to make their own positive and negative prediction for the year 2050, one using *will / shall*, the other using *going to*. Do a round the class check to make sure that the target language and negative contractions are being used correctly.

KEY

2 We are going to have the most successful product on the market. / We aren't going to have the most successful product on the market.
We will have the most successful product on the market. / We won't have the most successful product on the market.

3 Scientists are going to find new sources of energy. / Scientists aren't going to find new sources of energy.
Scientists will find new sources of energy. / Scientists won't find new sources of energy.

4 People are going to live to be 100. / People aren't going to live to be 100.
People will live to be 100. / People won't live to be 100.

5 Company employees are going to have more leisure time. / Company employees aren't going to have more leisure time.
Company employees will have more leisure time. / Company employees won't have more leisure time.

B Ask a student to read out the grammar section for making decisions, plans and setting intentions along with the examples. Get one pair to read out the first example sentence and the decision sentence using the target language *going to*. Instruct pairs to work on the exercise together and then do a class check.

KEY

2 He's going to do a lot of research.
3 CS employees are going to sign a confidentiality agreement.
4 They are going to work directly for CS.
5 CS are going to pay a big penalty if they don't reach the targets.

Extension activity. As a follow-up you might like to ask students to follow the model to write about a personal goal. Encourage them to make negative ones if they wish.

MODEL ANSWERS

I'm going to lose 10 kilos by next January.
I won't spend so much money on shoes / my car.

Instruct the class to mingle briefly until everybody has imparted their resolution to everyone else. Then set a subgroup competition to see which group can compile a complete and correct list of each student's resolutions, which they should read out to the class. Get class mates to say whether they remembered correctly or not. Do a last language review if necessary.

C Now explain that *will* can also be used in a rather more spontaneous way, to make requests and promises and to offer help. Ask a student to read out the examples with other uses of *will*. Ask pairs to come up with answers for C and do a round the class check.

MODEL ANSWERS

1 I'll see if I can find it on the computer system.
2 I'll just see if he's in his office.
3 I'll ask his manager to give him a formal warning.
4 I'll check the situation and phone you back.

Go round the class, collecting students' answers. Accept any answers which work and write them up on the board. Remind students to use the contracted form of *will*. Elicit that these are promises or offers of help.

Extension activity. Refer back to the example of a request in B on page 31. Give each student a statement or request card to read out. Going round the class, students read out their statement or request, to another student in the class. When a statement or request is put to them, students will have to give short negative or affirmative answers, or offer help.

INNOVATION UNIT 6

Do a couple of examples on the board as a reminder, eliciting a variety of appropriate responses.

Will you fix the photocopier for me?	Yes, sure. I'll do it in a moment.
I'm cold.	I'll close the window for you.
Will you make me a cup of coffee?	No, I won't. I'm very busy!

It might be useful at this point to explore the difference between abrupt and polite refusals!

▶ GRAMMAR REVIEW AND DEVELOPMENT ON PAGE 45 OF THE COURSEBOOK, CAN BE DONE AT THIS STAGE.

Communication

Socialising 2: Positive responses

We express our feelings partly through our body language (smiles, gestures and eye contact) and partly through the language we use. This section focuses on developing language to express positive responses.

▶ REVIEW THE COMMUNICATION NOTES FOR THIS SECTION ON PAGE 151 OF THE COURSEBOOK.

A Ask the class to open their Coursebooks at page 32 and go straight into this activity in pairs, one student doing the question/statement part, the other responding positively. Ask the questioners to listen to and watch their partners carefully when they are responding. Circulate, listening for good intonation patterns. When students have completed this exercise, you might choose a pair who used the most convincing and appropriate intonation patterns, to perform the exercise in front of the group. Audio recording students for review could be a useful aid. Ask the rest of the class to observe what happens to the performers' tone of voice. Write one or two of the exchanges up on the board and elicit rising and falling arrows. If you feel it would be beneficial, students could mark up all of the exchanges and practise the exercise again.

B AUDIO 6.2 Instruct the class to listen to this series of comments or questions to which they have to choose an appropriate response from the Key language box in A. Play the audio once straight through, for students to choose responses. Play it again, stopping after each sentence to invite a response from students.

AUDIO SCRIPT

1 I'd like you to have this small gift.
2 Could you send me the file when you get back?
3 I'm sorry, but I've lost the report.
4 Bye for now. Have a great weekend.
5 I hope we can work together again in the future.
6 Would you like to join us later for dinner?
7 My flight leaves at four o'clock. May I leave early?
8 Thanks for your support.
9 Why don't we take a taxi?
10 I saw King Kong on TV last night. I thought it was fantastic!

C Instruct students to practise this exercise in pairs. Ask students A to use the prompts on page 32 to make questions/statements to which students B should respond, choosing the appropriate positive responses from the Key language box. Afterwards, B should use the prompts on page 104 of the Coursebook. Circulate, and choose one or two confident pairs to perform their exchanges to the class. Audio recording them so that you can do a class review of appropriate intonation patterns to practise rising intonation patterns for questions and to show enthusiasm, afterwards, could provide a useful extension activity.

D Divide the class into small groups and name them Groups 1 and Groups 2. Tell the class that Groups 1 are going to prepare a short farewell speech for a departing colleague, using the notes on page 32. Groups 2 need to use those on page 104 to prepare their departing speech as they leave for a new job. Groups might divide up the writing of the speech or write the whole speech together, but they should each deliver the speech, which should be audio, or preferably, video recorded for fun, review and analysis. Either way, a pronunciation and delivery review could be useful. Inform students that they will be observed for the following items during their speeches; right speed, effective pausing, contractions, pronunciation, and any other considerations you deem to be important for your class.

▶ COMMUNICATION NOTES FOR THIS SECTION CAN BE REVIEWED ON PAGE 151 OF THE COURSEBOOK.

▶ COMMUNICATION REVIEW AND DEVELOPMENT ON PAGE 47 OF THE COURSEBOOK, CAN BE DONE AT THIS STAGE.

Business across Cultures

The culture of organisations

The attitudes towards power – who has it and how they deal with it – vary from company to company. This section focuses on how company cultures deal with power via the concept of **high power distance** and **low power distance** cultures. With the whole class review the culture notes for this section on page 154 of the Coursebook.

Direct students to open their Coursebooks at page 33 and to look at the picture. Elicit the word *organingram* and what organigrams represent. Ask students to consider where on the organigram scale they would place their organisation, (work place or college). Are there lots of layers or is the management structure relatively flat?

A AUDIO 6.3 Go into exercise A as instructed in the Coursebook. After the first listening get pairs to do a quick check together, before a final listening and class check. Other interesting items of vocabulary to point out and check might be the modifiers *pretty* and *fairly*. Ask students to identify which of the four companies is most like their own organisation in terms of size and management structure.

KEY

From left to right: The Metal Cooperative, Thorntons, TLC Ltd, National Health Service

AUDIO SCRIPT

1 I work for the National Health Service. It's a huge, bureaucratic organisation with a lot of management layers. The problem is that the top management are a long way from the reality of nurses and doctors working in hospitals.

2 I work for a small family company called Thorntons. There are only three layers in the company. We all know the boss, that's Mrs Thornton. She took over from her father a couple of years ago. Then there are the supervisors, who report to Mrs Thornton, and then the workers. It works pretty well. We don't need middle managers, really.

3 I work for a medium-sized company. It's called TLC Ltd. We don't have so many layers but we are still fairly structured. The managers have their own offices and they keep their distance. I guess there are around four layers but there are fairly big differences between the layers.

4 We set up our company nearly ten years ago – it's called 'The Metal Cooperative'. It's totally flat. Everybody is an owner. It's a registered limited company but all the members of the cooperative have the same number of shares, so we share the profits equally.

B This activity can be done individually or in pairs. Dictionaries should be used. Draw a table on the board and do a class check.

left: *flat, lean, transparent, network, bottom-up, climb the ladder, top-down*

right: *hierarchical, many-layered, bureaucratic, top-heavy, slow, complex*

If students already have experience of customer, supplier, or partner organisations, you could ask them to use these words and phrases to talk about organisations they know, in order to check their understanding of the vocabulary. Words such as *hierarchical* and *bureaucratic* will give many students pronunciation difficulties. Depending on the class, you might find that encouraging students to learn and make use of dictionary phonemic transcriptions helps their pronunciation and intonation patterns.

Word stress extension activity. Make some cards with business vocabulary containing similar stress patterns and suffixes to *hierarchical* and *bureaucratic*. Distribute a set to each subgroup. Ask each student to take a card and go round the group pronouncing their words, one after the other, before passing their card on to the person on their left. They can repeat the process until they are all proficient. This can be done with any set of difficult words. Examples:

hierarchical – economical – logistical

bureaucratic – diplomatic – problematic – pragmatic

C Having learned the vocabulary in exercise B, ask the class to read the text. Put the words: *gaps, place, communication, motivation, language* and *relationships*, on the board as prompts and then ask students to use these to explain the differences between *high* and *low power distance* cultures to the class. If they need further prompting, you might ask specific questions such as: *Which way do the channels of communication flow?*

D Divide students into subgroups. Ask each group to brainstorm a list of advantages/disadvantages of either flat or hierarchical organisations. Students with work experience might refer to the types of organisation they are most familiar with. A spokesperson should be chosen from each group to present the group's list to the class.

Checklist

As a review, ask students to refer to the checklist at the end of the unit and go over the items with them.

Extension activities. Ask each student to think of an important invention or system which has had an impact on their lives, their business, or the world. They should briefly explain who invented it and what impact it has had on modern life. In mixed nationality classes, students could be encouraged to choose something relating specifically to their own country.

This activity could take some time and generate a lot of interesting language which can be put on the board around the word *creativity*.

Review positive responses, which are often confusing as they are very culturally bound, and generally have to be learned as discrete blocks. Students could come up with a list of responses to the presented comments/requests, translated directly from their own language so that they become more aware of the differences between standard social responses in English and in their mother tongue and the confusion that simply translating out of their own tongue can cause. In a multi-cultural group this would also provide interesting insights into the differences in modes of expression between different cultures – which could be explored in terms of their differing use in English.

For further information on the culture of organisations, refer students to the website mentioned in the end matter for this section.

INNOVATION UNIT 7

7 Start-ups

PREVIEW

Listening and vocabulary	This unit deals with the vocabulary of start-ups, investment, and finance.
Grammar	**passives** The passive constructions of a variety of tenses are tackled. Generally used when the action, rather than the person performing it, is important. The use of the preposition *by* is introduced.
Communication	**running a meeting** The roles of the chairperson managing the purpose, the process, and the people in meetings, are explored.
Business across Cultures	**time** Cross cultural differences in attitudes to time are introduced, via the framework of monochronic and polychronic cultures.

Introductory activity

Write the word *start-ups* in the middle of the board. Ask the class what a start-up is. At the top left-hand side of the board, write: *What does a successful start-up need?* At the top right-hand side of the board write: *What are the dangers for start-up businesses?* Divide the class into two groups and ask each group to brainstorm answers to one of the questions. Note their ideas on the board in a class feedback, correcting and providing useful language. Give students time to write both sets of answers down. Ask them to estimate the percentage of start-ups in their country they think fail within the first three years.

Start-up

Tell students to turn to pages 34–35 of their Coursebooks. Direct students to the statistics on UK start-up failures at the top of the page.

A Ask students to read through the exercise and do a class check for vocabulary problems. Instruct pairs to discuss each point, then ask individual students to answer the questions in class, giving their reasons. Invite other students to add to their ideas or contradict them, explaining why they do so. Write up any useful language on the board around the word *start-ups*.

Listening and vocabulary

A AUDIO 7.1 Go straight into the activity as directed in the Coursebook. Inform students that they will hear the extract twice. The first listening should be for general understanding and in order to answer the first question. Ask students to make notes during the second listening. Get verbal answers to questions 2–7 and check for any vocabulary difficulties.

KEY
1 Business advisor and entrepreneur. They are talking about a business start-up.
2 A venture capitalist invests in new entrepreneurial ideas.
3 Because they hope that some will be very profitable and this will make up for the losses made on those ideas that fail.
4 A business angel invests in new businesses.

5 No, some just want to be a sleeping partner.
6 It should be brief and clear and awaken investors' interest in a couple of minutes.
7 It can be floated on the stock market.

B Play the audio excerpt again and ask students to complete the sentences.

KEY
1 The company is floated on the stock exchange in an IPO.
2 IPO stands for initial public offering.
3 Then the company is listed on the stock market.
4 Shares in the company are bought and sold by investors on the stock market.

AUDIO SCRIPT

Maya Newman: Come in, Mr Graham. Please sit down.
Jay Graham: Thank you.
Maya Newman: I've had a look at your business plan and it seems as if your idea has a lot of potential.
Jay Graham: I think so, too. I've been working on it for two years now. What I need now is some advice on where to go from here.
Maya Newman: Well, that's what I'm here for. This advisory service is intended for people just like you.
Jay Graham: That's great. Well, of course, I know I need a backer. Where should I go for financial backing?
Maya Newman: Well, you could try a venture capital company. These are organisations that invest in new entrepreneurial ideas. They know that some of the ideas they back will fail, some will do OK, and some, hopefully, will be very profitable. The profitable ones should make up for any losses on other investments.
Jay Graham: Are venture capitalists the only potential investors?

46

INNOVATION UNIT 7

Maya Newman:	*No, there are also business angels. These are individual investors, typically business people who've already made money from previous ventures and are looking for new businesses to invest in.*
Jay Graham:	*Right.*
Maya Newman:	*Some business angels may just want to be a sleeping partner – they won't want to get involved in the day-to-day running of the company. Others will want to get actively involved in your business. They will help you develop the business …*
Jay Graham:	*I see …*
Maya Newman:	*But whether you go to a venture capital firm or a business angel, a good pitch is essential.*
Jay Graham:	*A pitch?*
Maya Newman:	*Yes. You have to present your ideas to investors, and it's important to do it briefly and clearly. You should be able to awaken their interest in just a couple of minutes. If they're interested, they'll ask you to make a longer presentation.*
Jay Graham:	*So let's say I get some investment, everything goes well, and the company starts to grow. What about future expansion?*
Maya Newman:	*Hmm, if you succeed, and that's a very big 'if', you may reach a point where you need much more investment to expand. In that case, the company is floated on the stock exchange in an IPO – that's an initial public offering. Then the company is listed on the stock market. Shares in the company are bought and sold by investors on the stock market.*
Jay Graham:	*Right …*
Maya Newman:	*But that's a long way off yet! Concentrate for the moment on finding investors for your start-up!*

Extension activity. As quite a lot of new vocabulary has been introduced in this last exercise, you might like to recycle it immediately in context. Write the following words on the board and go round the class encouraging students to rebuild the main ideas of the audio excerpt, one by one.

business plan	potential backer / investor
financial backing	venture capitalist
company	new entrepreneurial ideas
loss	profit
business angels	individual investors
previous ventures	sleeping partner
day-to-day running	actively involve
develop	pitch
couple of minutes	longer presentation
investment to expand	float
stock exchange	IPO
list	stock market
shares	buy and sell

You might like to remove a few of the vocabulary items from the board and ask the class to run through the scenario once more, starting with the last student and working in the opposite direction.

Note that the audio excerpt and exercise B introduce passives. After the grammar section, this activity could be done strictly as a passives exercise.

▶ WORKBOOK START-UPS EXERCISE ON PAGE 28 CAN NOW BE DONE.

Grammar

Passives

Direct students to page 35 of their Coursebooks. Ask one student to read out the rules for forming and using passives. The class should identify the various tenses used in the example sentences. Where the form of the verb *to be* changes with the person or the plural (present and past simple tenses), it might be useful to check that students recognise the difference, such as in the case of the present simple, with one or two examples of your own.

MODEL ANSWER

Sake ---- made in Japan. I ---- overworked in Korea / Ireland, etc!

Elicit the fact that in the final example, a modal verb is used instead of *will*, to give more precise information, but the form of the sentence remains the same.

Instruct students to do exercises A, B and C individually. As several tenses are involved students may need some time. However you might find it useful to do a class check after each one, as the exercises become progressively more demanding.

A Ask students to match parts 1–5 to parts a–e to form sentences. Then, look at newly introduced vocabulary items such as *spin off*.

KEY

2 e   3 a   4 b   5 c

B Ask students to rewrite the sentences using the passive.

KEY

1 The company was founded by an entrepreneur.
2 The new product was developed by a mechanical engineer.
3 $75,000 was invested in the business by a business angel.
4 Sometime in the future, more investment will be needed by the company.
5 The company will be floated on the stock market by the founders.
6 More money could be raised on the stock market.

C Instruct students to complete the sentences by putting the verbs in brackets into the correct form. Do a class check. Highlight the use of modal verbs, other than *will*, in these sentences. Afterwards ask students to describe which function each modal verb serves in its corresponding sentence.

KEY

2 Large amounts of money could be made in this market in the next 10 years.
3 Forecasts of future sales can be found in our business plan.
4 Our profits could be affected by changes in the tax laws.
5 The company might be taken over by a stronger competitor.

47

INNOVATION UNIT 7

Extension activity. Write *take over/competitor* on the board. You might elicit or mention that there is a fairly strong collocation between this verb/noun combination, i.e. these words are frequently used together. Write up other word pairs from the listening passage and the grammar section such as: *make money / forecast sales*. Instruct pairs to use these verb/noun combinations to write two passive sentences in the tenses practised in the previous exercises, giving real life examples where possible, either from their company or from businesses they know about.

▶ GRAMMAR OVERVIEW ON PAGE 161 OF THE COURSEBOOK, CAN BE DONE AT THIS STAGE.

▶ REVIEW AND DEVELOPMENT EXERCISES A–C ON PAGE 46 OF THE COURSEBOOK, CAN BE DONE AT THIS STAGE.

▶ WORKBOOK PASSIVES EXERCISE ON PAGE 29 CAN NOW BE DONE.

Communication
Running a meeting

A lot of business is done in meetings, although in some cultures, the main decisions are made out of meetings. Performing effectively in meetings can make a big difference to your working life. This section focuses on the main elements of running a meeting, e.g. managing the purpose, process, and people.

Divide the class into two groups, or subgroups if it is a large class. Ask one half to imagine/remember the worst meeting they could ever attend/have ever attended. Ask the other half to imagine/remember a perfect meeting, which leaves/left them with a sense of achievement. After a couple of minutes of subgroup discussion, ask the *bad* group to put forward the cause of a bad meeting. Answers might include: *Some of the participants don't get a chance to express their opinion*. Ask the *good* group to provide the positive version of this situation. Answers might include: *Everybody is included in the meeting*. Allow groups to continue brainstorming. Then ask participants from one group to pair up with someone from the other group and compare ideas. Circulate, noting relevant language and write it up on the board. Ask a few students to mention some causes of unsuccessful meetings. A multicultural class might have conflicting views. Note them down and explain that this issue can be developed in a class discussion at the end of the *Business across Cultures* section on page 37 of the Coursebook.

A AUDIO 7.2 Inform the class that they are about to hear extracts from meetings, which they need to rearrange in the correct chronological order. Play the audio. Do a class check.

KEY
1 c   2 a   3 d   4 b

B Instruct the class to do the gap fill exercise individually. Then play AUDIO 7.2 again so that they can check their answers.

At this point it might be useful to check students' understanding of key vocabulary items such as *minutes / items / agenda*, as well as eliciting or highlighting typical meetings' collocations such as *attend a meeting*.

KEY
a *items*
b *fix*
c *attend*
d *circulate*
e *get*
f *minutes*
g *hold*

AUDIO SCRIPT

1 A: That brings us to the last item <u>on the agenda</u> – the budget for the maintenance programme. George, I think you've prepared some figures.
  B: That's right. I've got them here.

2 A: I'd like to <u>fix a meeting</u> for next week.
  B: Of course. When would you like to <u>hold it</u>?
  A: How about Thursday afternoon or Friday morning?
  B: Do you want all the team to <u>attend</u>?
  A: If possible. Could you email them and check their availability?
  B: OK. What about the agenda?
  A: I'll do that today and you can send it out tomorrow morning.

3 A: Did you get the <u>minutes</u> of the last meeting?
  B: No, I didn't.
  A: It's important that everyone reads the minutes. Peter <u>agreed to circulate</u> them after the meeting.
  B: He's been on sick leave.
  A: Well, there are some important actions to follow up …

4 Good morning, everyone. Nice to see you all. Let's <u>get down to business</u>, shall we? We have a lot to cover today. Have you all seen the agenda? Good. By the end of the meeting, I'd like to finalise our plans for the new product launch. Melanie, could you start, please?

Direct students to the Key language table. Introduce each stage of the meeting and go round the class, asking students to read out gambits in their most convincing style! Help with pronunciation difficulties and new language items. It might be useful to highlight that each language item has its own distinct intonation pattern. Some of the items are questions and therefore end in a slightly rising tone. You might find it useful to refer students back to the Communication notes for Unit 6 on page 151 of the Coursebook.

C Divide the class into groups of about three to five, depending on the size of your class. Ask them to read the rubric and make sure they understand. Set a time limit both for this task and the next. It might be useful to ensure that each student prepares a personal opinion on a number of causes of stress in the workplace and some suggestions for reducing it. A chairperson should be appointed.

D Instruct students to hold their meetings, following the instructions. If the class is large, you might choose to do this in two separate sessions, with the non-performing group acting as observers. Each observer should study a

INNOVATION UNIT 7

specific aspect of the meeting. Points to observe might include:

key language	effective management of the purpose
process and people	good and bad management moments
ideas discussed	actions agreed timing

Observers then report back to the rest of the class. Alternatively, if meetings are held in different rooms, they could be audio/video recorded for viewing and analysis, by the whole class afterwards.

▶ WORKBOOK EXERCISE A, PAGE 30, CAN BE DONE AT THIS STAGE.
▶ REVIEW AND DEVELOPMENT EXERCISE D, ON PAGE 47 OF THE COURSEBOOK, CAN BE DONE AT THIS STAGE.
▶ REVIEW BUSINESS NOTES FOR THIS SECTION ON PAGE 151 OF THE COURSEBOOK.

Business across Cultures
Time

This section explores how attitudes to time vary from culture to culture (more monochronic/measured or more polychronic/fluid) and how this difference in attitudes has an impact on business.

Direct students to read the opening rubric on page 37 of their Coursebook. Check that they understand the meaning of *measured* and *fluid*.

A Instruct students to do this quick quiz individually, briefly comparing and discussing the reasons for their answers in pairs. Ask one of the students to read out the Analysis section, checking for understanding of vocabulary such as: *virtue, punctuality* and *tolerate*. Do a class check on who falls into either category.

B Instruct pairs to read through the profiles of *monochronic* and *polychronic* cultures. Ask them to discuss and decide which one they relate most to. It could be useful to emphasise that these are extremes of a continuum. Students might not relate strongly to either.

Draw a horizontal line on the board.

monochronic ---------x-------------------------- *polychronic*

Ask students to tell you where on the line they place themselves. You could mark students' initials along the line. Ask them to give you examples from their working/college environment which support this. With a multicultural group the initials may well be more dispersed along the line, but either way it could give rise to an interesting discussion and some useful language items may appear for you to note below the line. Refer the class back to their discussions about features of good and bad meetings in the Communication section of this unit.

Ask students to think of another culture they are familiar with (either through work, college, travel or knowledge of people from other cultures living in their country) and to discuss it with a partner, pointing out the differences between this culture and their own. Invite students to report their partners' views. Where students have extensive knowledge of another culture, this can prove a very interesting subject, so you might find it useful to allow plenty of time for student to student questions, simply assisting with helpful vocabulary and so on, which could be written up on the board. Encourage students to place these cultures on the *monochronic ---- polychronic* continuum.

▶ CULTURE NOTES FOR THIS SECTION SHOULD BE REVIEWED ON PAGE 154 OF THE COURSEBOOK.

Checklist

Run through each point on the checklist with the class, asking questions to elicit key vocabulary relating to start-ups, including items brought up by students themselves, language for running meetings and key aspects of *monochronic* and *polychronic* cultures. If students are interested in reading further into the subject of attitudes to time, refer them to the reading matter mentioned in the end matter of this unit.

INNOVATION **UNIT 8**

8 Inventions

PREVIEW

Vocabulary and listening
This unit deals with vocabulary relating to the development and launch of new products onto the market.

Grammar
past perfect and past simple
The relationship between the past perfect and past simple is introduced. The main aim is for students to understand that past perfect events occur before the main past events in a sequence, and to be aware of useful time expressions for linking purposes.

Communication
participating in meetings
This section expands on the theme of the previous unit, reviewing the language students can use to exchange ideas and opinions in various types of meetings. It might be useful to review the concept of collectivist and individualist cultures in the *Business across Cultures* section in Unit 3, page 15, as it has an influence on the willingness of meeting participants to contribute ideas and express opinions.

Business across Cultures
developing a culture of innovation
The module subject of innovation is rounded off in this section, which explores how companies can develop a culture of innovation. The aim is to allow students to develop an awareness of and discuss the extent to which their particular company or national culture encourages or discourages the degree of uncertainty necessary for innovation.

Start-up
Direct the class to open their Coursebooks at pages 38–39. Ask them to read the statement by Thomas Edison. Check students' understanding of *perspiration* and *inspiration*. Elicit some inventions he was famous for.

Divide students into subgroups, as a certain amount of discussion at this stage should generate more ideas. As with any board work, it is useful for students to copy down anything written up.

A Ask the students if they agree with Thomas Edison's statement. Direct each group to discuss this for a few minutes, and then, to present their opinions. Any useful ideas and language can be written on the board.

B It could be useful to review the qualities needed by entrepreneurs in Unit 6. Ask: *Are any of these qualities important for inventors?* Give groups a few minutes to brainstorm any other qualities they think an inventor should have and write them up on the board.

C Elicit a few inventions from the class. Ask students to explain what they are/were used for. Alternatively, you could give each group different sets of magazine pictures of five or six common inventions and ask them to rank them in order of usefulness. Each group should appoint a spokesperson to explain the group's ideas to the class. Write up any useful expressions on the board for students to copy down.

Vocabulary and listening

A Ask students to do the exercise individually and then do a class check. Draw their attention to the key language items in bold, such as *apply for a patent*. Ask students to explain them giving real life examples, where possible, from industries or businesses they know or work for. Synonyms could be useful for describing vocabulary such as the word *patent*. Answers might include: *It's a kind of licence*.

KEY

1 f   2 c   3 a   4 e   5 g   6 d   7 h   8 b

B AUDIO 8.1 Direct students to look at the photo on page 38. Elicit the type of product the woman is holding, what it is made of, who it would be used by and what is special about it. If necessary, write the word *non-spill* on the board. Explain that they are going to listen to an interview with Mandy Haberman, the inventor of a non-spill cup for children, and that they should listen for any of the expressions in bold seen in A. Play the audio and do a quick class check.

KEY

a   d   e   g   h

C Ask students to read through the questions and answer them during a second listening. Play AUDIO 8.1 again and do a class check.

KEY

1 When she saw a little girl drop a cup and her mother dived to catch it.
2 In plastics.
3 No. She looked for companies to make her product.
4 When she exhibited at trade shows, she shook the cups over people's clothes.
5 She sent a non-spill cup full of fruit juice to a buyer at Tesco.

D Instruct students to do this exercise in pairs. Ask one pair to read out their list as a class check.

INNOVATION UNIT 8

KEY
1 b   2 d   3 e   4 c   5 g   6 a   7 f

AUDIO SCRIPT

Interviewer: How did you get the idea for the Anywayup cup?

Mandy Haberman: I first had the idea for a totally non-spill cup when I saw a little girl drinking from a conventional trainer cup. She dropped the cup and her mother dived to catch it before it hit the floor. This made me think that it must be possible to make a cup that would close and wouldn't spill or drip when the child wasn't drinking from it.

Interviewer: How did you go about producing the cup?

Mandy Haberman: Well, I had some experience of working with plastics, and, starting in my kitchen, I made a series of prototypes. After about a year I was ready to look for a financial backer to develop and sell the product.

Interviewer: How did you go about finding one?

Mandy Haberman: I had applied for a patent before I went to see possible backers, and over a period of a couple of years I showed my prototypes to about 20 companies.

Interviewer: Aha. How did companies respond when you went to see them?

Mandy Haberman: Responses varied. Typically, companies wanted to hold on to the prototypes while they assessed the product. Months would go by and I'd become very nervous about it until finally I would demand that they returned the product.

Interviewer: Mmm ...

Mandy Haberman: Those that were interested were either not prepared to invest enough money or were not prepared to commit to the sort of minimum sales figures that I considered possible.

Interviewer: So where did you go from there?

Mandy Haberman: I exhibited at trade shows. We showed prototypes which were convincing as real product samples. We demonstrated our samples by one moment drinking from them, and the next moment shaking them over people's clothes! Not a drop came out. The shows were a huge success. We took about £10,000 of advance orders.

Interviewer: What happened next?

Mandy Haberman: With the £10,000 from the advance orders, I set up my own company – The Haberman Company Ltd. – to make the cups, and we rocketed into business. Later on, I licensed my product to V & A Marketing Ltd. in the UK, and a company called 'The First Years' in the U.S.

Interviewer: How did you establish your routes to market?

Mandy Haberman: We realised that we needed to get the product into the supermarkets but this wasn't going to be easy – we had already been in contact with all the big chains, but they weren't interested.

Interviewer: Aha ...

Mandy Haberman: So we filled a cup with fruit juice and put it loose inside a white box and posted it to the buyer at Tesco, with a note to say that if it arrived without spilling, she should give us a call. A few days later, the telephone rang – we were into Tesco!

Extension activity. If any of the class work in the area of technical development or product marketing (even in a large industry such as in the automotive industry or pharmaceuticals) they could personalise the key language in A and B by describing some of these stages in their work to the rest of the group.

▶ WORKBOOK VOCABULARY EXERCISES A AND B ON PAGE 32 CAN NOW BE COMPLETED.

Grammar

Past perfect and past simple

The main aim in this section is for students to understand the chronological order of events expressed in the past perfect and past simple and be able to form more interesting and varied sentence structures using time expressions such as: *before, after, not until* and *already*.

Direct the students to open their Coursebooks at page 39, read the rubric, and underline the past simple and past perfect in each sentence.

KEY

When Mandy <u>developed</u> the non-spill cup, she <u>had worked</u> with plastics before.

She <u>didn't go</u> to see companies, until she <u>had made</u> a finished product.

<u>Had</u> Mandy <u>applied</u> for a patent when she went to see companies about her product?

A Go into this activity as in the Coursebook. Do a class check.

KEY
1 b   2 a

B Draw a timeline on the board.

before this event   past event   present

Ask the class which tense you use to describe an event in the past. Elicit the past simple. Write it up above *past event*. Ask them which tense we use to describe actions which happened before that event. Elicit past perfect and write it up above *before this event*.

KEY
1 a   2 b

C Write the rule with spaces on the board.

The past perfect is formed using _____ + the _____ _____ of the verb.

Elicit the rule from the class.

KEY

had

past participle

INNOVATION **UNIT 8**

D Instruct students to complete this exercise individually and do a class check, referring back to the timeline and rule. Ask students to identify the time expressions used in these sentences.

KEY

2	did not apply	had made
3	made	had seen
4	started	had already set up
5	sent	had contacted
6	started	had already met

E Ask the class to refer to the timeline and write sentences using both the *past perfect* and *past simple*. Do a class check.

F Ask students to draw a timeline like the one on the board, and interview their partner about events in their life and career, using the time expressions presented in D. Students might like to draw their partner's timeline on the board and present it to the class. Alternatively, they could write it up. The combined timelines and biographies could then be made into a class book.

▶ GRAMMAR OVERVIEW PAGE 162 CAN BE USED FOR REFERENCE, THROUGHOUT THE SECTION.

▶ REVIEW AND DEVELOPMENT EXERCISE A, PAGE 46 OF THE COURSEBOOK, CAN BE DONE AT THIS STAGE.

▶ WORKBOOK EXERCISES ON PAGE 33 CAN BE DONE FOR FURTHER PRACTICE.

Communication
Participating in meetings

As a general introduction to this section it might be useful to review the concept of *collectivist* and *individualist* cultures in the *Business across Cultures* section in Unit 3, page 15.

Direct students to the opening rubric on page 40 of their Coursebooks and ask a student to read it out to the rest of the class.

A AUDIO 8.2 Explain that students are going to hear three openings to meetings. Make sure they understand the instruction rubric. Play the audio, twice if necessary, and do a class check.

KEY

1 c   2 a   3 b

AUDIO SCRIPT

1 Thank you for coming to this meeting at such short notice. We have a small crisis and I want to make sure it doesn't become a big one. One of our packaging suppliers is in financial trouble and can no longer guarantee deliveries. We need to consider the options. Peter will present two alternative suppliers and Susan has costs for bringing the work back in-house. Peter, will you start ...

2 I'm delighted to welcome you all to our third meeting. Let me start by introducing a new member of the team. This is Pedro Rodríguez – he's the Marketing Manager in Venezuela – and he'll be representing our South and Central American markets. I've asked Pedro to start today's session with an overview of the market. Then we'll go around the table with the usual reports. Let's aim to stop for lunch around twelve thirty ...

3 A: Great to see you all today. Stephen is going to facilitate today's meeting. Stephen, let me hand over to you straight away.

B: Thanks, Sarah. We've got a fantastic new product and what we need now is a new name. We've had a few ideas but nothing really exciting. So let's see what we can come up with today. We have plenty of coffee and doughnuts, and I hope they'll help! I'll write your ideas up here first and then later we can see which ones we prefer ...

B Ask the class whether they go to these types of meetings, or any other type. Encourage them to describe what sort of objectives these meetings have. List any useful language items on the board.

C AUDIO 8.3 Ask the students if they have ever attended a trade fair, either as a visitor or an exhibitor. Elicit reasons for exhibiting or attending trade fairs. This should bring up some useful related language which you can note on the board. Answers might include: *improving company image / winning customers / taking orders for a product*. Ensure that students understand key vocabulary, e.g. *exhibition stand*. Then you could elicit some ideas on how to make a company's exhibition stand more attractive to potential visitors than the competition's stands. Answers might include: *bigger signs / brighter logo / simpler design*, etc.

Explain that students are going to hear an extract from a brainstorming session on improving the company's exhibition stand at a trade fair. Instruct them to make a note of the participants' ideas as they listen.

Play AUDIO 8.3 and do a class check on ideas heard, noting useful language on the board.

KEY

Use the audio script to check your answers.

AUDIO SCRIPT

Chairperson: As you know, we're going to the Electronica trade fair again this year. We want our stand to have a big impact. I want to hear your ideas on this. I'll list the ideas as we go. So, the topic is Electronica stand ... Susie, what do you think?

Susie: I think we need to change the colour. Last year, we used very boring dark colours. We need something light and bright.

Chairperson: OK. Cathy, what's your opinion?

Cathy: As I see it, the main problem is there's nothing for visitors to do on the stand, just read and talk. In my opinion, we should have something interactive ...

Doug: I don't agree. People come to the stand to learn about us and what we have to offer, and I think reading and talking are ...

Chairperson: Excuse me, Doug, you may be right, but at the moment we're brainstorming new ideas. Is there anything you think we should change?

Doug: Well, we could change the design and layout of the stand – to make it more attractive.

Danny: Yes, we could have one area where people sit and maybe have access to our website ...

Chairperson: Do you mean we could break the stand into two parts, Danny?

INNOVATION **UNIT 8**

Danny: Yes, that might be good. One area for talk and questions, maybe with something interactive, and another area to sit, read, access the Internet ...
Chairperson: Susie, do you have anything to add? No?
Susie: No, I don't think so.
Chairperson: This all sounds great. So let me summarise what we have so far ...

D Ask the class to read through the Key language box and practice saying the phrases with a partner so that they become more familiar with the language. Circulate, checking for any pronunciation difficulties. Play AUDIO **8.3** and tell the class to listen to the extract again and to tick any key language expressions that they hear. Do a class check.

At this point it is probably useful to get students to remember that whilst giving and listening to ideas and opinions is the 'meat' of the meeting, the chairperson needs to provide some very essential 'bones' too. Ask the class to focus on these once more, before they go into their brainstorming meetings. Elicit answers such as: *checking everyone understands the objectives of the meeting / summarising regularly / final summary / action points*, etc.

E Divide students into subgroups and ask each group to choose a topic from the list. You could add some more of your own. Ask each group to appoint a chairperson and to hold a short meeting to brainstorm these areas. Remind them to refer to the key language.

▶ COMMUNICATION NOTES ON PAGE 151 OF THE COURSEBOOK CAN BE READ AT THIS STAGE.

▶ REVIEW AND DEVELOPMENT ACTIVITIES D AND E ON PAGE 47 OF THE COURSEBOOK CAN BE DONE AT THIS STAGE.

▶ WORKBOOK EXERCISES ON PAGE 34 CAN BE DONE FOR FURTHER PRACTICE.

Business across Cultures
Developing a culture of innovation

Direct the class to the introduction rubric on page 41 of the Coursebook. Ask them if they agree with Peter Drucker's statement, or if they have any other ideas.

A Ask a student to read out the ideas suggested in this exercise. Check any vocabulary difficulties. Ask pairs to discuss these ideas, decide which ones work and which ones don't. Ask them to come up with one or two other ideas if possible. Do a round for the class feedback. Write any interesting language on the board.

B Ask students if they know the company *Google*. Find out from them what *Google* does, roughly how old it is, and where it operates. Find out if they have heard any stories in the news about it. This could prompt quite a number of interesting language items, which can be noted on the board.

MODEL ANSWER

It is one of the largest and most popular search engines, founded in September, 1998, by Larry Page and Sergey Brin. It scans web pages to find instances of the keywords people enter in the search box.

Ask students to quickly read the article about Google and how it tries to encourage innovation, for the ideas mentioned in the previous exercise. Do a quick class check and tackle any vocabulary or understanding problems at this stage. Then get the class to read it again and note any other ideas which are suggested in the article. Do a class check.

KEY

Reduce the number of layers in a company.
Recruit creative people.
Don't punish mistakes.

ADDITIONAL IDEAS

Google recruits a mix of risk-takers and people who know if something is too risky.
Project management rotates around team members.
It observes and listens with ten employees reading emails from users full-time.

It might be useful to ask the class some follow-up questions such as: *Do you prefer this management style to a more traditional one? Do you think everyone would be able to work this way? Do you think it would work in your company/college? Would you feel comfortable working this way? Are there any potential downsides to this style of management?*

C Refer the class to the previous brainstorming meetings on page 40. Ask them to briefly review the main points of a successful brainstorming session, e.g. *agenda, good people, time management, firm set of action points, resolutions*. Collect ideas from the class.

How you set this task, really depends on your students. If they all work for the same company or organisation, they could be divided into groups by department or by common interests. If they all work for different companies/organisations you could alternatively invent a few fictitious companies, providing students with specific roles. With a professionally inexperienced class, you may have to offer prompts.

Ask groups to appoint a chairperson. As subgroups hold their brainstorming meetings, go round the class collecting examples of both excellent and erroneous language items. Ask each brainstorming group to summarise the agenda and final decisions they reached as well as how well the purpose, process, people, and time were managed.

▶ CULTURAL BUSINESS NOTES FOR THIS SECTION CAN BE FOUND ON PAGE 154 OF THE COURSEBOOK.

▶ THE WORKBOOK WRITING EXERCISE ON PAGE 35 CAN BE DONE FOR FURTHER PRACTICE.

Checklist

Check off all the items on the checklist with your class. Ask them questions to elicit and revise key vocabulary from the vocabulary and listening section. Write the time expressions used in the grammar section up on the board and ask students to tell the class something about their life using one of the time expressions together with the past simple or past perfect. Go through the meeting language again, asking for opinions and ideas.

Extension activity. Biographies of famous people from magazines or internet articles could be distributed, and students asked to prepare a timeline for their famous person. They should then write short biographies using the past perfect and past simple. Students can then read their texts to the class or to a partner who should take notes and convey the information to the class.

BUSINESS SCENARIO 2

PITCHING FOR FINANCE

> This Business scenario rounds up all the elements of Module 2: entrepreneurship, creativity, the process of getting inventions off the ground and pitching for financial backing for a start-up. The class now has the opportunity to use the language they have learned in a very practical way which reflects the business environment in which they work, or will be working in, in the future. In terms of skills, the activities offer students the opportunity to participate in a brainstorming meeting, an open class discussion, to present ideas formally and then write an email of rejection.

INTRODUCTORY ACTIVITY

Replay and review AUDIO 7.1 from Unit 7, which introduces the idea of the *business pitch*. Write up the expression *business pitch* on the board and elicit its meaning. Ask the class to brainstorm items of information which should go into a good business pitch. Elicit the items on the list on page 42 of the Coursebook. Write them up around the central words.

In groups, ask the students to focus on these items and brainstorm a few convincing statements or claims that they could use to make a successful pitch. Answers might include: *We've got the best product. / There's nothing like it on the market. / It's certainly going to sell in millions. / It will revolutionise. / We've got the most experienced team.* Ask for ideas from each group and elicit language areas such as comparatives and superlatives, for selling their product and dismissing the competition and the language of positive forecasting for selling their chances of success. You could spend quite a lot of time, and have quite a bit of fun, eliciting, and feeding in boastful claims. Write them up on the board and allow pairs time to practise using them.

BACKGROUND

Read the rubric and all the instructions in class.

PROCEDURE

Preparing the pitch. Direct the class to open their Coursebooks at page 42. Ask a student to read the background information on TVC to the class. Explain that they are going to work in four teams. One team will represent Tiger Venture Capital, which is based in Amsterdam and invests €110 million every month in new business projects. They will consider pitches from the other three teams who are all looking for start-up capital.

Divide the class into four groups and run through the procedure as in the Coursebook. Assign start-up ventures to three groups. Direct them to their set of instructions and background information and instruct your TVC team to look at the background info and instructions on page 43 so that they can prepare some searching questions for the pitchers. Team A: page 104. Team B: page 111. Team C: page 112.

Entrepreneurs. Making sure everyone is clear about their role, it could be useful to remind the class that their recent experience of running and participating in brainstorming meetings will be useful as they have a limited amount of time to prepare their pitches and will need to be very organised. How each group divides up the exercise will depend on the class, but realistically, each group member needs to have a good understanding of every aspect of their pitch, and each member should ideally present part of it.

It could be useful to set strict time limits on pitch preparation and presentation and recommend that each team holds a brainstorming meeting to prepare their pitch/questions. You might circulate during this process to help groups with any language difficulties. Groups should also prepare adequate visual materials to support their presentation. These will aid the whole class review and discussion of each project idea.

TVC team. While the pitching groups prepare their pitches, the TVC team should brainstorm questions to ask each group. If you feel they need some extra help, you might suggest that they briefly review the entrepreneurs' information so that they are better prepared.

Making the pitch. Invite each group to make their pitch to the TVC team. Pitchers should support their main ideas visually, using slides or flip charts, to be reviewed afterwards. The TVC team should ask as many searching questions as possible in order to have the right information to make a decision on which pitch(es) to go

INNOVATION **BUSINESS SCENARIO 2**

with. Ask the groups which are not participating in the pitch to take notes about good use of persuasive language. If possible, audio or video record the pitches in order to aid an interesting class analysis session afterwards.

Class discussion. Display the visual support materials of each group's pitch, ask several students to summarise the main points of each pitch again and lead a short open class discussion on the viability of each project. This will allow as many ideas and opinions as possible to be aired.

Meeting to decide. Ask the TVC team to hold a short meeting to decide which project(s) to back. They should then have a short time to prepare a brief presentation of their verdict to the venture seekers. Both meeting and presentation can be audio or video recorded as before.

Reviewing the process. Do a class review (review audio/video recordings if you have them) for verbal and nonverbal language performance. Ask groups to comment on how they felt they managed their brainstorming meetings.

WRITING

Review correct email writing procedures with the class. Topics might include: *appropriate subject line, salutation, phrases for apologetic rejection, closing statement wishing every success, closing salutation.* The email could alternatively take the form of a formal letter, so in contrast, appropriate openings and closings for formal business letters could also be reviewed beforehand.

Get each group to work on an email as set out in the Coursebook instructions. They should review the reasons they gave for rejecting the business idea, referring back to the final points agreed in the TVC meeting. Review them afterwards in class for accuracy and appropriateness of language.

Review and development 5–8

Vocabulary: Personal characteristics

A Instruct students to look at the vocabulary on personal characteristics from Unit 5 and do the vocabulary matching exercise individually, as in the Coursebook. Do a quick class check.

KEY
1 e   2 f   3 c   4 d   5 a   6 g   7 b

B Ask the class to identify which characteristics in exercise A a job interviewer would be most interested in. Elicit that a–d are the positive characteristics.

In order to prompt students, you might find it useful to prepare a few interviewer/interviewee roleplay cards: job applied for with a few accompanying responsibilities and a few short bullet points covering the interviewee's relevant experience for this activity.

Instruct student pairs to interview each other for jobs to practise asking about and describing these positive qualities. Get one pair to read out the model example in the Coursebook first. Interviewees should really try to sell themselves. Give them a couple of minutes to check the prompts, answer any language queries in class and then go into the exercise. You might like to get one or two pairs to perform their interviews to the class, afterwards.

C Give the class time to review the noun forms in Unit 5 then come back to this exercise, check that they understand the rubric and ask them to do the exercise individually. Do a class check.

KEY
1 Strength
2 Innovation
3 Competitive
4 ✔
5 Persistence
6 ✔
7 Self-confidence

Grammar: Will and going to

A Ask the class to reread the rules and examples on page 31 of the Coursebook and to do the exercise individually. Do a concept check on the board.

KEY
1 c   2 b   3 a

B Check that students understand the rubric and get them to do the exercise individually. Do a class check.

KEY
1 won't be / isn't going to be
2 are going to cut
3 will lose
4 won't recover / isn't going to recover
5 will go up / are going to go up
6 will promote
7 are going to recruit
8 will finish
9 are going to increase

C Do this as an open class exercise.

KEY
1 a   2 c   3 b   4 a   5 a   6 b   7 c   8 b   9 c

Passives

A Instruct students to reread exercises and review rules for the passive structures on page 35 and to do the exercise individually as in the Coursebook. Do a class check.

KEY
2 An advertisement is placed on appropriate websites.
3 Candidates' applications are sorted and analysed.
4 A shortlist is drawn up.
5 Shortlisted candidates are interviewed.
6 References are checked.
7 The successful candidate is notified.

B In pairs get students to do the exercise as in the Coursebook. Circulate and correct any mistakes you note on the board afterwards.

C Go into the exercise as in the Coursebook and do a class check.

KEY
1 have been logged
2 have been cut down
3 might be planted
4 be developed
5 should be poured
6 will be made

Past perfect

A Invite a student to read out the rules and examples of the past perfect on page 39 of the Coursebook. Draw a timeline on the board and label it with a few events. Ask students to use the past simple and past perfect in contrast to describe these events.

Instruct students to complete the quiz in pairs and do a class check.

KEY
1 had, invented
2 had worked
3 had, been
4 had built
5 had developed

Extension activity. In advance ask students to research an inventor/innovator and their inventions on the Internet or from an encyclopaedia. They should write a few questions similar to the ones in the exercise for the rest of the class, relating to the inventor, date, country or invention. Depending on the number of questions produced, choose one or two from each student and create a class quiz. Students shouldn't answer their own questions.

Communication

Give students time to reread the Communication skills pages from Units 5 and 6 before completing activities A–D.

A Instruct students to complete this exercise individually and do a class check.

KEY
to share a flat
to apply for a job
to commute to work
to live with your partner
to be on a diet
to join a company
to move house
to keep in shape

B Ask students to write questions using the phrases in A, then to use them to interview a partner.

C Direct students to match questions or comments with an appropriate response. Then, as a class check, ask each student to direct a question to someone else who should reply.

KEY
1 c   2 e   3 h   4 a   5 f   6 g   7 d   8 b

Allow students time to review the two Communication sections from Units 7 and 8 before going into exercises D and E.

D This gap fill exercise reviews the vocabulary of meetings. Ask students to complete the text and check it in pairs.

KEY
1 hold
2 agenda
3 items
4 attend
5 fixed
6 copy
7 get down
8 taking
9 actions
10 circulate
11 follow up

E Invite one pair to read the example dialogue out to the class. Inform the class that they are going to practise *asking for*, *giving* and *clarifying* opinions. They should discuss the first topic for three minutes with a partner, and then move onto another partner to discuss a different subject.

Before doing this, it might be useful to model the exercise with a strong student.

For example:

You: Do you think it is a good idea to socialise with your colleagues regularly?

St: Yes, I think it is good for team building.

You: So are you saying that good teams should go out at least once a week together?

St: Well, perhaps not that often. Maybe once a month would be a good idea though.

MODULE 3

Promotion

MODULE OVERVIEW

AIMS AND OBJECTIVES

This module focuses on performance and the related themes include promotion of products and offering services to a range of target audiences. It also covers offering global advertising with local awareness and 'selling yourself'. A number of grammar and vocabulary items are reviewed and practised in the context of promotion. Each Communication section focuses on a different aspect of telephoning, such as leaving and taking messages, opening, structuring and ending a call. The Business across Cultures sections provide an insight into a range of areas. For instance, the 'silo mentality', customer service culture, corporate culture and 'work and play'.

At the end of this module, students should be able to:

- use countable and uncountable nouns relating to the theme of promotion with *much*, *many*, *a lot of*, *lots of* and *plenty of*
- open conversation and respond on the telephone
- leave and take telephone messages
- structure a call
- close a call effectively
- have greater understanding of corporate culture
- use a variety of adjectives and nouns to describe personal qualities
- form the negatives of adjectives using *not very* + positive adjectives and prefixes
- understand what it means to put a customer at the centre of a business
- use a range of verbs which are either followed by the infinitive form and/or the *-ing* form
- have an awareness of how social etiquette and attitudes towards 'work and play' contrast sharply in different cultures
- talk about actions or states which started in the past and continue up to the present using either the present perfect simple or the present perfect continuous
- understand the 'silo mentality' and the benefits of cross-functional teams

THEMATIC OVERVIEW

This module provides an insight into issues that are currently being debated and researched by marketing professionals and the news media alike. The new phenomenon of kids as consumers is investigated, focusing on the debate as to whether parents are the victims of *pester-power* when buying products, or whether parents and children simply make purchasing decisions together. In contrast, later in the module, we look at the *grey market*. This market is growing rapidly and will represent a significant portion of the market by the middle of this century, but do we really understand how this group makes its purchasing decisions? And do older consumers relate to advertising which is targeted at them? Another area covered in this module is global advertising, dealing with how consumers in different parts of the global market respond to advertisements. We also hear about one well-known bank which ran a creative advertising campaign to raise awareness of how its global presence was blended with local knowledge.

Products and services are not the only things that require promotion. The important issue of selling yourself is addressed in Unit 10 along with advice on improving your marketability and the secrets of success at work.

MAIN AUDIO CONTENTS

Unit 9: five short telephone dialogues which focus on the opening phase

Unit 10: an interview with a human resources specialist on the topic of 'selling yourself'; four individuals describe how they were helped by advice on how to sell themselves; messages left on the telephone and on an answer machine

Unit 11: two extracts from an interview with an expert on global advertising; a telephone conversation which demonstrates structuring a call; five brief extracts which feature key moments in social situations

Unit 12: two telephone conversations which demonstrate closing a call; four short extracts which feature people talking about their concerns within their departments

PHOTOCOPIABLE RESOURCES (PAGES 117-118)

3.1 can be used any time after Unit 10.
3.2 can be used any time after Unit 12.

BUSINESS AND CULTURAL NOTES

Kids as consumers. The ever-increasing purchasing-power of children may be good for business, but there are also important economic, social, health, and environmental factors to be considered. The topic of children as consumers is controversial in many countries and can be used as the basis of lively yet productive discussion in class.

The relationship between parents and children. Unit 9 deals with the relationship between children and parents and the amount of influence children have on family spending habits. In culturally diverse classes, teachers are likely to observe differences in the way in which parents and children interact.

Customer service. The concept of good customer service varies from culture to culture. The USA is renowned for its top quality service but the enthusiastic *Have a nice day!* and *Would you like to try that on?* style might be viewed as insincere and forceful by customers in the UK, even though friendly service is appreciated. Meanwhile, in Japan, a certain distance is expected between the shop assistant and customer; a shop assistant's attempt to make small talk would be considered over-familiar and disrespectful.

PROMOTION **UNIT 9**

9 Kids as consumers

PREVIEW

Reading

The reading exercise in this unit is based on a short article about *pester-power*, the way in which children nag their parents into buying certain products.

Grammar

count and uncount nouns

The nouns featured in this section relate to the themes of consumerism and promotion. There is a particular focus on using count and uncount nouns with words such as *many, much, a lot of, lots of* and *plenty of*.

Communication

telephoning 1: opening and responding

This section introduces phrases used to identify yourself, ask for a connection, and give reasons for calling. This is an essential area in forming positive first impressions.

Business across Cultures

understanding corporate culture

The elements and significance of corporate culture are investigated in this section. The aim of this is to help students analyse the different layers of a corporate culture that influence the behaviour and attitude of colleagues and associates.

Introductory activity
Module introduction.

The themes in this module include promotion to a range of target audiences, promoting oneself, and global advertising with local awareness. To introduce students to this area and to pool their promotion-related vocabulary and knowledge, create a 'promotion' wordfield in class.

PROMOTION
- types: children, families, young, mature
- TV
- campaigns
- what: brands? products?
- advertising
- market
  - verbs: to flood, to research, to break into, to tap into
- consumers
- tastes:
  - verbs: to make purchases, to purchase, to buy, to make decisions

To introduce the topic of this unit ask students to form subgroups and brainstorm commercials shown on TV in their country/countries. Give them five minutes, then put their examples on the board. Ask which commercials target children and families.

Next, get students to guess how many TV commercials children see every year in the USA.

Then tell them to open their Coursebooks and read the fact feature to find out.

Start-up

If you have different nationalities in your class, you are likely to identify cultural differences regarding the relationship between parents and children. If possible, put pairs or groups of the same nationality together to discuss these questions. Compare students' opinions in class and examine any cultural differences observed.

Reading

A Before reading the report and the related questions, direct students' attention to the photograph. Ask students what the children are doing. Possible replies might include verbs such as *persuade* and *convince*. Ask two students to share the text and read it out to the class. They should be able to guess the meaning of unfamiliar words from the context. However, if at the end of the reading, students are still unsure of the meaning of some words, ask others to provide definitions and examples. Ask students to answer the questions in pairs, then correct and compare in class.

KEY

1 Phrases that describe the way children persuade their parents to buy things.
2 Parents and children often like the same things.
3 Cookies, cars, video games, snack foods, the latest electronic gadgets, blockbuster film hits, evergreen food and drink brands.
4 International example: Coca-Cola / Heinz (canned foods) / Nestlé (various food products).
5 Students' own answers.
6 It means they can take advantage of the fact parents and children are making decisions together about what to buy.

Information exchange

Ask students to work in pairs and do the exercise as indicated in the Coursebook. Tell them to refer back to page 14, Building transparency, for language relating to checking, clarifying, and confirming information. After the exercise, provide feedback on errors, checking and clarifying skills, and positive interaction.

PROMOTION UNIT 9

Grammar
Count and uncount nouns

Ask students to close their Coursebooks. Write on the board:

New trends are emerging ...

Parents find enjoyment ...

Elicit which noun is countable and which is uncountable. Ask students to open their Coursebooks and read the grammar rules together. Warn students to be careful with *much* and *many*. *Much* is used with uncountable nouns, in questions and negative sentences. In affirmative sentences, we tend to use a *lot of*. *Many* is used with countable nouns and can be used with affirmative and negative sentences as well as questions. Write the following on the board:

Do you have _____ information?

I don't have _____ information.

I have _____ information. (a lot of / much)

Elicit where a *lot of* and *much* should be inserted.

A Instruct students, in pairs, to do the exercise as indicated. Tell students that they can refer to the way the nouns are used in the text to help them decide whether they are countable or uncountable. Check answers in class and ask whether the nouns can be used with *a/an, a lot of, lots of, plenty of, much* or *many*.

KEY

influence – both

enjoyment – uncount

power – both

popularity – uncount

decision – count

purchase – count

factor – count

gadget – count

advertising – uncount

information – uncount

B Do the first question together in class, then ask students to do the exercise as indicated, in pairs. Go through the answers in class.

KEY

1 *lots of*

2 *many*

3 *a lot of*

4 *a lot of*

5 *plenty of*

6 *many*

7 *much*

Extension activities. Ask students to talk about advertising in their country/countries using the nouns in exercise A. If you have a multinational class, ask students of different nationalities to work in pairs and interview each other, then summarise their findings in class. First, elicit an example sentence, such as the one below.

In Mexico, there is a lot of advertising on the radio, whereas in Sweden there is very little.

Children as consumers is a controversial issue and can be used as the basis of a discussion in which many of the count and uncount nouns above would be useful.

First, brainstorm objections to marketing to children. For example:

<u>Objections</u>

Makes children materialistic.

Many ads encourage children to eat unhealthy food.

Puts pressure on parents.

Creates peer group pressure.

Creates dissatisfaction (wishing you had more money).

Then, brainstorm how a marketer might respond to these objections. For example:

<u>Responses</u>

Advertising does not create desire. It simply promotes a choice.

Many children see ads as entertainment.

Parents are responsible for what they buy.

Parents are responsible for what their children eat.

Briefly review some discussion language (expressing opinions, agreeing, disagreeing, etc.) Set up the discussion activity by dividing the class into two groups: *parents* who are against advertising to children and *marketers* who wish to defend such activities. Next, form small groups consisting of both *parents* and *marketers*. Explain that the aim of this activity is for both parties to express their opinions and defend their actions as well as to respond to conflicting views. Encourage students to ask each other questions and respond to one another appropriately. Set a time limit and circulate, making a note of positive discussion language as well as errors. To provide more individual feedback, you could use an Accuracy Feedback Sheet (see Frameworks, page 121).

If you do this discussion activity, this would be a good stage at which to focus on the corresponding unit in the Workbook. This expands on the theme of children as consumers by dealing with the much debated issue of advertising in schools. It also features a letter of complaint to an advertising company. Any of these Workbook exercises can be set for homework.

▶ FOR FURTHER INFORMATION ON COUNT AND UNCOUNT NOUNS, REFER STUDENTS TO GRAMMAR OVERVIEW, PAGE 163 OF THE COURSEBOOK.

▶ FOR PRACTICE AND CONSOLIDATION OF COUNT AND UNCOUNT NOUNS, DIRECT STUDENTS TO PAGE 37 OF THE WORKBOOK.

▶ REVIEW AND DEVELOPMENT ON COUNT AND UNCOUNT NOUNS, PAGE 66 OF THE COURSEBOOK, CAN BE DONE AT THIS STAGE.

Communication
Telephoning 1: Opening and responding

With Coursebooks closed, ask students to work in pairs and list the types of calls they make and receive. Write on the board:

<u>Calls made</u>	<u>Calls received</u>
to get payment	enquiries about ...
to talk about ... meetings	a request for

Then ask students how they like to start their calls. Ask: *Do you make small talk? Do you get straight down to business?* In a culturally diverse class, you are likely to observe differences. Tell students to read the Communication overview on page 151.

Ask students to open their Coursebooks and read the introduction.

PROMOTION UNIT 9

A AUDIO 9.1 Check understanding of the phrase *to chase a delivery*. Brainstorm the kinds of phrases that might be heard during each call:

to chase a delivery – *I'm calling about a delivery* ...
to make a request – *Could you* ...
 I would like to ask you a favour ...

Play the audio and ask students to check their answers in pairs.

KEY
1 d   2 e   3 b   4 c   5 a

B Go through the Key language together in class. Tell students to look at the uses of *can* and *could* and ask how each is used:

could – polite request

can – offer

[N.B. *Can* used in a request, is informal in British English.]

Play AUDIO 9.1 again and check in class which phrases were used.

AUDIO SCRIPT AND KEY

1 A: *Marketing Department.*
  B: *Hi, Max. This is Patrick.*
  A: *Patrick, how are you?*
  B: *Not bad, and you?*
  A: *OK. What can I do for you?*
  B: *I want to ask you a favour.*
  A: *Fire away.*
  B: *Well, I was wondering if you could sit in on the project review meeting for me on Wednesday* ...
  A: *I suppose so. What time does it start?*

2 A: *International Properties. How can I help you?*
  B: *Could I speak to your General Manager, please?*
  A: *Who's calling, please?*
  B: *This is Gerard Manley from the Inland Revenue.*
  A: *Could you tell me what it's about?*
  B: *It's confidential but it's to do with your annual tax return.*
  A: *I'll see if I can connect you ... I'm afraid he's not answering his phone. I think he's in a meeting. Could you call back later?*

3 A: *Mo Jacob speaking.*
  B: *Hello, Mo. This is Helen.*
  A: *Hi, Helen. How are you?*
  B: *Fine, thanks. Listen, this is just a quick call. I thought you should know – Steve Johnson has got the job.*
  A: *Really? I don't believe it* ...

4 A: *Good morning. Key Supplies.*
  B: *This is Morgan Benton, calling from Bachelors. Could you put me through to Accounts, please?*
  A: *Just a moment* ...
  C: *Accounts.*
  B: *This is Morgan Benton. I'm calling about a payment.*
  C: *Hello, Morgan. I thought I recognised your voice. This is Jason. Can you give me the reference number?*
  B: *The date on the invoice is the 11th of January and the number is 2901.*
  C: *Have you got a purchase order number?*
  B: *I don't think so.*
  C: *Well, that could be the problem. All invoices have to have a purchase order number* ...

5 A: *Customer Service. How can I help you?*
  B: *I'm calling about a delivery.*
  A: *Can I take your name, please?*
  B: *It's Susan Freeman.*
  A: *One moment, please ... I'm afraid the line's engaged. Can I get them to call you back?*
  B: *Look, this is the third time I've phoned and* ...

Extension activity. Explain that the first call was informal. Play AUDIO 9.1 again and ask students to identify informal phrases. Play it more than once, if necessary, and then write the phrases on the board. Next, ask students for the more formal equivalent of the language used.

For example:

Informal	Formal
Hi, Max.	Good morning, Mr ...
Not bad ...	Very well, thank you.
I want to ask you a favour ...	I'd like to ask you if you could ...
Fire away.	Go ahead.
I suppose so.	Of course. / Certainly.

Erase the board, then ask students to turn to page 121 for the audio script. Tell them you will play the first call again and they should mark the intonation patterns on the script with an arrow. Do an example in class. Play AUDIO 9.1 and check for any patterns identified in class. Drill the key sentences and then ask students to practise the dialogue in pairs.

Tell students that the second call is a more formal dialogue. Ask them to look at the audio script and identify the intonation patterns while listening to the conversation. Once again, drill and get students to practise the dialogue in pairs.

C Students should work in pairs and do the exercise as indicated in the Coursebook. Ask them to sit back-to-back so that they cannot see each other in order to make listening more difficult. If you have a multinational class, ask people of different nationalities to work together so that they have the added challenge of dealing with a foreign accent. Tell students to make a note of any information received and to check that it is correct. Circulate during the activity, noting errors as well as positive opening and responding language, and clarification techniques. To provide more individual feedback, you could use a Telephoning Feedback Framework (see Frameworks, page 123). Go through the feedback sheet with the students prior to the exercise so that they are aware of the key factors upon which their performance will be assessed.

▶ FOR SELF-STUDY PRACTICE OF THE LANGUAGE USED IN OPENING CALLS, DIRECT STUDENTS TO PAGE 38 OF THE WORKBOOK.

▶ DIRECT STUDENTS' ATTENTION TO PAGE 151 OF THE COURSEBOOK FOR A SUMMARY OF THE POINTS COVERED IN THIS COMMUNICATION SECTION.

PROMOTION **UNIT 9**

Business across Cultures
Understanding corporate culture
With books closed, ask students what *corporate culture* means (dress, management style, values, internal style of communication, public image, etc.) Then ask: *Who or what creates a corporate culture?*

[N.B. Many founders or managing directors have succeeded in establishing a strong corporate culture, like Ricardo Semler of Semco mentioned in the article in this unit. However, research findings show that corporate culture is strongly influenced by national culture. In countries where people avoid uncertainty – high uncertainty avoidance cultures – there is more intense structuring of activities, greater resistance to change, and less risk-taking by managers. In cultures where uncertainty is not considered a problem – low uncertainty avoidance cultures – there is less structuring of activities, fewer written rules, more risk-taking by managers, and higher labour turnover.]

Tell students that they will read an article about an unusual manufacturing company based in Brazil. Write three facts taken from the article on the board:

Employees set their own schedules and choose their own salaries.
Employees choose their managers.
The company has no receptionists, secretaries, or personal assistants.

Ask students to discuss, in subgroups, the advantages, and disadvantages of such policies. Share ideas and opinions in class, and write some of them on the board.

A Tell students to open their Coursebooks and read the article individually. Once everyone has finished, ask two or three students to summarise the main points, and check for any comprehension problems.

B Ask students to discuss the questions in pairs, then check and briefly discuss answers in class.

KEY
1 It means that employees won't take advantage when deciding their own salaries.
2 They are motivated to make the company successful, and therefore keep budgets in line.
3–5 Students' own answers.

C Depending on your class, there are several ways of approaching this exercise. In a class consisting of students from a single company, ask them to work in subgroups, and to present their icebergs to the rest of the class. In a pre-work class, ask students to consider an educational institution or a company they have visited or know a lot about. Ask them to work individually and to present their iceberg to a partner or subgroup.

Before allowing students to begin the exercise, you could demonstrate the activity by presenting an iceberg relating to an organisation you belong to or one that you are familiar with.

▶ FOR A READING EXERCISE BASED ON A TEXT TITLED 'AVOIDING CORPORATE CULTURE SHOCK', SEE PAGE 39 OF THE WORKBOOK.

▶ REFER STUDENTS TO PAGE 154 OF THE COURSEBOOK FOR A SUMMARY OF THE POINTS COVERED IN THIS BUSINESS ACROSS CULTURES SECTION.

Checklist
As a review activity, ask students to refer to the checklist in their Coursebooks and go over the items with them.

For a brief review of some of the vocabulary that appears in this unit, write the following on the board with the possible answers underneath.

_____-power	pester
pop _____	nag
electronic _____	culture
_____ factor	trends
emerging _____	gadget
_____ consultancy	marketing

PROMOTION **UNIT 10**

10 Selling yourself

PREVIEW

Listening
The main listening activity in this unit features an interview with a human resources specialist in which she provides advice on ways of 'selling yourself'. There are also audio extracts in which people describe how the advice helped them progress professionally.

Vocabulary and speaking
This section focuses on nouns and adjectives frequently used to describe personal qualities. It also looks at the way in which negatives are formed through the use of prefixes and *not very* + adjective.

Communication
telephoning 2: leaving and taking messages
This section builds on the Communication section in the previous unit and concentrates on phrases used to offer and request help, give names and numbers, request action, check details and confirm action.

Business across Cultures
customer service culture
Various ways of putting the customer at the centre of your business are explored in this section. The aim is to make students consider elements of good and bad service based on their own experience, and to provide an awareness that what is considered *good service*, is not the same the world over.

Introductory activity

To get students thinking along the lines of promoting oneself, ask students what *networking* means. (Building up a pool of contacts who could help further your career or contribute to the success of your business.) Brainstorm how they could sell themselves to contacts/potential employers. For example:

offer a business card
know their goals / how they would like their career to evolve
know their strengths / skills
update their skills

Ask students to open their Coursebooks and look at the fact feature. Ask students in what ways they think personal coaches help people sell themselves. (Give advice on how to communicate their strengths and be persuasive.) Ask: *Do you think personal coaching is worth that much money? Why? Why not? Would you consider hiring a coach?*

Start-up

A Ask students to brainstorm their ideas in subgroups, then share their *secrets* with the rest of the class. Encourage students to ask questions and make comments.

Listening

A AUDIO 10.1 Read the questions and notes together. Ask students what they understand by *personal mission statement*, *psychometric tests* and *self-awareness*.

KEY
g f a e b c d is not mentioned

AUDIO SCRIPT

Interviewer: What do human resources specialists mean when they say that you should be able to sell yourself? Surely it's not like selling cars or washing machines?

Rebecca Sands: Well, in a way it is. In the same way that sales people have to communicate the benefits of their product and persuade people to buy it, someone in the job market has to communicate with potential employers and persuade them about what they have to offer.

Interviewer: I see ...

Rebecca Sands: Of course, in order to sell yourself, you have to know yourself. So self-awareness is where it all starts. For example, there are free psychometric tests on the Internet that you can take to check your skills – by answering the questions; you get feedback on how good you are at working with others, how well you manage stress, and so on.

Interviewer: Right ...

Rebecca Sands: This will help you write a personal mission statement – this states what you have to offer, and how you would like your career to evolve in the medium and long term. You can put this mission statement at the top of your CV.

Interviewer: So potential employers can see what your career goals are?

Rebecca Sands: Exactly. Another thing you can do is keep a work diary. Note down important things that happen to you at work and try to draw lessons from them.

Interviewer: We hear a lot these days about keeping your skills up-to-date ...

Rebecca Sands: Yes, that's very important. A lot of professions are changing constantly, so it's important to stay up-to-date, for example, through training. Some employers send their employees on courses, but training will increasingly be the responsibility of individuals, if they want to remain marketable.

Interviewer: Right. Any other tips?

Rebecca Sands: Yes. I know this will sound like a luxury to a lot of people, but getting a personal coach can be a good idea – someone who

64

PROMOTION **UNIT 10**

	can give you advice on developing your career, help you build your confidence, and so on.
Interviewer:	Aren't these coaches quite expensive?
Rebecca Sands:	*Well, a good personal coach will give you good advice on how to sell yourself, so you could see it as an investment for your future.*

B Play AUDIO 10.1 again. Ask students to do the task as indicated, and then to check their answers in pairs. As the audio is relatively long, you could pause after each piece of relevant information to allow students time to take notes. Use the audio script to check answers.

C AUDIO 10.2 Instruct students to do the exercise as indicated. Play the audio and ask them to check their answers in pairs.

KEY
1 d   2 a   3 c   4 e

AUDIO SCRIPT

1 It's very useful. I like the specialist journals and the articles in them. It's good to keep up with what's going on in the industry. Last month, I saw an advertisement for a job that I'd really like to get.

2 It's helped me focus on what I want to do in my career. Putting something on paper has helped me clarify my ideas. I think my CV will really stand out from the crowd now.

3 It's helped me build my confidence. I went for an interview last week and I felt much more confident than last time. We spent two whole sessions preparing for the interview. She went through the kinds of questions that they were likely to ask, we talked about how to sit, what to wear, and so on. It was so helpful.

4 It's made me see some patterns in the way I interact with other people. I wrote something down today that's almost exactly the same as something I wrote last year. It's helped me understand how I can avoid making the same mistakes next time.

Extension activity. There is some useful and interesting language in AUDIO 10.2.
Write on the board:

_____ what's going on in the industry
_____ what I want to do in my career
_____ the crowd
_____ my confidence
_____ the interview
_____ other people

Ask students to listen to the audio again and identify the verbs used in these phrases. Tell them that some may include more than one preposition. Pause after each extract and compare answers in class. Ask students to provide definitions or synonyms if some are not clear from the context.

D Ask students to work with someone new and discuss the questions together.

Extension activity. Write on the board:

REBECCA	INTERVIEWER
Making suggestions	*Questions*
	Comments
	Showing understanding

Tell the class you will play AUDIO 10.1 again. Ask half the class to listen for the phrases Rebecca uses to make suggestions and the other half to listen for the ways in which the interviewer asks questions, makes comments, and shows understanding. Play the audio, allow students to compare their answers, and then write the phrases on the board:

REBECCA	INTERVIEWER
Making suggestions	*Questions*
You can take ... (tests)	What do ... ?
Another thing you can do is ...	So potential employers can see what ... ?
It's important to ...	Any other tips?
... can be a good idea.	Aren't coaches quite expensive?
	Comments
	We hear a lot ...
	Showing understanding
	Right.
	I see ...

Focusing on the interviewer's questions, tell students that *So potential ...?* is a reflecting question. Ask: *Are these types of questions important in communication?* (They show that you are listening and trying to understand.) Also ask why the interviewer uses a negative question in: *Aren't coaches quite expensive?* (Because she already thinks/knows coaches are expensive and will be surprised if the interviewee disagrees.) Elicit the full question for: *Any other tips?* (Do you have any other tips?) Tell students that native speakers tend to shorten questions which include words such as *many, any,* and *much*. For example: *Much work to do?*

Ask students to turn to page 150 to review the different types of questions and encouraging comments which were introduced in Unit 2.

Now ask students to work in pairs and role-play the interview between Rebecca Sands and the interviewer. Encourage them to use a variety of questions and phrases for making suggestions. Provide feedback on the use of the target language.

▶ FOR A READING EXERCISE RELATING TO NETWORKING SKILLS AND HOW TO SELL YOURSELF, DIRECT STUDENTS TO PAGES 40 OF THE WORKBOOK.

Vocabulary and speaking

A Ask students to look at the first example and match the adjective to its definition. Before allowing them to embark on the activity, check that they understand the use of nouns and adjectives by eliciting an example sentence for each. For example:

Self-awareness is important when selling yourself.
Tim is very *self-aware*.

Get students to do the exercise in pairs, and then check answers in class. Elicit the pronunciation and main stress of each word, and drill if necessary.

65

PROMOTION UNIT 10

KEY

2	numeracy	numerate
3	motivation	motivated
4	flexibility	flexible
5	creativity	creative
6	energy	energetic
7	commitment	committed
8	cooperation	cooperative

1 h 2 d 3 f 4 b 5 c 6 a 7 e 8 g

B Ask students to work in pairs and do the exercise as indicated in the Coursebook.

KEY

1 energy
2 creative
3 committed
4 numeracy
5 motivated
6 Flexibility
7 cooperative

C Direct students' attention to the explanation. Tell students that using negative adjectives can, depending on the context, sound critical, direct and, of course, negative, so we use *not very* together with a positive adjective to avoid using negative adjectives.

Go through a few rules for *un-*, *in-*, *il-*, *im-* and *ir-* as negative prefixes:

There is no really firm rule distinguishing the prefixes *un-* from *in-*, except that words of Latin origin tend to take the *in-* prefix.
unclear   uncommitted   innumerate   inflexible

The *il-* prefix is used with words beginning with *l*:
illegal   illogical   illiterate

The *im-* prefix is used with words beginning with *b*, *m* or *p*:
impatient   impolite   imbalance   immoral

The *ir-* prefix is used with words beginning with *r*. Although, not all such words take an *ir-* prefix.
irresponsible   irreplaceable

[N.B. Latinate words often include the following:
-ex- -gred- -ject- -seq- -qui-

Many Latinate words begin with the following:
ad- qui- pro- in- com- re- cap- sub- form- oper- ex- app-

Examples of Latinate suffixes:
-ate -ation -it -ical -ient -eive -ite -ive -able -ible -al]

You could ask students to brainstorm words which include the above. You might also mention that such words are usually formal. If you have time, see if students can guess what their informal synonyms are.

Mention that some words such as *energetic*, cannot take a prefix. Ask students to do exercise C in pairs, and then check answers in class. Explain that the main stress of the word does not change position when a prefix is added.

KEY

1 He's inflexible. He's not very flexible.
2 He's not very creative.
3 He's not very energetic.
4 He's not very committed.
5 He's uncooperative. He's not very cooperative.
6 He's innumerate. He's not very numerate.

D Ask students to work with a partner and do the exercise orally. During feedback, ask students to tell the class two things their partner said.

▶ FOR FURTHER PRACTICE AND AWARENESS OF NEGATIVE PREFIXES, SEE PHOTOCOPIABLE RESOURCES ON PAGE 117.

Extension activity. Ask students what the purpose of a *mission statement* is. (It provides potential employers with a brief description of what you want to focus on, what you want to accomplish and who you want to become.) You could give subgroups a few sample mission statements, which are very easy to find on the Internet. Ask them to identify the main elements (core values, personal qualities, goals, etc.) You could then ask them to find nouns and adjectives which describe character and behaviour (responsibility, discipline, fairness, positive, enthusiastic, flexible, etc.). Finally, ask students to work in subgroups and write a mission statement (three to five sentences long) for a famous person. Alternatively, you could ask students to write their own mission statements for homework.

▶ FOR FURTHER INFORMATION ON USING ADJECTIVES, REFER STUDENTS TO GRAMMAR OVERVIEW, PAGE 164 OF THE COURSEBOOK.

▶ FOR FURTHER PRACTICE AND CONSOLIDATION OF USING ADJECTIVES AND PREFIXES, DIRECT STUDENTS TO PAGE 41 OF THE WORKBOOK.

▶ REVIEW AND DEVELOPMENT EXERCISES ON DESCRIBING PERSONAL QUALITIES, PAGE 67, CAN BE DONE AT THIS STAGE.

Communication

Telephoning 2: Leaving and taking messages

With Coursebooks closed, elicit a typical answerphone message and write it on the board:

Hello, you've got through to ... . I'm afraid I'm not available at the moment, but if you'd like to leave your name and number, I'll get back to you as soon as possible.

Read the message out loud and ask students to identify intonation patterns. Before asking them to practise it in pairs, check pronunciation of contractions (*you've/you'd/I'll*) and drill if necessary. If you have enough cassette recorders available, ask students to record their messages in groups, one person after the other, so they can hear how the message would sound.

Next, ask: *What should you include in an answerphone or voicemail message?* Answers may include: *name, date and time of call, reason for call or action required and when and how you can be contacted.*

Remind students that when leaving messages they should repeat any important information like telephone numbers and addresses.

Next, ask students to record an answerphone message. Write on the board:

You call Mr Smith to arrange a meeting, but you get through to his voicemail.

Ask students to decide in subgroups what kind of information they should include in their message. Then get each person to record their individual message.

PROMOTION **UNIT 10**

Circulate during the activity to identify good language and intonation as well as areas that could be improved. Give feedback after the exercise and analyse the language, pronunciation, and general tone of two or three of the recorded messages.

Ask students to open their Coursebooks and read the introduction.

A AUDIO **10.3** Go through the exercise together. Play the audio, pausing after each message, and then ask students to check their answers in pairs. It may be necessary to play the audio again.

KEY

1 Name of caller: Susan
   Message: would like to talk about the meeting this afternoon.
   Action: please call back.
   Contact number: 021 3567 2804

2 Name of caller: John Hacker
   Message: for Rosemary Finnigan. Needs to speak about software budget. Urgent.
   Action: Rosemary Finnigan to call him this afternoon.
   Contact number: 07882 393 978

3 Name of caller: Peter McEnery
   Message: for Gordon. Have won the contract.
   Action: Gordon to call.
   Contact number: Gordon already has it.

AUDIO SCRIPT

1 Hi, this is Susan. I tried calling you on your landline but I guess you must be out. I'd like to talk about the meeting this afternoon. Could you call me back? My number is 021 3567 2804. Speak to you later. Bye.

2 A: … Can I take a message?
   B: Yes, please. This is John Hacker.
   A: Could you spell that, please?
   B: H-A-C-K-E-R. I'd like to leave a message for Rosemary Finnigan. Could you tell her that I called and that I need to speak to her urgently about the software budget?
   A: Of course. Has she got your number?
   B: Let me give you my mobile number – it's 07882 393 978.
   A: Let me just repeat that – 07882 393 978.
   B: That's right. Could she call me back this afternoon? It's really urgent.
   A: I'll make sure she gets the message.
   B: Thanks.

3 A: Would you like to leave a message?
   B: Yes, could you tell Gordon that Peter McEnery called. Shall I spell that for you?
   A: Please.
   B: It's M-C-E-N-E-R-Y. I'd like Gordon to know that we've won the contract. And could you ask him to give me a call?
   A: Could I have your number?
   B: That's OK. He's got it.
   A: Fine. I'll tell him you called.
   B: Thanks.

B Go through the Key language in class. Draw students' attention to ways of spelling and giving numbers. Explain that some letters and numbers are difficult to recognise on the telephone, even for native speakers. Ask students how they can clarify and check letters. (Is that S for Spain?) Tell them they can use the international radio code to help them. Explain that sometimes it's difficult to differentiate between 13 and 30, 16 and 60 and so on, even though the main stress is on a different syllable. Ask students how they can check these numbers. (Is that three-zero or one-three?)

Ask students to work in pairs and do the exercise as indicated. Ask students to sit back-to-back throughout the activity and to make sure that they check and clarify details. Afterwards, give class feedback, underlining positive points as well as errors.

To provide more individual feedback, you could use a Telephoning Feedback Framework (see Frameworks, page 123). Go through the feedback sheet with the students prior to the exercise so that they are aware of the key factors upon which their performance will be assessed.

Extension activity. Ask students to work in pairs. Tell them that they are going to leave a telephone message for another student in the class. Their partners will take the message (the name of the caller, message, action, and contact information) and then pass it on to the intended recipient. To make the activity slightly more entertaining, ask callers to assume the role of an imaginary person.

▶ FOR SELF-STUDY PRACTICE OF THE LANGUAGE USED IN LEAVING AND TAKING MESSAGES, DIRECT STUDENTS TO PAGE 42 OF THE WORKBOOK.

▶ REFER STUDENTS TO PAGE 151 OF THE COURSEBOOK, FOR A SUMMARY OF THE POINTS COVERED IN THIS COMMUNICATION SECTION.

Business across Cultures
Customer service culture

Ask students to think of companies, retailers, and service sectors in their country/countries that are well-known for their customer service. Put their suggestions on the board, then ask why these companies are famous for their service. Next, ask which companies are well-known for their poor customer service and why.

Instruct students to open their Coursebooks and read the introduction to the class.

A Read through the rules together. Ask students if they think the statements are true and whether there is anything they would add.

B Ask students to discuss the statements in pairs, then check their responses in class.

KEY

c

C Ask students to do the exercise as indicated in pairs. When comparing their answers in class, they may come up with more than one opposite for each word or phrase.

KEY

to neglect a customer	to be uncompetitive
to lose a customer	to be unhelpful
to under-promise	to not smile / to frown
to treat a customer badly	to be rude

67

PROMOTION UNIT 10

D Before embarking on this exercise, write on the board:
What kind of service do you expect when:
you phone a utility company?
you enter a clothes shop?

Ask students to work in subgroups and come up with a list of points for each scenario.

Write their ideas on the board:

a utility company ▶ *to be dealt with very quickly (not put on hold), fast and efficient service*

a clothes store ▶ *friendly staff, offer of assistance*

If the class is multinational, ask the students if they identified any cultural differences during their discussions. For example, in North America, shop assistants are expected to be friendly and they often make small talk with customers. Meanwhile, in Japan, a certain distance is expected to be kept between the shop assistant and customer – a shop assistant's attempt to make small talk would be considered over-familiar and disrespectful. Direct students' attention to page 154 and read the Business across Cultures overview.

Direct students' attention to the exercise in the Coursebook. This exercise is best done in pairs. During feedback, ask each pair to briefly summarise the more interesting experiences mentioned during their discussion.

E Ask students to form new subgroups and do the exercise as indicated. Ask each subgroup to present their ideas to the rest of the class.

Extension activity. Ask students to imagine that they are business consultants who have to write a set of recommendations for the customer service department of an organisation which provides poor service. This should be one of the organisations discussed during the activity in exercise D. In their recommendations, they should explain what needs to be improved and how. Encourage them to use some of their ideas from exercise E. This could be set as a writing exercise for homework.

▶ REFER STUDENTS TO PAGE 154 OF THE COURSEBOOK FOR A SUMMARY OF THE POINTS COVERED IN THIS BUSINESS ACROSS CULTURES SECTION.

▶ THIS WOULD BE AN APPROPRIATE STAGE AT WHICH TO DO WRITING RESOURCE 19 WHICH FOCUSES ON LETTERS OF COMPLAINT.

Checklist

As a review activity, ask students to refer to the checklist in their Coursebooks and go over the items with them.

You may wish to expand on the vocabulary used to describe personal qualities. Provide subgroups with several job adverts and ask them to identify characteristics required for certain jobs. In addition, you could also elicit the opposite or negative form of the adjectives. For example:

Sales manager

driven ⟵⟶ not very driven

ambitious ⟵⟶ not very ambitious / unambitious

PROMOTION **UNIT 11**

11 Think global, act local

PREVIEW

Vocabulary and listening
The listening activity features an interview with an expert on global advertising in which she describes two very creative and popular advertising campaigns. Words which are frequently collocated with the word *global* are identified in the interview.

Grammar
infinitives and *-ing* forms
A range of verbs which are followed by the infinitive form, the *-ing* form or both forms are examined in this section.

Communication
telephoning 3: structuring a call
This section focuses on the process of making an effective telephone call and includes phrases for stating the purpose of a call, structuring, checking, deflecting, taking further action, making a final check, and making decisions. It also highlights the importance of preparation for a call in order to achieve effective and successful communication.

Business across Cultures
work and play
This section focuses on key moments in working and playing internationally. It also features advice on customs and social etiquette around the world. This raises awareness of the need for tolerance and sensitivity when entertaining foreign visitors or when being entertained in other cultures.

Introductory activity

In subgroups, ask students to brainstorm companies, corporations and organisations that have a global presence, (Nike, McDonald's, Volkswagen, Starbucks, BBC, Sky, Benetton, etc.) Allow two minutes, then put students' suggestions on the board. Ask: *Do these organisations tailor their products or services to local tastes and needs?* (McDonald's adapts its menu and ingredients according to local taste. / China took the Corsa and transformed it into a much more upscale model than the European version by slightly modifying the interior.)

Ask students to open their Coursebooks and look at the title of the unit, 'Think global, act local'. Ask students to put the title into their own words. (Companies that have a global presence also need to have local knowledge.)

Direct students' attention to the fact feature and ask what this suggests. (People around the world are increasingly buying the same products and perhaps they respond to advertisements in the same way.)

Start-up

A Ask students to read and answer the questions in subgroups, then compare their responses in class. Next ask: *In what ways do advertisements have to be adapted to the local market?* (Language, translation, appropriate images, etc.) You could bring in some print adverts and ask students to think of cultures in which they would be inappropriate and why. For example:

nudity / immodesty	▶ parts of the Middle East
people drinking beer with dinner	▶ France
eating food in front of the TV	▶ France, Southern Europe
scenes featuring large families	▶ China
men doing housework	▶ high-masculinity cultures

Listening and vocabulary

A AUDIO **11.1** Ask students to do the exercise as indicated in the Coursebook. Play the audio, and then check answers in class.

KEY
Company: HSBC bank
Countries: Egypt, Greece, Italy

AUDIO SCRIPT

Interviewer: Can you give us an example of a global advertising campaign?

Jane Williams: Yes, HSBC Bank ran a very interesting campaign recently. The slogan was 'Never underestimate the importance of local knowledge'. The advertisements demonstrated the brand idea of 'local knowledge' by looking at different customs and practices around the world.

Interviewer: Right ...

Jane Williams: For example, they looked at the meaning of gestures in different countries. One of these was the upturned hand with fingers closed. In Egypt, this means 'be patient'; in Greece, it means 'that's perfect'; in Italy, it means 'what exactly do you mean?'. They called this the 'cultural collisions' campaign.

Interviewer: I see ...

Jane Williams: The idea was to show that the bank has a global presence, but also has local knowledge. The strapline was 'HSBC: the world's local bank'. The message was that customers are treated as individuals, and that HSBC cares about them as individuals, and recognises their particular needs.

Interviewer: Was the campaign successful?

69

PROMOTION UNIT 11

Jane Williams: Yes, it increased global awareness of the HSBC brand. HSBC had been built up largely by the acquisition of banks in different countries and this was a great way of showing it as a global brand with local interests.

Interviewer: I see ...

B Check students' understanding of *slogan*, *outcome* and *strapline*. Elicit a few examples of well-known slogans.

Play AUDIO 11.1. Ask students to compare their answers to a partner's, and then check them in class. You may need to play the audio twice and pause after key information.

Ask students what they think of the campaign. Ask: *Is it a good idea? What other customs and practices could HSBC have used in its campaign?*

KEY

Slogan: Never underestimate the importance of local knowledge.

Brand idea: The bank has global presence and local knowledge.

Outcome: Successful. Increased global awareness of HSBC brand.

What the ad consisted of: Different customs and practices around the world.

Strapline: HSBC: the world's local bank.

C AUDIO 11.2 Before playing the audio make sure that students are aware that they are going to hear about a completely different campaign. Play the audio and ask students to check their answers in pairs. Again, you may need to play the audio twice and pause after key information. After the exercise, you could ask students which campaign they prefer and why.

KEY

Brand idea: The bank that values different points of view.

Media: TV, then website.

What the ad consisted of: Different views from around the world on different topics e.g. art, technology, food, sport.

Example from website: Choose from a list of words to describe your point of view on a topic such as modern art.

AUDIO SCRIPT

Jane Williams: They followed it up with a multimedia campaign that focused on the brand idea: 'the bank that values different points of view.' The first batch of 'different points of view' TV commercials was shown on global TV channels such as BBC World, CNN International, CNBC, Discovery, and National Geographic Channel. These ads present views from around the world on different topics, such as art, technology, food, sport, and so on. They aim to engage with viewers and send them to a website – yourpointofview.com – where they're asked to give their own views.

Interviewer: How do you mean?

Jane Williams: Well, on the website, you choose from a list of words that describe your point of view on a particular topic. So, for example on modern art, you have to say if you think it's 'fascinating', 'beautiful', 'confusing', 'rubbish', and so on. It's a very good way of engaging with people and encouraging the idea that HSBC is comfortable with different ideas and different ways of thinking about things.

Interviewer: And the Internet is, by definition, a global medium ...

Jane Williams: That's right. This website is not an advertisement in the ordinary sense, but it engages with, and involves people all over the world and makes them think about HSBC ...

Interviewer: Do HSBC intend to continue with ads like this?

Jane Williams: Yes. They'll have the same campaigns all over the world, but translated into the local languages of the countries where the campaign appears.

D Play the interview again. Compare answers in class, then ask students to match the words and definitions in pairs.

KEY

global advertising b	global brand c
global presence e	global TV channels f
global awareness a	global medium d

[N.B. You could draw students' attention to the website (yourpointofview.com) which is mentioned in AUDIO 11.2, so that they can do the survey at home if they are interested.]

▶ FOR READING ON THE TOPIC OF GLOBAL ADVERTISING MISTAKES AND WAYS OF AVOIDING THEM, DIRECT STUDENTS TO PAGE 44 OF THE WORKBOOK.

Grammar

Infinitives and *-ing* forms

Go through the information in the Grammar section in class. Although it mentions that *like* can be used with both the infinitive and *-ing* form, ask students what the difference is and write examples on the board:

I like eating fruit. (I enjoy it.)

I like to eat fruit. (I think it's good for me, but I don't enjoy it.)

A Ask students to do this exercise in pairs, then check their answers in class.

KEY

1 f　2 d　3 b　4 c　5 e　6 a

B Do the first question together in class, then ask students to complete the exercise in pairs. Check answers in class.

KEY

1 to run	2 producing	3 having worked
4 to do	5 producing	6 to make
7 to conduct	8 to design / designing	9 to wait

Extension activity. Tell students to write three questions using one of the verbs from each of the three groups in the grammar rules. They should then ask at least three people their questions. Do an example with one student in class:

What does studying a foreign language involve?

Would you consider working in a foreign country?

PROMOTION **UNIT 11**

▶ FOR FURTHER INFORMATION ON USING INFINITIVES AND -ING FORMS, REFER STUDENTS TO GRAMMAR OVERVIEW, PAGE 165.

▶ FOR FURTHER PRACTICE AND CONSOLIDATION OF USING INFINITIVES AND -ING FORMS, DIRECT STUDENTS TO PAGE 45 OF THE WORKBOOK.

▶ REVIEW AND DEVELOPMENT EXERCISES ON INFINITIVES AND -ING FORMS, PAGE 68, CAN BE DONE AT THIS STAGE.

Communication

Telephoning 3: Structuring a call

With Coursebooks closed, ask: *How do you prepare for a call with someone you have never met before to discuss travel arrangements?* Instruct students to write a checklist in pairs. Keep this brief and bring students' ideas together to create one checklist on the board. For example:

Checklist

Information about the person (surname, position).

Information needed during the call (reference numbers, dates, times, etc.)

Questions the other person may ask you and how you can answer these questions.

Your own contact information – in case he/she needs to call you back.

Erase the board, then ask students to open their Coursebooks and read the introduction together.

A AUDIO 11.3 Read the questions and check understanding of the points in class. Play the audio once and ask students to compare their answers to a partner's.

KEY

1 reason for call: new product launch
2 logistics
3 delivery date of headsets
4 promotion
5 point-of-sale material

AUDIO SCRIPT

Lucy: Lucy Chen speaking.
Mike: Hi, Lucy. This is Mike Brent here. How are you?
Lucy: I'm fine, Mike, and you?
Mike: Good, thanks. Listen, the reason I'm calling is to discuss the product launch next month.
Lucy: For the new headsets?
Mike: That's right. I'd like to cover two main points – logistics and promotion. Is this a good time to talk about this?
Lucy: Yes, it's fine.
Mike: Thanks. So firstly, logistics. We've decided to hold the main stock in our regional supply centres and ship to you locally on a weekly basis.
Lucy: Won't that lead to delays? I mean if it sells well, we could run out.
Mike: I don't think that will happen. The regional supply centre will have the headsets by the end of next week. You should receive the first shipment on the 4th of March. Is that OK with you?
Lucy: That sounds fine.
Mike: Good. Now on the promotion side, I'll email you the point-of-sale material later today. This will give you time to translate it, do any other local adaptations and get it to your printers by the beginning of next week.
Lucy: Fine.
Mike: OK, that's it for now. Is there anything else?
Lucy: I'd like to have a word with you about my transfer.
Mike: Don't worry, I haven't forgotten. I'll get back to you about that.
Lucy: OK, Mike.
Mike: Bye for now.
Lucy: Oh, Mike, before you go – could you send me an email to confirm the details we've discussed?
Mike: OK. I'll do that now.
Lucy: Then I'll let the team know about the schedule.
Mike: Great. I'll leave that to you. Lucy, I really must go now ...

B Direct students' attention to the key language and go through the different points. Ask students what the purpose of *deflecting* is. (Playing for time. / Delaying making an important decision.)

Depending on your class, you might focus on intonation patterns. (E.g. *Is that OK with you?* ▶ rising intonation.) You could also briefly examine sentence stress by asking which words are stressed in the following sentences:

First, I'd like to discuss ...

Finally I'd like to mention ...

Another thing is our promotion.

Mark the stress above the words *first*, *finally* and *another* on the board. Then ask where the speaker should pause. (After *first*, *finally*, and slightly after *thing*.) Mark the pauses on the board with a forward slash. (*First*, / *I'd like to ...*) Drill and ask pairs to practise together.

Listen to AUDIO 11.3 again and get students to check their answers in pairs.

KEY

a The reason I'm calling is ...
b I'd like to cover two main points ...
c Is this a good time to talk about this?
d So, firstly ...
e Now on the promotion side ...
f Is there anything else?
g I'll get back to you about that.

C Ask students to work with someone new and do the exercise as indicated in the Coursebook. Before beginning the activity, check that students understand their roles and remind them to check details such as times.

[N.B. Ask students for the most effective way of exchanging times in an international context. Explain that we use the 24-hour clock, particularly on the telephone, except in the USA where time is clarified by using a.m. and p.m. Ask students to briefly practise exchanging times in pairs: 18:30 ▶ eighteen–thirty, that's one–eight–three–oh or six-thirty p.m.]

Circulate during this activity and make a note of good language as well as errors.

To provide more individual feedback, you could use a Telephoning Feedback Framework (see Frameworks, page 123). Go through the feedback sheet with the students

PROMOTION UNIT 11

prior to the exercise so that they are aware of the key factors upon which their performance will be assessed.

Extension activity. Ask students to work in pairs. Tell them that Student A is visiting Student B's country to give a presentation. Write on the board:

B needs to know: flight number, arrival time, length of stay, facilities required for presentation

A needs to know: address of B's company, hotel telephone number

Student B should call Student A. Get them to make a note of the information received as each will need to send an email to their assistants providing information about the visit and presentation. Ask the students to write a short email after the activity.

▶ FOR SELF-STUDY PRACTICE OF THE LANGUAGE USED IN STRUCTURING A CALL, DIRECT STUDENTS TO PAGE 46 OF THE WORKBOOK.

▶ REFER STUDENTS TO PAGE 152 OF THE COURSEBOOK FOR A SUMMARY OF THE POINTS COVERED IN THIS COMMUNICATION SECTION.

Business across Cultures
Work and play

Read the introduction and answer the questions in class. In a multinational class, you are likely to observe differences in attitudes towards work and play. As we saw in the *Culture Clash* text in the Business across Cultures section in Unit 3, in collectivist cultures people value time spent socially with their colleagues, whereas in individualistic cultures people value their private life and free time away from work.

A AUDIO 11.4 Tell students that they will hear extracts from the situations listed. Ask students to do the exercise as indicated. Play the audio and get students to check their answers in pairs.

KEY

1 d   2 c   3 b   4 a   5 e

AUDIO SCRIPT

1   A: It's your shot.
    B: OK, here goes. ... Oh dear!
    A: Never mind. At least we can still see the ball.

2   A: Have you heard the one about the Englishman, the Welshman and the Scotsman?
    B: Probably, but go ahead.
    A: Well an Englishman, a Welshman, and a Scotsman form a lottery syndicate, and would you believe it, they win. It's a big payout – over ten million ...

3   A: You must let me get this.
    B: No way. It's my turn.
    A: No, I'd like to treat you.
    B: Well, if you insist. But next time, it's on me.

4   A: You really shouldn't have. Can I open it?
    B: Of course. Go ahead.
    A: Oh .... It's lovely. Is it from your part of the world?
    B: Yes, it is. In fact, it's made in ....

5   A: Cheers. Here's to a successful project.
    B: Yes, cheers. Umm ... That's good. I needed that.
    A: Me, too. It's been a long day. But I'm really pleased that ...

B Check pronunciation of the country names and mark the word stress on the board if necessary. Ask individual students to read each box out loud in class, and then ask where they can expect to find this behaviour. Make sure they give reasons for their opinions.

KEY

a Australia   d Japan
b Egypt   e Brazil
c China   f Poland

C Ask one student to read the advice out loud in class, then check understanding. Ask students to discuss the advice in subgroups for about five minutes.

D Before this activity, elicit areas that the students could provide advice on. For example:

Food   Drink   Business cards   Punctuality
Greetings   Clothing   Gifts   Discussion topics

If your class is made up of students of different nationalities, ask them to either work alone, in pairs or in groups of the same nationality. If you have a monolingual group, ask students to work in subgroups.

Give each group, or individual, a large sheet of paper or flipchart and ask them to list *Do's* and *Don'ts*. They will present their advice to the class. Provide an example based on your own country beforehand. For example:

The UK

DO	DON'T
Arrive 15–20 minutes after the stated arrival time for a dinner party.	Push in at the front of a queue.

Tell students that they should explain their advice, e.g. In the UK, people have a strong sense of fairness, which is why you should never push in.

Give students 10–15 minutes to prepare their tips. Encourage the other students to ask questions and make comments during the presentations.

▶ FOR A QUIZ AND A WRITING EXERCISE ON THE SUBJECT OF WORK AND PLAY, SEE PAGE 47 OF THE WORKBOOK.

▶ REFER STUDENTS TO PAGE 154 OF THE COURSEBOOK FOR A SUMMARY OF THE POINTS COVERED IN THIS BUSINESS ACROSS CULTURES SECTION.

Checklist

As a review activity, ask students to refer to the checklist in their Coursebooks and go over the items with them.

To review the infinitive and *-ing* forms, write the following verbs on the board:

agree   decide   offer   plan
promise   admit   mention   suggest

Then ask students to watch an interview or short scenario. (This could be a clip from a current affairs programme or even a soap opera.) While watching, students should make a note of things that were *agreed, mentioned, offered, promised* and so on. Show the clip as many times as necessary, then ask students to tell you what happened. For example:

He suggested going to the police.
He mentioned his boss.

PROMOTION UNIT 12

12 The grey market

PREVIEW

Reading and speaking
The reading exercise is based on extracts from an article about advertising to over 50s in the UK. The speaking activity involves preparing outlines for advertisements targeting different audiences.

Grammar — **present perfect simple and continuous**
Students are often confused by the difference between these two tenses. This section provides some simple rules and practice.

Communication — **telephoning 4: closing a call**
This is an area of telephoning that students usually find difficult. This section focuses on phrases used to signal closing, confirm and promise action, thank and close a call positively.

Business across Cultures — **working in cross-functional teams**
This section introduces the concept of the *silo mentality*, which can be defined as the failure to understand the concerns of colleagues in other departments, and ways of encouraging people to work in cross-functional teams.

Introductory activity
In order to get the class to think along the lines of targeting older consumers, write the following items on the board:

Car
Skin care cream
Holidays in Australia
Health food products

Then write two headings below:

<u>An Older Audience</u>   <u>A Younger Audience</u>

Ask students to form subgroups and discuss how advertisers would promote the products listed on the board to each audience. Do an example in class:

<u>A car</u>

an older audience → safety features, convenience, for visiting grandchildren, daytrips

a younger audience → speed, style, 'extras' such as a state-of-the-art stereo system

Write their suggestions on the board and invite comments from other groups.

Ask students to open their Coursebooks and ask what is meant by the *grey market*. Read the fact feature together and ask what impact the huge population of over 65s will have on businesses such as car companies, tour operators, etc.

Start-up

A Ask students to read and discuss the statements in subgroups. Then ask them to share their opinions in class, but keep it brief. In a multinational group, you may find cultural differences in terms of similarity between over 50s and younger people, which may be worth exploring.

Reading and speaking
Draw students' attention to the photograph and ask what they see. (Over 65s on a Harley Davidson.) Ask what this suggests about older people's tastes and outlook on life.

A Ask different students to read parts of the text out loud in class. Get students to answer the questions in pairs, and then compare their answers in class.

KEY

1 20 million. Yes, it is.

2 80 per cent.

3 A quarter.

4 They want it to be informative.

5 Older people have formed their tastes by the age of 40 and don't respond to advertising vs. older people are just as changeable as the young. The second view.

6 Students' own answers.

B Ask students to form subgroups and assign each group a different product to work on. Distribute large sheets of paper or flipcharts for the groups to write up the main points of their outline on. Set a time limit of 15–20 minutes for preparation. While students are listening to other groups' presentations, ask them to consider, in light of the article above, whether the ideas are appropriate for a younger/older audience and if that particular audience would relate to the advert.

During the presentations, note any useful language as well as errors, for feedback afterwards.

Extension activity. As an extension activity or variation of exercise B, you could ask students to actually produce an advertisement targeting a specific audience for one of the products already mentioned.

Prior to the exercise, distribute advertisements of a wide range of products and services, and ask the subgroups to identify comparatives and superlatives in the text, such as: *the best on the market, the most effective,* etc.

When you have written the identified sentences on the board, refer students to Unit 2 for a brief review of comparatives and superlatives.

Next, give each group large sheets of paper or a flipchart,

73

PROMOTION UNIT 12

on which to create a draft of their advert. Encourage them to include comparatives and superlatives in their product description. Set a strict time limit, and then ask students to show their adverts to the rest of the class. Invite comments and questions.

▶ FOR FURTHER READING ON THE GREY MARKET, DIRECT STUDENTS TO PAGES 48 OF THE WORKBOOK.

Grammar
Present perfect simple and continuous

Before presenting the present perfect simple and the present perfect continuous, it would be useful to review the differences between the present perfect and past simple tenses which were introduced in Unit 4. Refer students to the rules on page 17, then ask them to form questions using the following prompts:

How long / you / live / here?

What / you / do / last summer?

How long / you / have / your car?

When / you / leave / school?

What / you / do / last weekend?

What / you / do / since you left school?

Next, ask students to mingle and ask each other the questions. Encourage them to respond using complete sentences; demonstrate this by doing an example with a strong student. Circulate during the activity and make a note of grammatical errors. Provide feedback after the exercise.

With Coursebooks closed, introduce the present perfect simple and the present perfect continuous by writing the following sentences on the board:

A: I've read the report.

B: I've been reading the report.

Ask: *What is the difference between these two sentences?* Ask questions to help them, for example referring to A: *Have I finished reading the report?* (Yes.) and referring to B: *Have I finished?* (Probably not.) Then write on the board:

Focus is on result.   Focus is on continuous activity.

Ask students which sentence these statements describe.

Instruct students to open their Coursebooks and read the Grammar section. Go through it together and check understanding.

A Do the first question together in class, then ask students to do the exercise in pairs. While checking answers in class, elicit reasons for their choice of tense in each sentence.

KEY

1 've been studying	've decided
2 have been running	have increased
3 has been selling	have invested
4 have portrayed	have been considering

B Again, ask students to work on the exercise in pairs. Check their answers in class and get them to explain why some structures are not possible.

KEY

1✔ 2✘ 3✔ 4✘ 5✔ 6✘ 7✔

Extension activity. Tell students that both present perfect tenses are used a lot during social interaction. We use them to catch up with people we haven't seen for a long time.

Write on the board:

I haven't seen you for ages. What have you been doing?

Elicit possible responses:

I've been working in Peru.

I've written a book.

And ways of showing interest:

Have you? / Sounds interesting.

Drill the pronunciation of the contractions *I've, haven't* and *what've*. In speech, we nearly always prefer the contracted form of the auxiliary verb. When contractions are not used, a speaker can sound a little peremptory or even annoyed.

I have met him. (exasperation)

I have not seen the report. (anger)

However, at the beginning of a question or at the end of a clause, *have* cannot be contracted.

[N.B. Both *haven't* and *what've* tend to include the sound ə
▶ havən't and what'və. Awareness of contractions and the ə sound in the spoken present perfect will also help students to decode the speech of native speakers.]

Tell students that they are going to meet several people in the class and imagine they are catching up with each other. Allow one minute for students to think of some exciting news – the more imaginative or glamorous, the better. During this activity, stop students after they have spoken in pairs for two minutes and ask them to change partners. Allow them to speak to about six people. Circulate during the activity and note their use of the tenses and contractions, as well as natural dialogue. Before providing feedback, ask students who told them the most exciting news.

Alternative extension activity. Ask students to work in pairs and write a two minute speech, to be given to shareholders, about a very successful year in an imaginary company.

Prior to the exercise, brainstorm areas that the shareholders will be interested in hearing about:

Profits

Productivity

Public image – awards, public recognition

Expansion – new production sites, premises, etc.

Investment

Customer satisfaction

Also, briefly elicit ways of introducing the speech:

Good afternoon, ladies and gentlemen.

I'm very pleased to be here to tell you about ...

Then ask for one or two present perfect sentences relating to the topics above:

... profits have increased dramatically

... we have been expanding our operations

Allow students 20 minutes to prepare their speech, which can include as many outlandish and improbable claims as they like. They can also illustrate facts with one or two visuals (graphs, pie charts, etc.) if they wish.

After each speech, encourage the shareholders (i.e. the rest of the class) to ask questions and make comments.

▶ FOR FURTHER INFORMATION ON THE PRESENT PERFECT SIMPLE AND PRESENT PERFECT CONTINUOUS, REFER STUDENTS TO GRAMMAR OVERVIEW, PAGE 166.

▶ FOR FURTHER PRACTICE OF THE PRESENT PERFECT SIMPLE AND CONTINUOUS, DIRECT STUDENTS TO PAGES 49 OF THE WORKBOOK.

PROMOTION UNIT 12

▶ REVIEW AND DEVELOPMENT EXERCISES ON THE PRESENT PERFECT SIMPLE AND CONTINUOUS ON PAGE 68, CAN BE DONE AT THIS STAGE.

Communication

Telephoning 4: Closing a call

Direct students' attention to the introduction and exercise.

A AUDIO 12.1 Ask students to do the exercise as indicated, play the audio and check answers in class.

KEY

1 Double deliveries for the next two months – one midmonth and one at the end of the month.
2 Delivery of preliminary report by the end of the week, full report by the end of the month.

AUDIO SCRIPT

1   A: It's been good to talk to you.
    B: Yes, it's been very helpful. We should do this more often. Talking things through is so much better than emailing.
    A: That's true. Anyway, can I just confirm that we've agreed to double deliveries for the next two months?
    B: Yes, we've agreed that there will be one delivery midmonth and another at the end of the month. We can adjust these with two weeks' notice.
    A: That's right. Would you like me to put that in writing?
    B: An email would be good, and then I can forward it to the relevant people.
    A: Fine, I'll do that.
    B: OK, Pete. Nice to speak to you.
    A: You, too. And thanks again.
    B: You're welcome. Goodbye.

2   A: Let me just go over that. You'll let me have a preliminary report by the end of the week and then the full report at the end of the month.
    B: That's right. I'll get on with it straight away. Is there anything else?
    A: No, that's it. Thanks for your support on this.
    B: No problem. See you at the meeting on Monday.
    A: See you then. Bye.
    B: Bye.

B Go through the various language items in the Key language box together. Point out that *Anyway*, *Right* and *OK* are usually used to signal closing. Say them out loud and elicit the intonation pattern. (Falling.)

Ask students to listen to AUDIO 12.1 again and check their answers in pairs, then in class.

As students often find it difficult to end calls and can sound quite stilted, the audio can be used again to provide awareness and practice of intonation patterns and sentence stress. Tell students that they are going to listen to the end of the first dialogue in AUDIO 12.1 again and that they should write out the full dialogue. Play the dialogue from *Fine, I'll do that*, as many times as necessary. Then ask students to listen again and identify intonation patterns and sentence stress. Check for patterns then play it again, pausing after each sentence, and ask individual students to listen and repeat. Finally, get students to briefly practise the end of the call in pairs.

C Ask students to do the exercise as indicated in pairs. Encourage them to use the phrases in the Key language box and to end each call as positively as possible. Circulate during the exercise, making a note of good use of target language and of natural exchanges.

To provide more individual feedback, you could use a Telephoning Feedback Framework (see Frameworks, page 123). Go through the feedback sheet with the students prior to the exercise so that they are aware of the key factors upon which their performance will be assessed.

▶ PHOTOCOPIABLE MATERIALS ON PAGE 118 CAN BE USED TO REVIEW ALL OF THE ASPECTS OF TELEPHONING COVERED WITHIN THIS MODULE.
▶ FOR SELF-STUDY PRACTICE OF THE LANGUAGE USED IN CLOSING A CALL, DIRECT STUDENTS TO PAGE 50 OF THE WORKBOOK.
▶ REFER STUDENTS TO PAGE 152 OF THE COURSEBOOK FOR A SUMMARY OF THE POINTS COVERED IN THIS COMMUNICATION SECTION.

Business across Cultures

Working in cross-functional teams

With a class of work-experienced students, you could begin this activity by asking: *How much does your department communicate with other departments? How much do you understand about what goes on in other departments?*

Ask students to open their Coursebooks and direct their attention to the photo of a grain silo and the figure showing different departments in separate silos. Ask students what this suggests about communication between departments and discuss what the heading means.

Read the introduction in class.

A Ask students to match the departments to their roles in pairs.

KEY

1 e   2 d   3 f   4 a   5 c   6 b

B AUDIO 12.2 Ask students to listen to the audio and check their answers in pairs.

KEY

1 Human Resources   2 Finance   3 Marketing   4 R&D

AUDIO SCRIPT

1 Of course, people are our most important asset. We need to encourage and develop them. This is the only way to ensure the success of our company. We have to retain talent, not lose it to our competitors.

2 In the end, it comes down to the bottom line. We need to have tight control over the business. This means monitoring transactions, especially cash flow. If we become too exposed, we could easily become the target of a takeover bid.

3 If you haven't got any customers, you haven't got a business. Our job is to match the company's products to the needs and aspirations of consumers. The customer is the king and the sooner we realise that the better.

4 In my view, the key competitive advantage comes from innovation. We can't compete on price but we can use our know-how to develop solutions for the future.

PROMOTION UNIT 12

To extend this listening exercise, ask half the class to listen to 1 and 3 again and the other half to listen to 2 and 4. Ask students to make a note of each person's key concerns relating to their area of work. Play AUDIO 12.2 and check students' answers together. For example:

1 retain talent, not lose it to competitors

2 if too exposed, we could become the target of a takeover bid

3 need to realise that the customer is the king

4 can use know-how to develop solutions for the future

C Before embarking on this exercise, check students' understanding of *stereotype* by getting them to brainstorm nationality stereotypes. Ask students to work in subgroups on exercise C. Check understanding and pronunciation of words beforehand. Allow a maximum of ten minutes to discuss and add to the list of adjectives. Share ideas in class.

D Depending on the professional experience of your class, there are different ways of tackling this exercise:

With experienced students from the same company, ask them to discuss exercise D in the context of their own company.

With experienced students from different companies and industries, get them to discuss and compare the roles of different departments in the various companies.

With pre-experience students, ask them to think of well-known companies (e.g. IBM, General Motors, Starbucks), and get them to discuss the roles and importance of different departments within those companies.

[N.B. The role and importance of various departments will vary in different types of business or industry.]

Get students to discuss this issue in subgroups. Ask them to briefly share their ideas with the rest of the class.

E Ask students to read the problem individually, then check understanding of the context by asking one person to summarise the situation. Then ask: *What are the risks to the company?* Next, write on the board:

R&D   Logistics   Production   Finance Marketing

And ask: *How will each department react to the problem?*

Ask students to work in groups of five. If this does not suit the size of your class, ask some students to share roles. Set a strict time limit for the discussion. You may wish to review the language of meetings beforehand. Refer to the Communication sections in Units 7 and 8.

Make a note of any common mistakes and positive exchanges, and, if possible, record the discussion for feedback and analysis. To provide more individual feedback, you could use an Accuracy Feedback Framework (see Frameworks, page 121).

Extension activity. In class, brainstorm the advantages and disadvantages of cross-functional teams:

Advantages	Disadvantages
avoid competition	time-consuming (lots of cross-functional meetings)
goal awareness	getting 'buy in' from all departments
can maintain the same standards throughout the organisation	depends on having a strong company culture
information sharing (greater access)	
no repetition / duplication of exercises in different departments	
coordination	

Now ask subgroups to consider ways in which a company with a *silo mentality* can encourage its departments to work cross-functionally. Write students' suggestions on the board. For example:

team building seminars

ask the best managers to rotate into different functions

reward collaboration

communicate transparently

▶ FOR FURTHER READING AND VOCABULARY EXERCISES RELATING TO SILOS AND CROSS-FUNCTIONAL TEAMS, SEE PAGE 51 OF THE WORKBOOK.

▶ REFER STUDENTS TO PAGE 155 OF THE COURSEBOOK, FOR A SUMMARY OF THE POINTS COVERED IN THIS BUSINESS ACROSS CULTURES SECTION.

Checklist

As a review activity, ask students to refer to the checklist in their Coursebooks and go over the items with them.

Extension activity. To round off this unit and module as a whole, if you have a fairly imaginative and extrovert class, you could ask subgroups to produce a one-minute TV commercial targeting either families, younger audiences or older audiences.

Give each group an ordinary object, such as a pen, a watch, a candle, a bag or a notebook, and tell them that their exercise is to make it sound appealing to the target audience.

Allow 20 minutes for preparation and practice. Then ask each group to *perform* their commercial. Video each one for feedback, if possible.

MODULE 3 PROMOTION

BUSINESS SCENARIO 3

BOLTON BIKES

> This section focuses on nouns connected with skills and qualities. These relate to a job advertisement which will be referred to in the Group interview section. The communication activity directs students to simulate an informal group discussion between three job candidates and a consultant. This will provide the opportunity to use language for describing strengths and weaknesses. In the Writing section, students are required to write an email relating to the discussion in the Communication section.

INTRODUCTORY ACTIVITY

Before opening the Coursebooks, ask: *What types of European/North American companies are transferring their operations to China?* (Car, clothing, and manufacturing companies.)

Why? (Cheaper production costs, more efficient procedures, and Chinese government actively encourages and enables foreign investment.) *In your opinion, is the transfer of production to China likely to continue in the long-term? Why? Why not?*

BACKGROUND

Ask students to open their Coursebooks and read the background information.

THE RIGHT QUALITIES

A Read the job advertisement in class. Then write four language items from the text on the board:

to oversee =

to ensure =

to reach targets =

in conjunction with =

Ask students what their synonyms are and write them on the board.

KEY

to oversee = to manage

to ensure = to make sure

to reach targets = to achieve targets

in conjunction with = in cooperation with

B Read through the skills/qualities in class and ask students to provide definitions for those who don't understand.

Instruct students to do the exercise as indicated in pairs. Compare opinions in class and ask students to give reasons for their opinions.

Then ask: *What challenges do you think a manager being transferred from Canada to China would face?* Brainstorm different ideas and put them on the board:

Transferring family (if has family)

Language constraints

Adapting to the local culture / business style

Next, ask: *How can transfers and relocations be made easier for employees?* Write students' suggestions on the board:

Orientation trips prior to actual move

Language courses

Provision of mentors

Intercultural training

Finally, brainstorm adjectives to describe the type of person who would suit the position being advertised. Possible adjectives:

flexible   bilingual   skilled   open   tactful

patient   driven   sensitive   stable   experienced

GROUP INTERVIEW

Ask students to read the introduction. Ask: *Why do you think she has asked him to hold a group discussion rather than looking at the candidates' CVs?* (Perhaps because she wants him to find out how they come across in person more than how they appear on paper.)

Ask all students to read Tim's role. Elicit a few examples of the kinds of questions he might ask:

77

MODULE 3 PROMOTION
BUSINESS SCENARIO 3

BOLTON BIKES

Could you tell me about ...
I'd be interested to know ...
What are your main strengths?

Divide the class into groups of four and assign a role to each person. If you have an uneven number of students in the class you could eliminate one of the candidates' roles. Ask the 'candidates' to study their roles carefully and consider how best to present their strengths and underplay any weaknesses (refer them to page 6 in Unit 1 for language used to describe strengths and weaknesses). As well as forming questions, Student As should consider ways of welcoming the candidates and ending the discussion. Allow plenty of time for preparation (up to ten minutes). The actual discussion should also have a strict time limit (twenty to thirty minutes depending on your group). If you have more than one group, run the discussions simultaneously and, if possible, record each one in order to analyse during feedback. To provide more individual feedback, you could use an Accuracy Feedback Framework (see Frameworks, page 121).

WRITING

Ask students what information they could include in Tim's email. For example:
- *Method of assessment*
- *Each candidate's strengths and weaknesses*
- *Choice of candidate*
- *Reasons*
- *Recommendations*

Elicit ways that he could express his opinions:
- *In my opinion ...*
- *I feel that ...*
- *It was clear that ...*
- *There is no doubt that ...*

Ask which phrases are weak, neutral or strong. Then elicit ways of offering recommendations:
- *It is strongly recommended that ...*
- *You should ...*
- *You could ...*
- *You might consider ...*
- *I would suggest that you ...*

Ask which are weak, neutral, strong and personal/impersonal.

Set the writing exercise for homework and correct/check them out of class. You could use two or three emails to highlight weaknesses and strengths common to the group.

Review and development 9–12

Grammar: Count and uncount nouns

A Go through the rules and examples on page 49 together in class. Exercise A can be done in class.

KEY

influence – both   experience – both   employment – uncount
progress – uncount   information – uncount   behaviour – both

---

B This exercise should be done in pairs, and then corrected in class.

KEY

1 employment	4 information
2 behaviour	5 experience
3 influences	6 progress

C Before embarking on the exercise, elicit which words on the left can go with which nouns. Elicit the rules relating to *much* and *many*. *Much* is used with uncountable nouns and is used in questions and negative sentences. In affirmative sentences, we tend to use *a lot of*. *Many* is used with countable nouns. It can be used in affirmative and negative sentences as well as questions. Write the following sentences on the board:

Do you have _____ time?
I haven't got _____ time.
I have _____ time.
(a lot of / much)

Elicit where *a lot of* and *much* can be inserted.

Ask students to do exercise C as indicated in the Coursebook. Remind them that, as in the example in exercise C, they should offer more information than simply *Yes* or *No*. Circulate during the exercise and make a note of the use of countable and uncountable nouns. During feedback, ask students to tell the class two things they learned from their partner.

Extension activity. To build on students' awareness of count and uncount nouns, write the following words, which appear in Units 10, 11 and 12 of the Coursebook, on the board:

self-awareness (U)	motivation	diary
slogan	flexibility	training
cooperation	creativity	coach
mission statement	energy	psychometric test
advertising	taste	consumer
research		

Elicit which are countable or uncountable. Then, to remind students to use the correct verb forms and articles with the nouns, write on the board:

Trainings are offered.
Coach is helpful.

Ask students to correct the sentences. Then, tell them to work in pairs and write definitions for five of the words on the board. Do an example yourself beforehand. For example:

It is a type of book in which you make a note of future arrangements and plans.

Ask students to guess what you are describing. (A diary.)

While students are writing their definitions, check that they are using the correct verb forms with the nouns. Once they have finished, ask them to read their definitions to a different partner who has to guess what they are describing.

Vocabulary: Personal qualities

A Look at the vocabulary on page 53 together in class. Remind students of the correct use of nouns and adjectives by writing the following on the board:

John is very _____.
His _____ as a team leader was outstanding.
(capable / capability)

Ask students which word fits into each sentence.

Elicit the pronunciation and main stress of each word in the box, and drill if necessary. Instruct students to do the exercise as indicated in pairs, then check answers in class.

KEY

1 commitment	4 honesty
2 responsibility	5 maturity
3 literacy	6 capability

B Ask students to do this exercise in pairs. Check answers in class as well as pronunciation of the adjectives.

KEY

1 committed	4 honest
2 responsible	5 mature
3 literate	6 capable

C Review the rules for using negative prefixes, then do the first example in class. Ask students to do the exercise in pairs, and then check answers in class.

KEY

1 inflexible	4 illogical
2 impatient	5 disloyal
3 uncreative	6 irreplaceable

D Again, do the first example in class. Ask students to do the exercise in pairs, and then check answers in class. Check and drill pronunciation of all of the adjectives in the table. Remind students that the main stress of the word does not change position when a prefix is added.

KEY

dis-	il-	im-
disloyal	illogical	impatient
dishonest	illiterate	immature
in-	ir-	un-
inflexible	irreplaceable	uncreative
incapable	irresponsible	uncommitted

79

E This is best done in pairs with the teacher circulating and listening carefully to the use of adjectives.

Extension activity. Ask students to work in pairs and describe different personalities. Their partner has to guess what the appropriate adjective is (it can be positive or negative). Do an example in class:

He doesn't think in a sensible way. ▶ *He must be illogical.*

Grammar: Infinitives and *-ing* forms

A Read through the rules and examples again on page 57.

B Ask students to work in pairs and complete the email. Check their answers in class.

KEY

1 c   2 c   3 b   4 a   5 b   6 a   7 c   8 c

Extension activity. Tell students to read through the email again, and then close their Coursebooks. In pairs, each person should summarise the contents of the email in their own words, with prompting from their partner. To help, write on the board:

fail / take off
get / results
send / results
abandon / projects
put / money
involve / bring in lawyers
talk / to lawyers
delay / take action

Present perfect simple and continuous

A Go through the rules and examples on page 61 together in class. Ask students to do the exercise individually then compare their answers with a partner. Check answers in class and ask why they chose the particular tenses.

KEY

1 have finished
2 have worked
3 has had
4 have been learning
5 have been talking   haven't decided
6 have known

B Ask students to do the exercise as indicated with a partner. Remind students that the present perfect tenses are very 'social' tenses. When we haven't seen someone for a long time, we often ask: *What have you been doing?* Check and, if necessary, drill pronunciation of the contracted forms (haven't / what've / I've).

Communication

Review the communication skills language in Units 9–12 together in class.

A Ask students to do the exercise as indicated in pairs, then compare answers in class.

It may be necessary to review and clarify certain language and pronunciation points. For example, ask: *How are requests and offers made?* (Using could/can.)

You could also ask why the receptionist and Jim use *will* in some sentences. (We use *will* to confirm and make promises.)

You might elicit the intonation patterns for the various questions:

Can I get her to call you back? ▶ Rising
How can I help you? ▶ Falling

Finally, get students to act out the dialogue in pairs.

KEY

Receptionist:	Good morning, Crystal Lighting. How can I help you?
Peter:	Could I speak to someone in Sales?
Receptionist:	Of course. Who's calling, please?
Peter:	It's Peter Menzies from Galtons.
Receptionist:	Just a moment, Mr Menzies. I'll put you through.
Jim:	Sales, how can I help you?
Peter:	This is Peter Menzies from Galtons Appliances. I'm calling about an order I placed last week.
Jim:	Do you have the reference number?
Peter:	Yes, it's 456/IND/MC.
Jim:	Oh yes, that's one of Maggie's. I'm afraid she's out of the office at the moment. Can I get her to call you back?
Peter:	Yes, please. Could you tell her that we were expecting delivery this morning and nothing has arrived.
Jim:	I'm sorry to hear that. I'll get her to call you as soon as she gets back. Has she got your number?
Peter:	I'm sure she has, but just in case – it's 0355 634 4577.
Jim:	OK. I'll make sure she gets the message. Goodbye.
Peter:	Goodbye.

B Ask students to do the exercise as indicated in pairs. Get them to do the exercise sitting back-to-back and remind them to clarify and check any new information and note it down correctly. Circulate during the activity and make a note of areas such as language, pronunciation, and intonation that could be improved as well as examples of positive interaction. Provide feedback after the exercise.

MODULE 4

Investment

MODULE OVERVIEW

AIMS AND OBJECTIVES

Module 4 explores the area of investment, through unit themes centred around well-known industries such as the car industry, newspaper industry and film industry, which will be of common interest to most students and provide valuable material for discussion. A large vocabulary bank relating to a variety of aspects of the subject of investment is introduced, through discussion of geographical and environmental issues, personal investment choices, development of new markets and the success or failure of overseas ventures depending on the ability to use local knowledge and to adapt the product accordingly. The grammar and functions reflect elements of these themes. Students consider possible business ventures using the second conditional, analyse the reasons for past failed ventures and possible remedies using *could have* and *should have* and produce more complex vocabulary strings through the use of compound structures. This module's Communication sections focus students' attention on different elements of giving presentations so that they will have had a very comprehensive training in giving presentations by the end of the module. The Business across Cultures pages deal with general cultural communication variations in body language, degree of directness, as well as more specifically corporate management issues, such as leadership and decision-making style.

At the end of this module, students should be able to:

- use a range of financial investment terms
- use a range of vocabulary relating to the car industry
- use compound forms for more succinct sentence structures
- use a range of vocabulary relating to the newspaper industry
- speculate about the past using *could have* and *should have*
- discuss overseas expansion and business failure
- consider possible future investment decisions using the second conditional
- discuss the film industry and film making
- open, develop and close presentations effectively, using a range of visual aids
- have an understanding of some important aspects of communication styles, such as body language, which can vary greatly between cultures, as well as the degree of directness, through the concept of high and low context cultures
- discuss the variation in attitudes to leadership and the decision-making process between different company and national cultures
- present and discuss the viability of a number of investment options and write an explanatory email about the final choice

THEMATIC OVERVIEW

In the age of globalisation, foreign markets are becoming increasingly important to large industries and organisations, both from a production and sales perspective. Local knowledge is vital. Even experienced corporate giants can make fundamental errors when expanding overseas. What are the factors for success or potential pitfalls, when entering a new geographical market?

MAIN AUDIO CONTENTS

Unit 13: an interview with James Evans, car industry expert, who discusses key current and future market issues; three presentation openings; a presentation giving advice on the use of body language during a presentation

Unit 14: six short extracts of people describing how they get news; presentation extracts demonstrating the use of linking and organising language in presentations

Unit 15: an interview with Robert Dussollier, a French business school teacher, about Carrefour's failed attempt to enter the Japanese market; presentation extracts illustrating the language used to describe visual aids; three short extracts of people giving opinions about the qualities needed for leadership

Unit 16: an interview with Bharat Mistry, an Indian film producer, about the Bollywood film industry; three presentation closings; three presentation openings

PHOTOCOPIABLE RESOURCES (PAGES 119-120)
4.1 can be used any time after Unit 15.
4.2 can be used any time after Unit 16.

BUSINESS AND CULTURAL NOTES

Units 13–16 focus on communication skills for making effective presentations. The student is given extra support in terms of background tips which should underpin the skills developed in the module. These relate to body language, particularly important for making an impact and establishing a rapport with the audience, the importance of transparency of structure and rehearsal for added confidence, the way visual aids should be used to make them as clear and effective as possible, and a final five point checklist which the student should consider to ensure they have met their presentation objectives. Units 13–16 focus on interactions across business cultures.

Communication style. The notes in Unit 13 highlight the difference between 'neutral cultures' in which people are expected to guard their emotions and others, where close

MODULE 4

Investment

physical contact and showing feelings through facial expression is essential. Unit 14 develops this theme through the concept of *high-context* and *low-context* cultures, which can have a big impact on the transparency of a message. Emailing is highlighted as being a relatively *low-context* medium, and tips are given to avoid misunderstanding through overuse of this means of communication.

Management communication style. The distance between senior management and the workforce is discussed. Different cultures, both national and corporate have differing attitudes to hierarchy in organisations. As companies become increasingly international, this can give rise to misunderstanding in organisations, which can be crippling. Equally, in the decision-making process, formality can vary greatly from one organisation to another. These differences are explored through the concept of task-oriented versus relationship-oriented cultures.

INVESTMENT **UNIT 13**

13 The industry of industries

PREVIEW

Reading
In the reading section students develop language for discussing the car market and purchasing decisions.

Listening and speaking
In the listening and speaking section students discuss plant investment, production issues and future innovations.

Vocabulary
The vocabulary section focuses students' attention on specific investment vocabulary.

Communication
presentations 1: opening
By the end of this module, in which the Communication sections focus entirely on presentations, students should have a very comprehensive understanding of effective presentation skills. This unit introduces the first of four Communication sections dedicated to presentations. This unit aims to help students make a strong and vital impact at the beginning of their presentations in order to focus the attention of the audience and give students confidence.

Business across Cultures
body language
Body language, and the way it communicates different information in different cultures, is explored in this unit. Awareness of this subject is of vital use to students in order to avoid accidental communication of negative messages during business encounters with other nationalities.

Introductory activity

Direct the class to pages 70–71 of their Coursebooks. Elicit that the thematic overview of the module is the subject of investment. Divide the class into subgroups and ask one half to brainstorm industries, and the other half to brainstorm geographical regions which are currently receiving large amounts of investment. Do a class feedback and board review. As an extension to this you might like to encourage students to match up the industries identified with corresponding geograhical regions, where appropriate. Answers might include: the automotive industry, mobile phone technology, bio technology, India, China, Eastern Europe, etc.

Start-up

A Ask the class to look at the car photos on page 70. Elicit car makes and models and a ranking in order of price. Find out which car students would prefer to drive, and why. Check understanding of new vocabulary in question 2 and get pairs to discuss questions 1 and 2. You might like to encourage one or two students to report on their discussion to the class.

Direct the class to the statement at the top of the page. Elicit any alternative fuels that students might know of and ask for a poll of agreement with the statement. This could lead to a short class discussion on the future of fuel.

Reading

A Instruct the students to match the statements to the cars and then to check their answers with a partner. Do a class check, particularly for newly introduced vocabulary items such as *criterion*, *manoeuvrable* and *consumption*.

KEY
1 a   2 d   3 c   4 e   5 b

B Ask students to read the text again, underlining the reasons why each person chose a specific car. Get pairs to discuss which of these reasons is most applicable to themselves, or would be in the future, if they don't currently own a car.

KEY
1 It goes very fast.
2 It has to have space for as many children as possible.
3 It's the manoeuvrability that I really like.
4 I need a vehicle I can use off-road.
5 I like to drive in comfort.

C Again, instruct pairs to discuss the questions and report back to the class. If you have a multinational class, it might be most productive to pair up students with someone of a different nationality. As a round up, you could ask one student of each nationality to give a brief summary of the car industry in their country.

Listening and speaking

A Instruct students to do this exercise individually and do a quick class check.

KEY
1 b   2 e   3 d   4 c   5 a

B AUDIO **13.1** Explain that they are going to hear the first part of an interview with James Evans, a car industry expert. Ask them to read the four statements and to predict in pairs what his views will be. Check their predictions, then ask them to listen to the interview to see if their predictions were correct. Do a class check.

83

INVESTMENT UNIT 13

KEY

1 F. It's also because car manufacturing is one of the most complex industrial activities.
2 T
3 F. There is overcapacity.
4 T

AUDIO SCRIPT

Interviewer: The management guru, Peter Drucker, said that car manufacturing is the 'industry of industries.' What did he mean exactly?

James Evans: It's to do with the fact that cars are among the most desirable consumer products, and making them is one of the most complex industrial activities – a typical car contains 20,000 parts. To do this successfully requires a high degree of planning and organisation.

Interviewer: Right ...

James Evans: Of course, the car industry is an important employer in advanced countries and in developing countries, too, such as Turkey, Brazil, and China. And, of course, this means not just the people who are directly employed in the industry, but also the jobs created among parts suppliers as well.

Interviewer: Yes ...

James Evans: But the problem is overcapacity – there's too much capacity – there are too many plants turning out too many cars – output is too high in relation to demand. Already some of the big players like Ford and General Motors are cutting back investment and closing plants.

C AUDIO 13.2 Ask students to read through the questions then play the second extract. Get pairs to check answers and do a second listening, if necessary, with feedback.

KEY

1 $20 a barrel a few years ago. $100 a barrel predicted for the future.
2 When there is no more oil.
3 The technology is still not advanced enough to produce electric motors for cars. You have to charge the battery too often and the maximum speed is not very high.
4 Cars that run on petrol some of the time and electricity the rest of the time.
5 Up to $8000 more expensive.
6 Toyota.
7 No. The engines are made in Japan.

AUDIO SCRIPT

Interviewer: What about the future? We hear a lot about air pollution and traffic congestion, and the increasing price of oil ...

James Evans: That's right. Cars aren't the status symbols they once were but car owners still find it difficult to accept limitations on their freedom to drive. However, some cities, such as Singapore and London, have introduced congestion charges which have helped to cut traffic and reduce pollution levels.

Interviewer: And the increasing price of oil is a concern ...

James Evans: That's right. A few years ago, oil was $20 a barrel. Now industry analysts are predicting as much as $100 a barrel. And of course, people are beginning to think about a time when oil runs out completely.

Interviewer: How are car manufacturers responding to that?

James Evans: Well, for a long time electric cars seemed to be the future. But after many years of investment and development the technology is still not advanced enough to produce electric motors for cars. You have to charge the battery too often and the maximum speed is not very high ...

Interviewer: Right ...

James Evans: But we are beginning to see what are called hybrid cars – cars that run on petrol some of the time and electricity the rest of the time. These hybrid cars are really taking off, especially in the U.S., despite the higher prices – up to $8000 more for the hybrid version of some models.

Interviewer: Who are the big investors in the development of hybrid cars?

James Evans: Well, as so often, the Japanese are taking the lead. For example, Toyota said they're investing $10 million to start manufacturing the hybrid Camry model in Kentucky, with the engines supplied from Japan. They're making a massive investment there ...

D These are ideal questions to put to the class to round up the subject of cars in the form of an open discussion, which could be audio recorded for review and analysis. Alternatively, subgroups could each be given one of the questions to discuss, with a quick class feedback. A board review and correction/noting down of persistent language errors could be useful at this point.

Vocabulary

A Ask students to do this exercise individually and do a quick class review.

KEY

1 a   2 e   3 b   4 c   5 d

▶ REVIEW AND DEVELOPMENT EXERCISE A IN THE COURSEBOOK, PAGE 88, CAN BE DONE AT THIS STAGE.

▶ WORKBOOK VOCABULARY QUIZ AND READING AND WRITING EXERCISES UNIT 13, PAGES 52-53, CAN BE DONE FOR FURTHER PRACTICE.

Communication

Presentations 1: Opening

Ask students to think about presentations they have attended or given. Prompt questions might include: *Do you enjoy listening to or delivering them? Have you had any bad experiences?* Elicit one or two examples of presentations which haven't worked well or students haven't enjoyed. *What was wrong with those presentations?* Answers might include: too long / subject not adapted to the specific needs of the audience / difficult to follow / speaker didn't speak clearly, etc.

INVESTMENT **UNIT 13**

Divide the class into subgroups. Instruct each group to brainstorm essential features of a good presentation. Ask them to consider all aspects: body language, voice, subject, audience, structure and organisation. Get them to report their ideas to the class. Allow some time for discussion and other ideas. Write up ideas on the board. Make sure they note board items down and remind them to review these regularly over the course of this module.

Ask them which parts of a presentation they are most likely to remember and in which parts of a presentation is it vitally important to have a great impact. (The first and last few minutes. The introduction and conclusion.)

Direct students to read the opening rubric in their coursebooks on page 72.

Ask the class to give you specific examples for the first five points. These might include: name, organisation, department, role, responsibilities, etc. Write all ideas on the board under the headings given in the Coursebook.

A AUDIO 13.3 Ask the class to listen to the two following presentation openings for the five elements mentioned. Do a class feedback.

KEY

Presentation 1 includes all five elements.
Presentation 2 does not include a clear objective or timing.

AUDIO SCRIPT

1 *Good morning. I'm very pleased to see you all here this morning. I'm going to speak for about thirty minutes, and I'd be happy to answer any questions. My name is Grigory Spanek. I'm responsible for regional development in this part of the country. I was born here and I grew up here and perhaps I am biased, but I think this is a beautiful part of the world. This morning I aim to give you an overview of the region – its main landmarks, something about the economy, and also future infrastructure plans. By the end of this presentation, I hope that you will be convinced that this is a great area for investment.*

2 *Ladies and gentlemen, welcome to STS Solutions. It's a pleasure to see you all here and to have this chance to show you around. First, let me introduce myself. My name is Victoria Sanchez and I'm in charge of PR. This is an exciting business to be in right now and this new joint venture is a great opportunity. Before we take a look around, I'd like to tell you a little about the company and how it's organised, just to give you an idea of how we work. Of course, if you've got any questions, please ask. Then I'll hand you over to my colleague, Miguel Pires, who will show you around the facility and explain everything in more detail.*

B Ask the class to listen again and answer the question.

KEY

They both start with a welcome.

Ask the class to comment on how this adds impact to the presentation opening. (It instantly involves and focuses the attention of the audience on the speaker and subject.) Check understanding of *rhetorical*. Ask the class to think of any other interesting techniques for opening presentations. Answers might include: short anecdote, real question, amazing fact, etc. However the style of presentations varies greatly depending on corporate and national cultures.

C Instruct the class to read through and practise the phrases in the Key language box in pairs. Then play AUDIO 13.3 again and do the exercise.

KEY

Use the audio script to check your answers.

As a short follow-up activity to improve students' understanding of the importance of pausing for clear presentation delivery, you could ask the class to listen to AUDIO 13.3 again, marking the places in the script where the speaker paused for emphasis or punctuation. Ask a student to read out each presentation opening. Do a class review.

D With closed books, elicit and review the five main points of presentation openings mentioned.

Ask students to prepare a short presentation opening on one of the subjects presented in the exercise. Depending on your class, you might like to personalise the exercise by encouraging students to choose their own subject. A quick review of the use of interesting opening sentences or very short anecdotes could be useful here. Direct students to the checklist as an aid.

Do a quick class brainstorm on key points to observe during presentation openings. Items might include: *Was the opening well sequenced? Did they use the target language?* Audio or video recording their introductions could add value to the review, during which you might like to invite individual students to assess the key aspects of their own presentation before giving your own feedback. Presentations can be highly stressful situations and self assessment can be a good method of diffusing embarrassment and encouraging students to give and receive constructive feedback (which might otherwise feel like criticism) on their personal performance. It can be very useful to focus on highlighting positive aspects of performance and to present areas to be improved, as learning opportunities. However, your style of feedback will depend largely on the culture of your class. Depending on your class, you might like to appoint observers to make notes on their impression of each student's opening. Ask: *Did they speak clearly? Was their intonation engaging? Was their speed appropriate? Did they pause in the right places?* Do a class review and give your own feedback.

▶ WORKBOOK COMMUNICATION EXERCISE PAGE 54, CAN BE DONE AT THIS STAGE.

▶ COMMUNICATION NOTES FOR THIS SECTION CAN BE REVIEWED ON PAGE 152 OF THE COURSEBOOK.

Business across Cultures

Body language

In subgroups, ask the class to brainstorm any gestures or elements of body language which have a special meaning in another culture. Do a class feedback. Are there any gestures in students' culture(s) which could be impolite in another culture? Ask the class if they have ever experienced any cross-cultural misunderstandings due to body language.

Read the opening rubric on page 73 of the Coursebook with the class and check understanding.

A Ask students to do the exercise in pairs. Do a class feedback.

85

INVESTMENT UNIT 13

KEY

Body Language	Country	Meaning
Smile	All countries	I'm pleased.
Tip head back, suck air in	China	That's difficult.
Bow very low	Japan	Shows great respect.
Males stand close and make contact	Saudi Arabia	Shows trust.
Males go though door first, ahead of women	Korea	Shows males are dominant.
Palm facing in, index finger moving	USA	Come to me.
Constant eye contact in one-to-one communication	UK	I'm interested.

B Ask subgroups to go back over the examples of body language in A and discuss how they would react to this body language. Appoint one person from each group to present their conclusions briefly, pointing out any differences in opinion within their group, if it is a multicultural one.

C Body language checklist

Monocultural groups: Instruct subgroups to use the ideas in C to develop a body language checklist for foreign visitors. They will each need to have a copy of this list and be able to talk about it. Then reorganise the groups, so that the new groups contain one person from each of the original groups. Each newly formed group should compare and discuss their list and come up with a final list. Do a class feedback.

Multicultural groups: Organise the groups according to cultural background and get each group to present their checklist to the class.

D AUDIO 13.4 Go into the exercise as in the Coursebook. Play the audio twice if necessary and do a round the class feedback on the items they heard. Check understanding and write up any useful language items on the board.

KEY

Use the audio script to check your answers.

AUDIO SCRIPT

Giving a presentation to an international audience isn't easy but my advice is just to be natural and be yourself. However, there are also some useful guidelines you can follow.

Gestures with the hands and arms are very important in some cultures. In Egypt, where I come from, we use our hands and arms a lot to get our message across. In some cultures, this isn't so acceptable so it's probably a good idea not to use your hands and arms too much. Maybe if you want to emphasise a point – for example, if you have three points to make, you could use your fingers to indicate which point you're talking about.

Wherever you are, don't fold your arms – this looks defensive or even aggressive. Also, even though the British do this quite a lot, I wouldn't advise you to put your hands in your pockets. Try to keep your palms open and hold up your hands sometimes so that the audience can see them.

Some people walk around during their presentation. I wouldn't advise too much movement but, on the other hand, it's good to move a little so you don't look like a statue. We used to say it was good to stand up for a presentation – that it's better for delivering your message. But nowadays, it's sometimes more appropriate to stay sitting down, like your audience.

E Ask students to prepare a short presentation. It might be a good idea not to do one directly about body language as this would involve lots of gestures students might not ordinarily use! Students could have a chance to recycle their presentation openings from the previous section as this would involve minimal extra input at this stage and they would be able to focus on the body language aspects of their presentation. Otherwise, new topics will depend on your class. Again, video recording would be useful from the point of view of analysis, but whether you have these facilities or not, the class should observe and give feedback on each student's body language.

▶ WORKBOOK EXERCISES ON PAGE 55, CAN BE DONE AT THIS STAGE.

Checklist

Go through each item on the checklist with students and ask questions to recycle the key vocabulary in this unit.

Extension activity. To recycle language from the first section and to work on key pronunciation aspects of presentation delivery, divide the class into two. Give the audio script of AUDIO 13.1 to one half and the audio script of AUDIO 13.2 to the other half of the class. Model a couple of sentences from page 70, such as: *It's what they call a saloon …*, on the board, eliciting sentence stress patterns from the class and marking them up above the correct words in the chosen sentence(s). Elicit intonation patterns (rising and falling tones) where appropriate. Ask students to go through their script, marking sentence stress over the key words which should be emphasised in each sentence. Then get each group to review their sentence stress patterns together. Finally, ask students to pair up with a student from the other group and swap scripts. After they have studied and practised these, ask pairs to perform these interviews together. You might like to ask a couple of pairs to perform the scripted interview in front of the class.

INVESTMENT **UNIT 14**

14 Something for nothing?

Reading and speaking
This text develops language relating to the newspaper industry and its target market.

Listening and speaking
Students listen to people talking about how they keep informed with the news. Students further discuss different types of news media and how they relate to them.

Vocabulary
This section focuses on the use of compound structures to produce a more succinct and natural sentence style.

Communication
presentations 2: developing the message
This section deals with developing the main part of a presentation. Students will acquire useful language for structuring and linking ideas cohesively.

Business across Cultures
communication style
This section explores cross cultural differences in directness of communication style via the concept of high-context (indirect) and low-context (direct) cultures. Students benefit from focusing on the potentially positive or negative impact their spoken and written communications may have on the recipient.

Start-up

Ask the class to describe the most popular newspapers in their country. Possible answers might include words such as: number, type, cost, political bias, quantity of pictorial content, hard news, serious, gossip, scandals, circulation, readership, bought or delivered. It could be useful at this point to elicit or revise basic related vocabulary. Examples might include: broadsheet, tabloid, circulation, daily, weekly, national, regional, distribution, format, editorial.

Instruct the class to open their coursebooks at page 74 and read the statement about America's leading newspapers. Ask the class for reasons why circulation might be decreasing. Possible answers might include: the Internet, TV, news channels, free newspapers, busy lives, depressing news, etc.

Ask the class if they know or read any free newspapers. You might ask further questions such as: *What are they called? What type of news do they report? Are they any good? Why/Why not? Are they different in their format to other newspapers?*

Reading and speaking

A Do the exercise as instructed in the Coursebook and do a class answer check.

KEY
1 5983
2 5.1m
3 From $9.6m in 1995 to $302m.
4 Young urban professionals.
5 Its strict editorial formula and its scientific approach to success.
6 It is distributed to 'high commuter traffic zones.' It is delivered by trucks to hand distributors and racks.
7 No. There were problems in the Czech Republic because old women were taking 100 copies at a time from railway stations to sell on.

At this point it might be useful for students to identify recycled key vocabulary items from the text such as: freesheet, edition, urban professionals, editorial formula, teething problems, distribution system and commuter. Ask students to use this vocabulary to describe freesheets, if they have them, in their countries. Do this as an open class exercise. Ask: *Have you experienced similar problems to the ones in the Czech Republic?*

B Divide the class into A's and B's and put the students into pairs. Instruct pairs to read the question and discuss it briefly. Do a class feedback. Then ask students A to look at page 108 and students B to look at page 110. Tell students to exchange information. Choose one pair to answer the questions in class in order to check understanding and vocabulary.

Listening and speaking

A AUDIO 14.1 Tell the class they are going to hear a series of comments about how people keep up with the news. They need to complete each *beep* with one of the items (a–f). Play the audio twice if necessary. Do a class check and elicit the meaning of PDA. (Personal digital assistant.)

KEY
1 f   2 d   3 a   4 c   5 e   6 b

AUDIO SCRIPT

1 I travel a lot. I don't have time to read newspapers, so I catch up on the news when I'm in my hotel room or at the airport waiting for my plane. I usually watch [beep] like CTV – I like the presenters and the programmes.

2 I look at the news on the [beep] – I never buy a newspaper. I like the BBC site – it's very well organised. The amount of information on there is absolutely incredible.

87

INVESTMENT UNIT 14

3 *I listen to the news on the [beep] when I'm in my car. The hourly news bulletin on a pop music station is more than enough for me!*

4 *I like old-fashioned [beep], the ones you pay for! I really like the book reviews in the New York Times, for example. They're excellent.*

5 *I pick up a [beep] at the underground station – the journalism's pretty good, just as good as you get in newspapers that you pay for.*

6 *I pick up the news on my [beep], you know, personal digital assistant. The Internet sites have special versions for people with mobile phones and you get the top stories very quickly. The Financial Times is my favourite.*

B Instruct pairs to discuss the questions and to say which speaker(s) they relate to most and why this way of getting the news suits them. Do a class feedback on choice factors.

Vocabulary

Explain that a typical problem for foreign language students is the importation of mother tongue language structures, resulting in somewhat unnaturally complex sentence structures. You might like to demonstrate this by writing up one or two of the students' own examples (collected previously). Ask the class to consider how they could make these more succinct, but don't gather any answers until later in the lesson.

A Instruct the class to read through the vocabulary types. Write the five statements on the board and ask the class to identify the grammatical forms without looking at the book.

B Ask pairs to do the exercise in the Coursebook and then do an open class review. Check understanding of the terms.

KEY

Type 1 – local newspaper – public transport – huge operation – international expansion	Type 2 – distribution system
Type 3 – combined circulation	Type 4 – shopping malls – teething problems

C You might like to set this exercise as a class race!

KEY

high commuter traffic zone

D Get pairs to do the exercise in the Coursebook and then ask different pairs to read out each question to the rest of the class, giving feedback where necessary.

MODEL ANSWERS

2 A: *Do you expect continued international expansion?*
  B: *Yes, we're opening five new plants in three different countries this year alone.*

3 A: *What's the distribution system?*
  B: *Our trucks deliver products overnight to supermarkets all over Europe.*

4 A: *Were there teething problems?*
  B: *Only small ones. Our first plants didn't operate with 100 per cent of potential output at the beginning, but this was soon solved.*

5 A: *Are young urban professionals among your customers?*
  B: *No, our products are targeted mainly at older people living in the country.*

As a follow up get the class to correct the examples you gave them at the beginning of the exercise, on the board. When correct, elicit the types of compound structure used.

▶ REFER STUDENTS TO GRAMMAR OVERVIEW PAGE 167.
▶ REVIEW AND DEVELOPMENT EXERCISES ON PAGE 89 OF THE COURSEBOOK CAN BE DONE AT THIS STAGE.
▶ READING AND WRITING AND VOCABULARY EXERCISES, ON PAGES 56-57 OF THE WORKBOOK, CAN BE DONE AT THIS STAGE.

Communication

Presentations 2: Developing the message

Direct the class to read the opening rubric on page 76 of the Coursebook.

It might be useful to run briefly through the main points of the last communication presentation session in Unit 13.

A AUDIO 14.2 Instruct the class to listen to Maggie Peters giving a presentation about her company. Ask them to make notes on the main points of each part as set out in the exercise. Do a class review.

KEY

Objective: to give an overview of the organisation
Part 1: the organisation and how it works
Part 2: the people in the organisation
Part 3: the local community
Summary: have changed organisation to meet needs of customers; developed unskilled workers into highly skilled workforce; local community has supported the business

B Play AUDIO 14.2 again and go into the exercise as in the Coursebook.

KEY

Use the audio script to check your answers.

AUDIO SCRIPT

In this presentation, I aim to give you an overview of the organisation. To do this, I'm going to cover three areas. Firstly, we'll look at the organisation and how it works; secondly, the people who work here; and thirdly, the local community. So, let's start with the organisation. As you can see from this slide, there are four departments …

… As I mentioned earlier, we are in the middle of a major restructuring and that brings me to the second part of my presentation – the people …

… So it's important to remember that most of our employees live in this area. Let's move on now to the third and final part of my presentation – the local community. It's a critical part of our success …

… On the one hand, we have a good relationship with the town and its people but on the other hand, we are

INVESTMENT **UNIT 14**

sometimes seen as being too dominant. I'll come back to that later ...

... OK, so let me just summarise. We've changed the organisation to meet the needs of our customers, and we have developed our people from a group of mainly unskilled workers into a highly skilled workforce. And finally, we can thank the local community for continuing to support our business ...

Extension activity. Instruct pairs to work through the Key language box, practising linking and structuring phrases, adding their own subjects where appropriate. Write an example on the board.

As I mentioned earlier, these are only the forecast sales figures.

Do a round the class check of linking sentences. At this point, it could be useful to work on the stress and intonation of the sentences, as these pronunciation factors are important in using signposting language during the presentation.

C Ask students to prepare a presentation using the table in their Coursebooks and the phrases in the Key language box, to help them. They might find it helpful to review AUDIO 14.2 too. It could be useful to develop the subject introduced in the previous unit, particularly if students had previously used personalised subjects. It could be a good idea to set a fairly short time limit (up to five minutes) for each presentation. The point of the activity is more to use the target language effectively than to become too involved in the subject of the presentation.

D Ask each student to deliver their presentation. Audio or video record the presentations for analysis, if possible. As in the last unit, depending on your class, you might wish to appoint observers to comment on whether the objectives were clearly stated and whether they were delivered as per exercise C. Get feedback on this and on the extent the target language was used. Audio or video review will enable you to work on the pronunciation and intonation aspects of the presentation. Particularly that of the target language, but also of the key business subject items which may be of particular interest to individual students.

▶ REVIEW THE COMMUNICATION NOTES ON PAGE 152 OF THE COURSEBOOK.

▶ EXERCISE A ON PAGE 58 OF THE WORKBOOK, CAN BE DONE AT THIS POINT.

Business across Cultures

Communication style

Direct the class to open their Coursebooks at page 77 and read through the opening rubric with them. Check understanding of the phrase *getting to the point*.

A Ask students to look at the two emails and to describe any stylistic differences they notice. Elicit the phrase *exercise oriented*. Elicit the phrases which make the second email less direct.

MODEL ANSWER

The first email is very short and direct. It is very task-oriented.

The second email is more direct. It asks about the addressee and uses very polite language.

B Instruct students to read about the low-context and high-context cultures, in pairs. Ask them to discuss which type of culture they belong to. Do a quick class check to find out if there are differences amongst your students. Get feedback from the class on why they place themselves in a certain category. If you have students in both categories, you might develop a discussion on one category before the other or do a point by point comparison of the two. This could lead to an interesting class debate on how misunderstandings in the workplace, particularly in the international business field, can arise from low-/high-context cultural differences. Encourage students to give examples from their own experience.

C Ask subgroups to discuss these points and do a quick class feedback. Encourage concrete examples of students' experiences.

KEY

saying 'no'	low-context
being very polite	high-context
pleasing everybody	high-context
saying 'yes'	high-context
criticising	low-context
disagreement	low-context
getting to the point quickly	high-context
reading between the lines	low-context
packaging the message with a nice beginning and end	high-context

D Go into this activity as in the Coursebook. Do a class review and ask students to point out which types of phrases make their emails more high-/low-context.

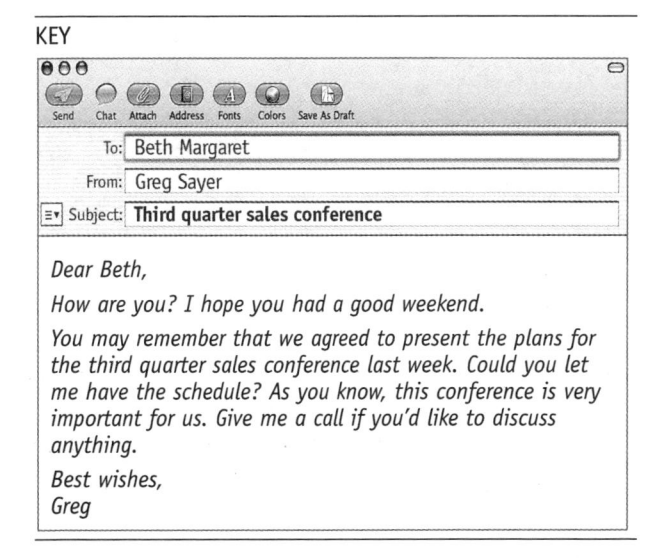

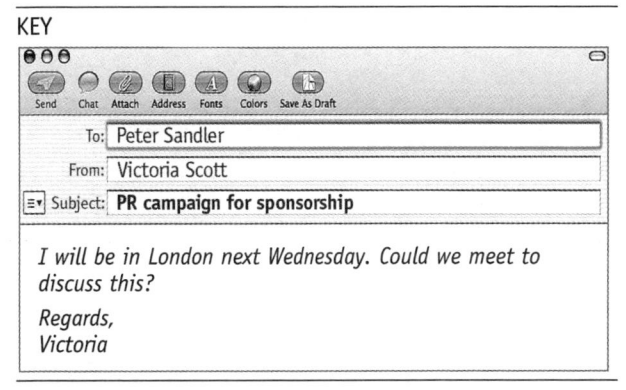

KEY

```
To: Beth Margaret
From: Greg Sayer
Subject: Third quarter sales conference
```

Dear Beth,

How are you? I hope you had a good weekend.

You may remember that we agreed to present the plans for the third quarter sales conference last week. Could you let me have the schedule? As you know, this conference is very important for us. Give me a call if you'd like to discuss anything.

Best wishes,
Greg

KEY

```
To: Peter Sandler
From: Victoria Scott
Subject: PR campaign for sponsorship
```

I will be in London next Wednesday. Could we meet to discuss this?

Regards,
Victoria

89

INVESTMENT UNIT 14

E Assign email situations to individuals or pairs, depending on the size of your class. Ask half of the students to write *direct* emails and the other half to write *indirect* emails. Get students to pair up with a student who has adopted the opposite style to compare emails. Ask them to give feedback on these differences to the class.

Extension activity. Look at the three email situations with the class. Ask them which style (direct or indirect) would be more appropriate for each situation. They should consider the context of their own culture and the relationship they have with the person they are writing to. Emails for b and c are likely to be less direct. There might be more room for variation in email a, depending on the culture.

▶ CULTURE NOTES FOR THIS SECTION CAN BE REVIEWED ON PAGE 155 OF THE COURSEBOOK.

▶ EXERCISE A ON PAGE 59 OF THE WORKBOOK, CAN BE DONE AT THIS POINT.

Checklist

Go through each item on the checklist with the students and ask questions to recycle the key vocabulary in this unit.

Extension activity. This exercise can be set as homework. Ask students to write a short article about the industry they work for (if they are job-experienced) or an industry they have learnt about (if they are still in education). Instruct them to use one or more examples of each of the five compound structures in exercise A of the vocabulary section. After review and correction, you might like to ask students to swap their articles with a partner's, and identify and list the target structures used.

INVESTMENT **UNIT 15**

15 In search of new markets

Listening and speaking
The vocabulary of entering new geographical markets is dealt with in a case study of Carrefour's unsuccessful move into Japan.

Speaking
In this section students use language from the previous section to advise an international supermarket chain on how to enter their local market.

Grammar should/shouldn't have, could have
Students are introduced to the use of modal verbs *should/shouldn't have* and *could have* when speculating about the past. This is set in the context of talking about failed business ventures and bad business decisions.

Communication presentation 3: using visuals
This section improves students' ability to use and describe visual aids to support a presentation.

Business across Cultures leadership
This unit looks at leadership styles and how they vary from culture to culture. Students are encouraged to consider what style of leadership they favour and what type of leader they would like to be.

Start-up

Ask the class to describe supermarket chains in their country (if they have them). You might ask questions to elicit some of the following information: number of different chains, names, annual turnover, approximate number of stores, age of chain, national or regional, part of an international group, family owned, cooperative, publicly owned food, non-food, differences in price, quality of product, etc. If there are no supermarket chains, it could be interesting to find out how food is sold. Ask students to guess how much the global food retail market is worth annually. Then direct them to the statement in the box at the top of page 78 of the Coursebook, to discover whose answer was closest to the correct one.

Listening and speaking

A AUDIO **15.1** Do the exercise as in the Coursebook and do a class check. If useful for your class, you might follow up with a review of pronunciation and abbreviation aspects of numbers and dates. For example: Two thousand and two, ten (per) (a) hundred thousand, abbreviations bn/m, currency sign before the number, etc.

KEY

Year Carrefour entered Japanese market: 2002
Year Carrefour withdrew from Japan: 2005
Price paid by Aeon for Carrefour's stores: ¥ 1 bn / € 70 m
Company whose success Carrefour wanted to copy: Renault
Reasons for Carrefour's failure in relation to customers: didn't offer anything new, quality of goods was nothing special
Number of shops per 100,000 people in Japan: 90
Number of shops per 100,000 people in USA: 55
Reasons for Carrefour's failure in relation to Japanese business culture: they wanted a quick return
Market that Carrefour is now trying to get into: Korea

B Instruct students to do the interview exercise in pairs as in the Coursebook. Then, ask different pairs to act out the questions and answers as an accuracy check.

C Replay AUDIO **15.1** and ask students to fill in the gaps individually. Do a class check. Highlight that the negative form of *should* is contracted.

KEY

1 should have studied
2 shouldn't have assumed
3 could have done
4 could have paid
5 should have expected

Extension activity. At this point it could be useful to do a short exercise on the use of the contracted form of the verb *have* ('ve) in spoken English. Write up *should have studied* and then say it quickly, crossing out the *ha-* of *have*. Repeat it and get the class to follow suit. Ask them to do the same with the other four answers to C. Number 2 may well cause amusement!

AUDIO SCRIPT

Interviewer: Carrefour is one of the world's leading retail chains, with operations in many parts of the world, but it didn't do too well in Japan. Can you explain some of the reasons for this?

Robert Dussollier: Yes, of course. As you know, Carrefour withdrew from the Japanese market after three years by selling its eight stores to the Japanese chain Aeon for one billion yen – that's about 70 million euros, and much less than they paid for them. I think they failed in Japan because they

91

INVESTMENT UNIT 15

	misunderstood the business culture and they misunderstood their clientele. They should have studied the market more carefully.
Interviewer:	*Right.*
Robert Dussollier:	*Carrefour was encouraged by what had happened with Renault. Renault bought a large stake in Nissan – the car maker which had been making heavy losses but Renault turned it round. However, Carrefour didn't realise that these two markets are very different. They shouldn't have assumed that the car industry and the retail industry were the same.*
Interviewer:	*Of course …*
Robert Dussollier:	*When Carrefour opened their first store in the suburbs of Tokyo in 2002, they thought they would benefit from the crisis in Japanese retailing – at that time some chains had gone out of business completely. But what Carrefour offered didn't appeal to Japanese consumers. They could have done more research into the Japanese retail market.*
Interviewer:	*What do you mean?*
Robert Dussollier:	*Japanese consumers are very demanding, but they are also price-conscious. Carrefour didn't offer anything new, except perhaps a slight 'French' flavour. They didn't offer lower prices and the quality of their products was nothing special. They could have paid more attention to product quality.*
Interviewer:	*What about Japanese shopping habits? Do they drive to the supermarket once a week for the big family shopping expedition, like in Europe or the U.S.?*
Robert Dussollier:	*No, Japanese consumers tend to go shopping more frequently, and buy smaller quantities. There are a lot of small local shops, many of them open 24 hours a day. In Japan, there are 90 shops per 100,000 inhabitants, compared to only 55 in the United States.*
Interviewer:	*Aha …*
Robert Dussollier:	*And another problem was that Carrefour wanted a quick return on its investment in Japan. They didn't realise that to make a profit in Japan you need to be in for the long haul. They weren't prepared to wait. They should have expected to wait longer for a return on investment.*
Interviewer:	*So has this affected Carrefour's plans for the rest of Asia?*
Robert Dussollier:	*No, they're now trying to get into Korea.*
Interviewer:	*Have they learnt any lessons from their Japanese experience?*
Robert Dussollier:	*Yes, but of course the lessons learnt in Japan may not be applicable elsewhere …*

Speaking

A Ask the class to go through the audio script on page 126 of the Coursebook, picking out the factors which led to the failure of Carrefour's entrance into the Japanese market. Give students time to prepare advice for their partner on how best to open an international supermarket chain in their country, taking into account business factors and the local food culture. If possible, pair up students from different cultures. Before going into the exercise you might find it useful to do a class review of phrases for giving advice and making suggestions: *could/should/shouldn't/it would be a good idea to,* etc.

B Ask each student to describe the most important factor their partner mentioned. Note useful ideas and market related vocabulary on the board.

C Divide the class into subgroups (by nationality if applicable). Ask each group to brainstorm essential business and cultural factors to be taken into account for one of the three markets stated in the exercise. Then, get students to pair up with someone from another group in order to exchange advice. In a class round up, ask for feedback on the advice given for each market, while making corrections, giving ideas, etc.

▶ EXERCISE B ON PAGE 61 OF THE WORKBOOK, CAN BE DONE AT THIS POINT.

Grammar

Should/shouldn't have, could have

Ask a student to read out each rule together with the corresponding example. Check for understanding.

A Allow students time to write down their answers to this exercise before eliciting the answers in a class review. Try to encourage the use of the contracted form of the verb *have* as well as *shouldn't*.

KEY

2 *Coca-Cola should have kept its traditional formula. Coca-Cola shouldn't have dropped its traditional formula in 1985.*

3 *British Leyland should have used just one brand name. British Leyland shouldn't have used two brand names for the same car.*

4 *Elf should have expanded abroad more slowly. Elf shouldn't have expanded abroad so rapidly.*

5 *Siemens should have entered the mobile phone market with a partner who knew the market. Siemens shouldn't have entered the mobile phone market on their own.*

6 *Gerald Ratner shouldn't have said that the jewellery he sold in his shops was rubbish. Gerald Ratner should have kept quiet!*

B Ask students to write down a few sentences about their own experiences as in the Coursebook. Do a class review.

C Go into the exercise as in the Coursebook and check answers out loud in class.

KEY

2 *They could / should have used a market research company.*

3 *They could / should have talked to people who knew the market.*

INVESTMENT **UNIT 15**

4 They could / should have worked with a local partner.
5 They could / should have advertised in the local press.
6 They could / should have listened to what people were telling them.

▶ REVIEW AND DEVELOPMENT MODALS EXERCISE ON PAGE 90 OF THE COURSEBOOK CAN BE DONE AT THIS STAGE.
▶ THE GRAMMAR EXERCISE ON PAGE 61 OF THE WORKBOOK, CAN BE DONE AT THIS POINT.

Communication

Presentation 3: Using visuals

Direct the class to open the Coursebook at page 80 and read the opening rubric.
Ask the class to think of presentations they have seen. Elicit a few advantages and disadvantages of using visuals in a presentation. Answers might include: fewer words needed, easier to process and remember information, more interesting, visuals can dominate, can be too complex, presenters simply read visual text, etc.

A Ask pairs to do the matching exercise and then do a quick class review.

KEY
1 d   2 a   3 e   4 g   5 f   6 b   7 c

At this point you could ask the class to give you any other names of visuals they have heard of or used, and put them up on the board. (E.g. table.) You might elicit specific types of information favoured by specific visuals such as: A pie chart is useful for describing market shares.

B AUDIO 15.2 Run through the Key language box in class then instruct the students to listen for details about the visuals described in the audio. Do a class review.

Extension activity. Replay AUDIO 15.2, then invite students to illustrate the parts of each visual, as described, on the board. Distributing visuals from Internet or press materials and getting pairs to practise the target language could be useful.

KEY
Presentation 1: mind map, flow chart
Presentation 2: pie chart, bar chart

AUDIO SCRIPT

1 So, we've brainstormed what your customers have in common and here, on this chart, you can see the connections. They are very much around quality and brand image. Can I draw your attention to these two customers, which, as you know, represent around 25 per cent of your business.
Now here on this chart you can see the typical route to market they use – following their customer trials, they move on to a local launch and then, if this is successful, they start to roll out nationwide.

2 I've prepared some charts to illustrate my points. Here, on this chart, you can see the main segments in the market. By far the largest slice is the personal security sector. Not only is it the largest but it's also growing the fastest, which you can see on this chart. Here are the three main segments, showing total sales over the last three years. If you look here, you can see the corporate sector remains stagnant and the industrial sector is actually declining, but the personal security sector has grown by nearly 20 per cent over the last three years.

C Ask students to give a short presentation, or at least part of one (possibly useful to recycle part of their previous one), using visuals. Do a review after each presentation on the use of the target language. It might also be useful to review related phrases, such as: *at the top of/bottom of, on the left hand side,* etc.

▶ COMMUNICATION NOTES FOR THIS SECTION CAN BE REVIEWED ON PAGE 152 OF THE COURSEBOOK.
▶ WORKBOOK COMMUNICATION EXERCISE B ON PAGE 62, CAN NOW BE DONE.

Business across Cultures

Leadership

Direct students to open their Coursebooks at page 81 and read the opening rubric. Elicit the differences between *top dog* and *one of the people*. Do a quick class poll of which style each student relates to or has experienced.

A Instruct the class to do the exercise individually, having first read it through and checked students' understanding of the vocabulary. Get pairs to compare answers. Then, ask them to summarise any similarity or difference in leadership style preferences to the rest of the class. Pairing up students from different nationalities, depending on your class, may create more discussion between pairs. Write up any useful language on the board.

B AUDIO 15.3 Instruct the class to listen to the audio for the points about leaders, mentioned in exercise A. Do a class check. Do a second listening for additional points followed by another class check.

KEY
Speaker 1: a good listener (6)
Speaker 2: lonely, decisive and vision (4, 5, 9)
Speaker 3: none (+ managing change)

AUDIO SCRIPT

1 I think the most important quality for a leader is to be able to understand people. You need to be in touch with them, understand their concerns, needs, and ambitions. If you understand them, you can then motivate them, direct them, and get great performance from them. It's important for a leader to stay close to people.

2 Being a leader is a lonely job. You have to make difficult, sometimes unpopular, decisions. You also have to have a vision – to know where you're going and to take your people with you. It's hard but you need to keep your distance. This is what allows you to make the right, but difficult decisions.

3 Nowadays, the key factor is how you manage change. Do you recognise what needs to change, when it needs to change and how it needs to change? Are you able to implement these changes? It's no good having a great vision, if you can't push through change.

C Building on the vocabulary already supplied, get subgroups to brainstorm words and phrases useful for describing leaders. Tell them to think of well-known leaders in order to

93

INVESTMENT **UNIT 15**

prompt ideas. Reorganise the students so that the groups are now made up of one member of each of the original groups. Get students to pool ideas. Do a class feedback, providing help and correction. In pairs, get students to describe one national or company leader they know, using the vocabulary previously established. They can make notes. Ask one or two students to tell the class about the leader described by their partner. Repeat this process as many times as you like.

D Ask students to write a profile of the sort of leader they would like to be. After correction, they could be displayed. Alternatively, the class could give short speeches, using their written profiles, for extra presentation delivery practice and to add interest.

▶ WORKBOOK EXERCISE B ON PAGE 63, CAN NOW BE DONE.

▶ REFER STUDENTS TO THE REVIEW BUSINESS NOTES ON PAGE 155 OF THE COURSEBOOK.

Checklist

Go through each item on the checklist with students and ask questions to recycle the key vocabulary in this unit.

Extension activity. Ask each student to remember or devise three life/work problems. Ask students to mingle and talk about their problems. Partners should offer advice. Before this activity is carried out, it could be useful to review the contracted form of *have*. At the end of the exercise, ask each student to talk about one of their problems and to report the best piece of advice they received. For example:

A: *I didn't get the job because I didn't have the right IT skills.*

B: *You should have done an online IT course in the evenings to improve your chances.*

INVESTMENT **UNIT 16**

16 Bollywood goes global

Vocabulary — The overall theme of this unit is the Bollywood film industry. There is a specific focus on the international film market, including production and financing issues. This section introduces the theme, focusing on general film-making language.

Listening and speaking — In this section students hear Ruby Bennet interview Bharat Mistry, an Indian film producer, about the difference between making a Bollywood film for the home market and making a Bollywood film for the overseas market. Issues such as financing and return on investment are discussed.

Grammar — **second conditional**
This unit tackles the structure and use of the second conditional.

Speaking — Students practise using the second conditional for making suggestions within the thematic context of the film industry.

Communication — **presentations 4: closing**
This section is the last of the four Communication sections dealing with presentations. It aims to help students make a strong and vital impact on listeners in the closing part of their presentations.

Business across Cultures — **decision-making**
This section looks at the influence of country and company cultures on the decision-making process in organisations.

Start-up

Ask the class to describe their favourite types of films. Elicit different film genres and write them up on the board. Elicit the most famous film-making place in the world as being Hollywood. Ask students to guess how much global annual cinema ticket sales are worth. Note the answers on the board and ask the class to open their Coursebooks at page 82 and check the box at the top of the page to find out who made the most accurate guess. Direct students to look at the photo. Elicit that it is a scene from a Bollywood film. Elicit that these films are made in India and that India has a fast growing film production industry. As a follow-up, you might like to ask students to think of a recent film that was a success in their country. Prompt questions might include: *Was it made in Hollywood or Bollywood? Was it locally filmed? Has it won any film awards? What type of film was it? How much profit has it made? What were the reasons for its success?*

Vocabulary

A Instruct the class to go straight into the matching exercise and then do a class check.

KEY
1 c   2 d   3 b   4 a   5 f   6 e   7 h   8 g

As a follow-up and in order to personalise the exercise, you might ask students to use the vocabulary listed to tell you about films that were written, produced, directed, or filmed in their country.

Listening and speaking

A AUDIO 16.1 Ask the class for ideas on why Indian films are becoming so popular around the world. Note their ideas on the board and check how accurate they are after listening to the audio. Instruct the class to read the rubric and statements. Do a quick check for understanding and go into the exercise as in the Coursebook. Check answers. Then play the audio a second time and ask students to note down and explain the reasons for their answers in more detail, in order to recycle language from the audio text.

KEY
1 T
2 F. *No, they are in English, have fewer songs and a more complex story.*
3 F. *Some film-makers are raising money on the Mumbai stock exchange.*
4 T
5 T
6 F. *Scriptwriters have never had much status in Bollywood.*
7 F. *The training school will teach many aspects of film production including budgeting, scheduling and planning.*

AUDIO SCRIPT

Ruby Bennett: There's increasing interest in Indian films around the world. Why do you think that is?

Bharat Mistry: Well, I think there is a market among international audiences for the singing and dancing, the colourful costumes, and the storylines that you find in Indian films. International audiences and Indian audiences are very similar in that respect.

Ruby Bennett: But there are some differences, too?

INVESTMENT UNIT 16

Bharat Mistry: That's right. For a film aimed at overseas markets, we would produce versions in two languages – Hindi and English – for release in India and in Europe. In the international version, there would be fewer songs and the story would be more complex. And the international version might have one big climax, whereas for Indian audiences we would have a series of climaxes throughout the film. That's what they expect.

Ruby Bennett: What about finance for Bollywood film productions?

Bharat Mistry: Finance has traditionally been informal, through family contacts and cash flow from earlier films. But some Indian film-makers are raising money now on the Mumbai stock exchange. A big international Bollywood production would need to gross between $25 and $30 million overseas in order to make a profit. But that's possible, if global audiences can relate to the content. That's what we have to get right.

Ruby Bennett: What else are you doing to make Bollywood a global industry?

Bharat Mistry: Well, we need to promote higher standards of production to meet the demands of an international audience.

Ruby Bennett: How is that being achieved?

Bharat Mistry: Traditionally, we've relied on natural talent, but now we're introducing training in all areas of film-making. One important development is a new $3 million training centre at Film City, just north of Mumbai, called Whistling Woods International.

Ruby Bennett: Whistling Woods?

Bharat Mistry: Yes, it's a training school for the entertainment industry, where film-makers can learn their trade. The school will place great emphasis on scriptwriting. Scriptwriters have never had much status in Bollywood, but the screenplay should be the foundation of a professional film production. And the whole industry needs to become more cost-effective – in terms of budgeting, scheduling, planning locations and working out the entire logistics. The training school will address all of that, and more.

Ruby Bennett: Before we finish, can you tell me about your latest film project?

Bharat Mistry: Well, I have very provisional plans for a film about an Indian woman who ...

▶ THE READING AND VOCABULARY EXERCISE ON PAGE 64 OF THE WORKBOOK CAN BE DONE AT THIS STAGE.

Grammar

Second conditional

Ask a student to read out the grammar rules on the second conditional to the rest of the class. Give students time to write one second conditional sentence about their own lives and then ask them to read it out to the class.

A Direct students to do the exercise as in the Coursebook and do a class check.

KEY

1 would you cast	would use	was / were
2 would you shoot	would go	didn't cost
3 would you choose	would ask	accepted
4 would you pay	would give	
5 would we	would start	

B Ask the class the question and give them time to reflect on it and write down an answer before doing a round the class check. Remind students that they need to work on the second clause of the *if* sentence (*would* + base form of the verb) and refer them to the grammar reference at the top of the page.

Speaking

A Instruct the class to read the instruction rubric and divide them into pairs or small groups. Ask them to do this exercise using the second conditional form. Circulate, providing help where necessary.

B Ask each group/pair to present their ideas to the class. Encourage the rest of the class to ask questions about detail, using the second conditional form.

▶ REVIEW AND DEVELOPMENT EXERCISE A ON PAGE 90 OF THE COURSEBOOK CAN NOW BE DONE.

▶ EXERCISE A ON PAGE 65 OF THE WORKBOOK CAN BE DONE AT THIS STAGE.

Communication

Presentations 4: Closing

As a start-up exercise it might be a good idea to review the Start-up discussion in Unit 13. Elicit that it is most important to make a strong impact in both introductions and conclusions and that the conclusion is obviously the last thing an audience remembers. Elicit from the class some important features of an effective presentation conclusion. Put them up on the board. As a check, run through the objectives at the beginning of the section on page 84 of the Coursebook. Then get pairs to come up with appropriate phrases for these features, and write them up too, providing correction where necessary.

A AUDIO 16.2 Do the exercise as in the Coursebook. Ask the class to note down which objectives are achieved in each case. Do a class check.

KEY

Presentation 1 does not include objective 4.
Presentation 2 does not include objective 5.
Presentation 3 meets all the objectives.

B Run through the Key language box in class. Get pairs to practise the phrases with each other and do a check for understanding. Ask the class to listen to AUDIO 16.2 again for phrases from the Key language box. Use the audio script to check answers. Get the students to say which features, if any, are missing from the presentation conclusions. Divide the class into three groups. Ask pairs from each group to use the audio scripts on page 127 of the Coursebook to rewrite one of the conclusions. Ask one student from each pair to read out their conclusion and do a quick review of the target language.

INVESTMENT **UNIT 16**

AUDIO SCRIPT

1 That brings me to the end of my presentation. I said at the start that I wanted to convince you to invest in this area and I hope I've done that. This is a great region with a big future. Thank you for your attention. I've prepared a folder with more information about the region. Please pick one up as you leave.

2 That's all I have to say as an introduction to STS Solutions. I hope that gives you a good overview of the business. There are some handouts here, which I'll pass around. Please help yourself. There will be a chance to ask questions during and after the tour. So, shall we get started ... ?

3 So to sum up, for us, our workforce is the key to the future. That's why we invest so much in training and recruitment. Are there any questions? No? Well, if you would like to know more, please contact me – you all have my email address. You've been a very attentive audience. Thank you.

C Assign presentation prompts 1 or 2 to small groups. Give students time to make notes to help them deliver the closing speeches to each other. Get one person from each group to deliver theirs to the whole class. Check intonation and pronunciation features. Write up one or two phrases on the board and get the class to practise correct stress and intonation patterns.

D AUDIO 16.3 Ask students to listen to the audio and make notes. Divide the class into three groups and get students to prepare their closing speeches individually. Go round the class listening to them and providing correction on the board where necessary.

MODEL ANSWERS

1 That brings me to the end of my presentation. I hope that gives you a good overview of how to set up a project. I have some handouts here, if you'd like to take one. Thank you very much for your attention. I'd be happy to answer any questions.

2 I said at the start that I wanted to convince you to upgrade your system. I hope I have done that. I've prepared a folder which goes into more detail. Are there any more questions? You've been a very attentive audience. Thank you and goodnight.

3 That covers everything I wanted to say. I hope that gives you a good overview of the company and our product range. I'm happy to take any questions now and as we look around the factory. Any questions? Let's take a look around now.

AUDIO SCRIPT

1 In this presentation, I aim to show you how we set up a new project. I'll cover three main areas: the selection of personnel, the use of software, and the project reporting system. By the end of this presentation, you should be able to start setting up your own projects. Right, let's start with the selection process.

2 My objective today is to convince you to upgrade your system. I've had a look at your current system and there is no doubt that it needs upgrading. I'll look at this from two points of view – firstly, user needs and secondly, system design. Please ask any questions as I go along. When I started this survey, I ...

3 Welcome to Castle Electronics. It's a pleasure to have you here. Before we have a look round, I'd like to take ten or 15 minutes to explain a little about the company. I thought it would be helpful to give you a short history and tell you something about our product range. After I've finished, we'll start the factory visit, which will take about an hour.

▶ COMMUNICATION NOTES FOR THIS UNIT CAN BE REVIEWED ON PAGE 152 OF THE COURSEBOOK.

▶ REFER STUDENTS TO THE REVIEW AND DEVELOPMENT EXERCISES ON PAGE 91 OF THE COURSEBOOK.

▶ EXERCISES A AND B ON PAGE 66 OF THE WORKBOOK, CAN BE DONE AT THIS STAGE.

Business across Cultures

Decision-making

A Instruct the class to open their Coursebooks at page 85. Read through the opening rubric with them. It might be useful to elicit various elements in the decision-making process. Answers might include: by whom, when, how quickly, and in which way, decisions are communicated to an organisation. Ask students to read the situation box and with a partner, to discuss who they would involve in the solving of this problem. Do a class feedback on ideas, eliciting reasons for their decisions. Elicit key words *individualist* and *group*. This could lead to a class discussion on who is involved in the decision-making process both in your students' organisations and in organisations they know well. (*Top-down* or *consensus* driven.) Encourage students to give input on different countries and industries, depending on your class.

B Again get the class to read the situation box. Ask pairs to decide how this decision should be made and communicated to the rest of the organisation. Get feedback from the class.

C Focus on the difference between *exercise oriented* and *relationship oriented* cultures. Ask students to assess which end of the spectrum they are closest to, giving their reasons. Depending on your class, draw a line on the board. Label each end and ask the class where they would place other countries/cultures on the continuum. Get the class to read through the situation box. Do a class check on understanding. Ask subgroups to discuss what went wrong and prepare some advice (using the second conditional) on how to win a contract in this culture. Get feedback from each group.

KEY

The Swedes took a task-oriented approach to winning the contract. They assumed they would get it and did not pay enough attention to building a personal relationship with the Venezuelans whose culture is person-oriented.

They should not have expected a decision during the meeting as in more person-oriented cultures decision-making is less structured.

The Swedes need to take time to build the relationship, and not focus immediately on the task.

They should not try to force a decision but accept that this will be made by those in a more person-oriented culture in their own time.

INVESTMENT UNIT 16

- ▶ EXERCISE A ON PAGE 67 OF THE WORKBOOK, CAN BE DONE AT THIS STAGE.
- ▶ REFER STUDENTS TO THE REVIEW CULTURE NOTES ON PAGE 155 OF THE COURSEBOOK.

Checklist

Go through each item on the checklist with the students and ask questions to recycle the key vocabulary in this unit and to review the second conditional.

Extension activity. Get each student to think of a second conditional question about life and work. Then ask them to mingle, putting their question to other students. At the end of the activity, each student should tell the class the most interesting answer they received.

MODULE 4 INVESTMENT

BUSINESS SCENARIO 4

SENIORSERVICES

> This business scenario involves three teams, each presenting a potential business investment opportunity to Brisbane-based, Seniorservices Chief Executive, Janet Townsend. Seniorservices is a holiday company for the fast-growing over 60s market. In a meeting led by Janet, the whole class consider each potential opportunity and decide on the one they consider to be most profitable. The final exercise is the writing of an email to an absent colleague, in order to explain the reasons for their choice.

BACKGROUND

Instruct the class to open their Coursebooks at page 86 and look at the pictures and photos. Ask the class to describe what they see in the photos. Answers might include: older people having fun outdoors, possibly on holiday in Australia, etc. Ask them to read the background information on Seniorservices and Janet Townsend, as well as the information on the grey market. Do a vocabulary check on key items which might include: grey market/baby boomers/significant segment/affluent/disposable income.

Ask the class to give ideas about how they would like to enjoy their older years and where they might like to go on holiday.

EXPANDING THE BUSINESS

A quick review of Key language from the Communication sections on meetings, from Units 7 and 8, and presenting, from Units 9–12, might be a useful exercise at this point.

There could also be a quick focus on comparatives, superlatives, *will* and *going to* for forecasting, and a look at key investment vocabulary from Units 9–12.

Appoint a Janet/John Townsend and ask her/him to read student A information and prepare some relevant questions.

Divide the rest of the group into three teams, A, B and C.

Ask Team A to look at the information on page 108.

Ask Team B to look at the information on page 110.

Ask Team C to look at the information on page 113.

Give the class a fairly short time scale in which to prepare their investment opportunity presentations. Circulate, helping with vocabulary problems and Janet/John Townsend's questions.

Appoint someone to make notes for use in the writing exercise.

You might like to appoint one or two observers to take notes on good presentation techniques and appropriate meetings' language, used to manage the people and process. Video/audio recording would allow for useful feedback material.

Let Janet/John Townsend open, lead and close the meeting, giving the reasons for the final decision. Do a class review of language and on how well the exercise was managed. Encourage the class to review themselves and their performance.

WRITING

An explanatory email to an absent colleague on the chosen project giving reasons for the decision.

Ask the note-taker from the last exercise to run through the main points raised and discussed during the meeting, with reasons for the final decision. Get him/her to write them up on the board. Ask the class to note these down.

Do a short review of email formalities and set this exercise for homework. After individual correction, do a class review pointing out useful language items/repetitive grammar problems, etc.

Review and development 13–16

Vocabulary: Car industry and investment

A Students can complete their own crossword with a partner. Alternatively, you could divide the class into two, giving them crossword copies, with one half of the clues blanked out. Group A works on the across questions, while group B does the other half, checking their answers as a group. They then dictate their clues to a partner from the other group, giving them hints where necessary, until both partners have completed the crossword. This second part can also be done as a group exercise with a timer, no hints and a winning team!

KEY

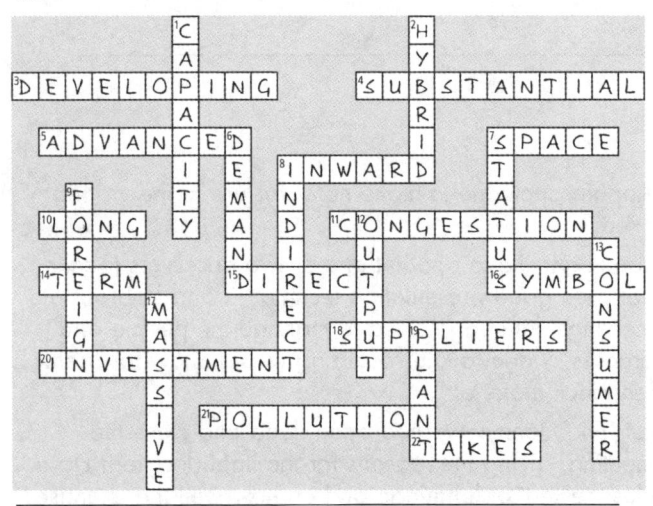

[Crossword grid with answers:
3 DEVELOPING, 4 SUBSTANTIAL, 5 ADVANCED, 7 SPACE, 8 INWARD, 10 LONG, 11 CONGESTION, 14 TERM, 15 DIRECT, 16 SYMBOL, 18 SUPPLIERS, 20 INVESTMENT, 21 POLLUTION, 22 TAKES; Down: 1 CAR, 2 HYBRID, 4 STRICT, 6 DECENT, 9 FRY, 12 ENDING, 13 CONSUMER, 17 MASSIVE, 19 LACE]

B Instruct students to work on this exercise individually and to compare their answers with another students'. Do a class review. You might elicit which type of compound students have formed, using the grammar box on page 75 of the Coursebook.

KEY

1 domestic expansion
2 reduced growth
3 private transport
4 combined sales
5 advertising rates
6 shopping catalogues
7 ongoing problems
8 complex operation
9 distribution network
10 national newspaper
11 restaurant chain

C Ask student pairs to create sentences as in the exercises. Do a round the class check for each compound, making a note of correct grammar on the board as you go, but keep the main focus on correct use of the compounds.

Grammar: Should/shouldn't have, could have

A Review the rules and examples on page 79 with the class and ask students to do the exercise individually. Do a class check.

KEY

1 c   2 c   3 b   4 a   5 b   6 b   7 a

B Read through the rubric with the class and get one pair to do the first example. At this point, it might be helpful to review the extra pronunciation item, relating to this grammar point, the contracted form of *have* – *'ve*. Ask pairs to alternately explain the problem and offer advice to each other. Invite pairs to do the examples out loud in class as a grammar check.

MODEL ANSWERS

2 You could have / should have asked for promotion.
3 You could have asked for an office.
4 You should have taken your full four weeks' holiday.
5 You should have asked for a car.
6 You shouldn't have agreed to do all the worst jobs.
7 You shouldn't have worked so late / should have left at six every evening.

Grammar: Second conditional

A Review the rules on page 83 with the class again and instruct pairs to do the exercise as in the Coursebook.

MODEL ANSWERS

2 A: What would you do if the computer system crashed?
   B: I'd call the computer manager.
3 A: What would you do if one of the sales people left to go to work for a competitor?
   B: If one of the sales people left to go to work for a competitor, I'd be very angry.
4 A: What would you do if the photocopier broke down?
   B: If the photocopier broke down, I'd contact the photocopier company.
5 A: What would you do if the company was taken over?
   B: If the company was taken over, I'd leave.
6 A: What would you do if you invented a new product for the company?
   B: If I invented a new product for the company, I'd ask to be the product manager for it.
7 A: How would you feel if the company went bankrupt?
   B: If the company went bankrupt, I'd be very upset.

Communication

A Instruct the class to do the exercise as in the Coursebook.

KEY
1 b	4 j	7 g	10 e
2 f	5 k	8 c	11 i
3 h	6 d	9 a	

B Review the four main tips for effective presentations with the class. You might find it useful to set a fairly short time limit for student presentations, depending on your class. Do a post presentation final review on progress made over the module's Communication sections. Your class should feel considerably more competent by now!

MODULE 5

Writing resource

MODULE OVERVIEW

AIMS AND OBJECTIVES

This section is a resource which gives students further practice in writing letters, CVs, faxes, and emails. It also provides reading practice and some model examples. Each unit in this module relates to the themes and language of one of the other four modules, in logical order, so it is advisable to begin each one only after students have covered the relevant units.

PEDAGOGICAL NOTES

Each unit includes introductory or follow up activities which are linked to the information and questions. Oral activities to elicit relevant vocabulary and ideas are suggested. Usually a particular type of exercise exploitation is suggested (i.e. individual, pair or class). Most *open* writing exercises are suggested as individual (possibly homework) exercises. Where possible, it could be useful to ask students to submit these pieces of work, for correction, before the next lesson. As with any other exercise in the Coursebook, adaptation of the writing exercises to the students' own work/study situations would be beneficial from the point of view of relevance and student motivation.

Before embarking on this module, it might be useful to review the differences between letter writing and emailing. Elicit that whilst many typical business letter phrases are used in emails, the degree of formality is generally less formal than in a traditional business letter, particularly in opening and closing salutations, and they are generally shorter and more direct. It could also be useful to stress that in appropriate situations, formal letters can be sent in email form, but should still follow formal letter writing conventions.

Unit 17: Nice job

This unit prepares students for job hunting; particularly relevant to pre-work learners, although no doubt equally useful for employees preparing to look for jobs in companies whose official business language is now English. It could be useful to review related items from Module 1, such as the Communication section on page 6 of Unit 1. Here students talk about themselves, their hobbies and interests, and listen to excerpts of people discussing their strengths and weaknesses in terms of their people, organisation and communication skills. Unit 2 provides language relating to motivation, useful for letters of application. Unit 3 builds up vocabulary for employee compensation and benefits, useful for reading job advertisements. Supplementary exercises can also be found in the relevant Workbook units.

Students are provided with a model of both a job advertisement and a CV. They read and answer questions on the required skills and benefits offered in the job advertisement and use the model to write their own CV. A job application email gap-fill exercise provides them with standard job application phrases.

Unit 18: Getting the go-ahead

This unit follows the Module 2 theme of innovation. It is set in a multinational electronics company, Diretto, and comprises a series of email exchanges, between Susan Wang, an entrepreneur, and Diretto's management team. Students complete one gap-fill email exercise and then follow instructions to write two more, so that by the end of the unit they will have had practice in writing emails for a variety of internal business scenarios. It could be useful to encourage students to identify the relationship between the different characters and to reflect on how this could affect their degree of politeness, formality, etc.

Unit 19: Unhappy customers

This unit, which focuses on letters of complaint and customer service, corresponds with the Business across Cultures section (customer service culture) of Unit 10. It begins with a letter of complaint from a passenger on a cruise organised by Seniorservices. Students use notes to write a formal response to the customer. Finally, they write a short reply from the customer either accepting or refusing a suggested refund. The Teacher's Resource book, makes suggestions for highlighting the differences between formal and informal writing.

Unit 20: Local partners

The main theme of this unit is the expansion of a supermarket chain abroad. This should be done after Unit 15, as it is based on a similar topic. The first task involves completing a letter of enquiry in which a French supermarket chain writes to the Turkish Retailing Association to ask if they can recommend a joint venture partner in Turkey. Students then write responses from the Turkish Retailing Association and from a potential joint venture partner. The skills developed in this unit can be applied to other letters of enquiry, for example, in relation to unadvertised vacancies and asking for advice. The Teacher's Resource book provides instructions on ways of eliciting and presenting the order and content of letters of enquiry.

REVIEW AND DEVELOPMENT

This section revises various aspects of the four main units in the module. Students read a transcript of Serguei Bronovski, a young London-based engineer, talking about his educational background, hobbies and interests and career to date. They can use this as a basis for writing his CV. Finally, the theme moves back to that of Unit 2, Diretto, and students complete a gap-fill email rejecting a product development project, and a counteroffer from the CEO, Roberto Campi.

WRITING RESOURCE **UNIT 17**

17 Nice job

- a job advertisement
- a CV
- an email of application

Start-up
Inform the class that they are going to work on job ads, CVs, and emails of application.

Elicit that the compensation for a job often includes both salary and benefits. Get subgroups to brainstorm the sorts of benefits they get or would like! Do a class feedback, writing up useful language on the board.

Job advertisement

A Ask the class to open their Coursebooks at page 92 and read the job advertisement. Check for any vocabulary problems.

B Ask students to do the exercise as in the Coursebook.

KEY
1 a   2 b   3 b   4 b   5 a   6 a   7 a   8 c

Extension activity. Get groups to reread the ad and to produce a bullet point profile of the personal characteristics of the employee this company is looking for. They could also provide synonyms for some of the terms in the ad. Answers might include: innovative, creative, imaginative, autonomous, team player, etc.

CVs

A Ask the class to read the CV on page 93. Check for vocabulary problems. Ask subgroups to decide whether Rosario Gomez would be a suitable applicant for the job. Do a class feedback on her skills and personal qualities, as stated on her CV, in relation to the job ad.

B Set this exercise as homework, followed by an individual feedback session.

Job application

A This gap-fill exercise could also be set as homework and reviewed briefly in class.

KEY
1 c   2 c   3 a   4 c   5 b   6 a   7 c   8 b

B It could be useful to do a class review of typical phrases, like the ones in exercise A, used in letters and emails of application. Briefly review the personal characteristics and experience needed for this job. Instruct subgroups to brainstorm skills, qualifications and experience that could be brought to this position from a car design background. Do a class feedback, writing up interesting ideas on the board.

Set the email for homework. Encourage the use of the ideas generated in class. It could be useful to mark students' emails individually before reviewing any particular difficulties in class.

MODEL ANSWER

To: johann.schmidt@scirocco.ch
Subject: Phone designer, ref: PD1

Dear Mr Schmidt

I am writing with reference to your ad for phone designers. As you can see from the attached CV, my background is in car design, but I would now like to move to another area of design. I think that car design and phone design have a lot in common.

As my CV indicates, I have worked for more than seven years at Renault, of which the last five have been in its design office outside Paris. Now I would like to move to a hi-tech company. I am willing to move to Switzerland; I can do this at any time from September onwards.

I am available for an interview at any time except during the last week of March, when I will be on holiday.

I look forward to hearing from you,

Best regards,
Jens Jensen

Extension activity. Ask students to swap CVs with a partner. Ask them to write a job ad suited to the applicant whose CV they are reviewing. After these job ads have been corrected individually, put all the CVs and job ads on the wall/table and get students to select a suitable candidate for each job. A round the class feedback on, the reasons for each choice, could round off the exercise and unit. This exercise can be set as homework.

WRITING RESOURCE UNIT 18

18 Getting the go-ahead

- an email to congratulate, assign roles and responsibilities and to request a meeting
- an email of thanks, giving information and confirming arrangements
- an email of apology, alternative suggestion and offer

Direct the class to open their Coursebooks at page 94. Read the start-up rubric with them and check for understanding. Elicit the meaning of *navigation device* from students and ask them to explain its use.

Email exchange

A Ask the class to do the exercise as in the Coursebook. Do a class review.

At this point, it might be useful to do a review of appropriate opening and closing remarks, the fitting register and stock phrases such as: *I am delighted to tell you / we discussed the possibility of ...-ing / to discuss the project further*. Also look at the difference between commonly confused words such as: *delighted, amused* and *enjoy / argue, talk* and *discuss / possibility* and *potential*.

KEY
1 b
2 a
3 c
4 c
5 c
6 c
7 b
8 c
9 a
10 b

B Ask the class to describe the probable relationship between Richard Long and Susan Wang. How will this affect the language register used in their emails? It might be useful to review:

Thanking formalities

Expressing happiness / enthusiasm: *I'm delighted/very pleased*

Apologies: *I'm sorry/afraid / Unfortunately*

Signalling attachments

You might wish to set the exercise for homework and do a class review of recurring errors, after correction.

MODEL ANSWER

Dear Richard

Many thanks for getting the go-ahead for my project. I am very happy to be working on it. I have prepared a detailed development plan with a schedule, which I am attaching here.

I will try to be in your office at 10:00 am, but I might be slightly late, if that's OK, as I'm seeing a supplier at 9:00 am for an hour, and it may run over slightly.

Best wishes
Susan

C It could be useful to review phrases used for making suggestions and requests.

Again, set the email for homework and do a class review of any particular problems, after correction.

MODEL ANSWER

Hi, Richard.

Thanks for asking me to come to your meeting with Susan tomorrow. Unfortunately, I can't make it – I have an important meeting with an advertising agency. My apologies for this.

Please have the meeting without me and let me know what you discuss.

Best regards
Paola

WRITING RESOURCE **UNIT 19**

19 Unhappy customers

- a letter of complaint
- a response to a complaint
- a response to an offer of a refund

As this unit focuses on letters of complaint and customer service, it would be appropriate to do it after the Business across Cultures section (customer service culture) of Unit 10.

Introductory activity

Ask: *What are common causes of complaints to organisations?* Brainstorm ideas and write them up on the board. Then ask: *How should companies deal with complaints?* Write students' suggestions and useful vocabulary on the board (product replacement, a refund voucher, written apology, etc.) Tell students that they are going to read a letter of complaint to a travel company. Ask: *Have you ever experienced a bad holiday? Did you complain?* Allow students to exchange a few anecdotes, but do not spend too long on this. Make a note of any useful vocabulary (or words that appear in Unit 19) on the board.

Letter of complaint

A Ask students to open their Coursebooks. Write vocabulary items from the letter on the board (cruise, holiday of a lifetime, scheduled stopover, stomach bug, cabin, to play out of tune, etc.) and elicit definitions or synonyms. Ask students to read the letter individually, then answer the questions in pairs. Compare answers in class.

KEY

1 b   2 c   3 a   4 a   5 b   6 c   7 b

B Before embarking on this exercise, write the following on the board:

Informal	Formal
Sorry about …	?
Can you send me …	?
Thanks for your letter.	?
I don't mind helping you.	?
Let me know if this is OK.	?

Elicit more formal versions of each sentence. Students may come up with a variety of appropriate suggestions; write the most common on the board. Ask students how the formal and informal styles differ.

For example in formal letters:

do not contract words (I'm, don't)

write full sentences

use more formal vocabulary
(sorry ▶ apologise, OK ▶ acceptable)

'I' often becomes 'we' when writing from a company

Ask students to read the instructions for exercise B and do the first sentence (*Thank you / letter / 8 September* …) together in class. Ask students to work on the exercise in pairs. Compare answers in class. Ask students whether the letter is formal or informal, then ask what makes it formal.

MODEL ANSWER

> Dear Mr Kinnear,
>
> Thank you for your letter of 8 September. We have looked into your complaints.
>
> We are aware of the late departure of the cruise ship from Colombo and we apologise for this.
>
> The stopover in the Seychelles was cancelled because the engines were not working properly and the ship was getting behind schedule. We are sorry for any disappointment that this caused.
>
> We have had no complaints from other passengers regarding the food and the dance band.
>
> We are willing to make a refund of 10 per cent of the cost of the cruise because of its late departure and the lack of a stopover in the Seychelles. Please let me know if this acceptable to you.
>
> Yours sincerely,
>
> Amanda Grayson
> Customer Care Manager

C Ask students to do the exercise as indicated either for homework or individually in class. Tell them to write between 50 and 100 words. Remind them to begin and end their letters suitably and use the right level of formality. To provide in-depth feedback, you could use a Writing Feedback Framework (see Frameworks, page 124). Go through the feedback sheet with the students prior to the exercise so that they are aware of the key factors upon which their written performance will be assessed.

MODEL ANSWER

> Dear Ms Grayson,
>
> Thank you for your letter of 1 October, offering 10 per cent of the cost of our cruise in compensation for the problems that occurred. Although this is less than the 50 per cent I was hoping for, I have decided to accept this offer. I look forward to receiving your cheque.
>
> Yours sincerely,
>
> George Kinnear

MODEL ANSWER

> Dear Ms Grayson,
>
> Thank you for your letter of 1 October, offering 10 per cent of the cost of our cruise in compensation for the problems that occurred. However, this offer is totally inadequate. You will soon be hearing from my lawyers.
>
> George Kinnear

Extension activity. Ask two to three volunteers to describe a bad customer service experience they've had. Ask the other students to take notes while they listen and to write a response to one of the complaints from the customer service department in question.

105

WRITING RESOURCE UNIT 20

20 Local partners

- a fax of enquiry
- a response to a fax of enquiry

The main the theme of this unit is the expansion of a supermarket chain abroad. This should be done after Unit 15 as it relates to a similar topic.

Introductory activity

Ask students why people write letters of enquiry. (To find out if companies have job vacancies, to find business opportunities, to ask for advice, to get information concerning a product or service, etc.) Tell students that they are going to read a fax in which the writer is enquiring about joint venture opportunities abroad. Elicit a definition of *joint venture*. Then ask students for the advantages of setting up a joint venture with a local partner abroad.

Fax exchange

A Ask students to read the fax and do the exercise as indicated in pairs. Go through the answers together in class, and be prepared to provide or elicit example sentences for the other words.

KEY
1 b   2 a   3 c   4 a   5 c   6 a   7 c   8 b   9 a

Extension activity. Write the following on the board:

Thanking for help in advance
Purpose of fax
Introduction of self and reasons for interest
Reference to recipient's response
Showing you are prepared to take action

Ask students to refer to the fax and put the points on the board in the order they appear in the fax. Also ask them to note down key phrases that relate to the points.

1 *Introduction of self and reasons for interest*
  (I am the ... We are now ...)
2 *Purpose of fax (I am writing to ask if you can ...)*
3 *Showing you are prepared to take action*
  (I would be more than willing to ...)
4 *Thanking for help in advance*
  (I would be very grateful for any advice ...)
5 *Reference to recipient's response*
  (I look forward to hearing from you.)

B Instruct students to do the exercise either individually or in pairs. Get students to write fax responses on overhead transparencies. Circulate, checking for common errors, and providing assistance where necessary. Supply feedback after the exercise showing some of the faxes on an OHP.

MODEL ANSWER

Dear Mr Bertrand,
Thank you for your fax of 2 May. I have been in touch with a member of our association, Ms Dilek Saray, who is based in Izmir. I have asked her to contact you with reference to your enquiry and she will be in touch with you soon.
I hope she is able to help you with your enquiry.
Best wishes,
Mehmet Emin

C Ask students to do the exercise for homework. As in the above activity, writing could be done on overhead transparencies which can be used during feedback and analysis. To provide in-depth feedback, you could use a Writing Feedback Framework (see Frameworks, page 124). Go through the feedback sheet with the students prior to the exercise so that they are aware of the key factors upon which their written performance will be assessed.

MODEL ANSWER

Dear Mr Bertrand,
Mr Mehmet Emin of the Turkish Retailing Association has given me your name. He has told me that you wish to find a local partner in Turkey.
My company, Saray Markets, is a small but successful chain of supermarkets. The company was founded by my father in 1945. He started with one shop in Izmir, and the chain now has seven supermarkets in various towns in western Turkey.
We are currently looking for an international partner to expand further. Would it be possible for you to come to Izmir next week to discuss things? How about Wednesday 22 May? Please let me know if this is suitable.
I look forward to meeting you.

Yours sincerely,
Dilek Saray

Extension activity. Ask students to write a letter/fax of enquiry to a large international company to either find out whether there are any job vacancies or any joint venture opportunities. Elicit the elements and order of a letter/fax of enquiry for an unadvertised position in a company. For example:

Introduce yourself and refer to the position you are interested in.

Explain your interest in working for the company and why you want to be considered for that particular post.

Describe your qualifications, experience, and personal qualities that are relevant to the job and company.

Refer to your CV which is enclosed/attached.

State your availability for an interview.

Thank them for their consideration.

Express your interest again.

Close the letter.

Review and development 17–20

This unit reviews and extends the writing activities covered in Units 17–20. Activities include:

Reading a transcript of a young Russian engineer, talking about himself.

Writing a CV.

An email reply to request funding to develop a project.

Before completing the exercises in this unit, it would be useful for students to review the last four units, particularly Units 17 and 18.

A Direct the class to look at the photos on page 100 of their Coursebooks. Ask questions to elicit that the man has a job connected with high rise buildings/steel.

Ask the class to read the transcript and do a vocabulary check.

B Before doing this activity it might be useful to review the CV on page 93. Other items to review might include compounds on page 75, and the use of these to describe one's personal skills and qualities.

In pairs or individually, instruct students to do this exercise as in the Coursebook. This could be a useful point at which to review students' writing skills individually.

MODEL ANSWER

SERGUEI BRONOVSKI

Career goals:	Looking for stimulating research and development work in a US construction company.
Skills:	• Enthusiastic self-starter
	• Good at independent research
	• Native Russian speaker; fluent English; good German
Qualifications:	<u>1995–1999</u> Degree in civil engineering, Moscow University
	<u>1999–2003</u> PhD: High-strength Steel in Wind-exposed High-rise Buildings, University of London
Experience:	<u>2003-now</u> Research engineer, Astrup Engineering, London
Interests:	Ice hockey

C Instruct students to do the gap-fill exercise as in the Coursebook. In a class review, it could be useful to ask students to compare the reply to Roberto Campi's product development proposal with that of the reply to Susan Wang (page 94). Ask students to highlight the typical letter writing phrases used in both. Answers might include: Thank you for your memo of (date). / Unfortunately, I have to inform you... / I am delighted to tell you... / Please don't hesitate to get back to me.

KEY

1 funding
2 unfortunately
3 inform
4 products
5 energy
6 developing
7 benefit
8 working
9 hesitate

Extension activity. Ask the class to write their own CV following the model set out in exercise B.

Photocopiable resource

INTRODUCTION

MODULE 1
Performance

The main aim of this activity is to review comparatives and superlatives. Briefly review the various structures covered in Unit 1 of the Coursebook (... than ... / ... (not) as ... as ... / slightly / nearly / much, etc.)

1.1 is an information exchange activity where students ask their partner for the missing information. Before starting the activity, ask students: *What do you know about teambuilding activities? Have you ever taken part in a teambuilding event? What did you do? Was it effective?* You may need to pre-teach some vocabulary such as: *paintball, rock climbing, and popularity rating*. You may also need to review the language for checking and clarifying.

Activity 2 requires participants to use comparative structures. You could set students a time limit of five minutes to make as many comparisons as possible. This should be done in pairs and then checked in class.

Extension activity. This provides the opportunity for free practice of comparative structures. Tell students that they are responsible for organising a teambuilding event for a department of twenty-two staff and that they are going to hold a meeting to discuss, and finally choose, one of the events. It would be best to create subgroups for the meeting if your class is large. Select chairs beforehand to ensure that the meeting is well structured and everyone gets a chance to express their views. Allow students five minutes to prepare their arguments in favour of one event (assign roles by giving each student an event to support during the discussion) and their objections to the others. Set a time limit of twenty minutes for the meeting. Make a note of students' use of comparatives and superlatives (which should arise naturally in this type of discussion) and any errors. Provide feedback after the meeting.

1.2 is a pair work role-play and should be done after Unit 3. Before beginning, review the structure and use of the first conditional. The situation involving an employee negotiating a benefits package with his/her boss includes some new vocabulary, which may need to be pre-taught *(subsidised, contributions, crèche)*. Give students enough time to read through the notes and prepare their ideas before conducting the meeting.

MODULE 2
Innovation

2.1 reflects the theme of start-ups, which is part of the module's theme. A Spanish tax consultant advises the finance director of a large German company how to set up a Spanish company and register it for tax purposes. She explains the process, with the aid of a flow chart, to help her client understand.

Students should put the verbs in brackets into the suitable passive form to exchange information with their partner, in order to complete the flow chart. A review of any vocabulary difficulties might be useful after the exercise.

2.2 is designed to allow students to practise asking for and giving information about the past, using the past simple and the past perfect. Based on a series (by no means exhaustive) of Sir Timothy Berners-Lee's (inventor of the World Wide Web) milestones, it follows the theme of innovation and entrepreneurship. A longer biography of Sir Timothy Berners-Lee can be found at www.w3.org.

After a review of the relationship between the uses of the past simple and past perfect to talk about past events, it could be useful to start this exercise by eliciting that he invented the World Wide Web.

Students should fill in the gaps in their Tim Berners-Lee timelines by asking their partner questions formed in the correct tense, depending on whether they are asking about main past events, or events which preceded these. They should then answer their partner's questions.

MODULE 3
Promotion

3.1 increases familiarity with adjectives that share the same negative prefixes. It should be used after Unit 10 of the Coursebook.

Review the rules for *un-, in-, il-, im-* or *ir-*, as negative prefixes.

Before the game, give subgroups sets of the photocopiable cards, which feature a variety of adjectives, and ask students to group them according to whether they take the *un-, in-, il-, im-* or *ir-* prefix. Check the answers in class.

Extension activity. Snap. The object of this game is to win all of the cards. Two or more people can play. The dealer should deal out all of the cards. Each player puts his/her cards, without looking at them, in a pile, face down in front of him/her.

The player on the dealer's left turns over the top card of the pile and puts it face up in the middle of the table. Play continues clockwise around the table, with each player placing one card face up on the pile. If a card placed on the pile matches the previous card (i.e. it shares the same prefix), students must shout *Snap*! It is a race to see which player can shout *Snap* first. The player who says *Snap* first, wins all of the cards in the pile only if he/she can say which prefix the adjectives share.

This player adds the cards to the bottom of his/her pile. The game continues where it left off with the player to the left of the winner starting the next round. The game ends when one player has won all of the cards.

[N.B. A player who shouts *Snap* at the wrong time must give up his/her top card to the player who played before.]

3.2 should be used at the end of Module 3 to review all of the elements of telephoning. The aim of this activity is to give students practice at responding spontaneously to telephone calls. In our working lives, we frequently receive calls that we are not expecting.

For this exercise, students should work in pairs. Give each pair a set of cards and tell them to put them face down on the table. Explain that they are to take it in turns to pick up one card and to use the information on it so as to assume their role and make a call to their partner. Tell callers that they must make it clear who they are, and what they want, in order to help their partner understand the context. Encourage them to use their imagination to expand on the information provided on the card. Their partner has to respond appropriately to the caller and deal spontaneously with any requests, complaints, messages, invitations or cancellations. Remind both callers and recipients to use the right level of formality depending on the context. Demonstrate the exercise with a confident student. Circulate during the exercise and make a note of errors, as well as good use of telephoning language.

To provide individual feedback, you could use a Telephoning Feedback Framework (see Frameworks, page 123). Go through the feedback sheet with the students prior to the activity so that they are aware of the key factors upon which their performance will be assessed.

MODULE 4

Investment

4.1 incorporates many of the elements of the module's theme. The grammatical aim of the exercise is to practise the structures *should, shouldn't have* and *could have* as presented in Unit 15 so the exercise probably should only be attempted after Unit 15.

Before beginning this activity, depending on your class, you might find it useful to review previous units from Module 4 and elicit key investment vocabulary items.

Pairs should read through the introductory paragraph together. In order to build up a more complete background to the business scenario, pairs should ask their partner the questions on their card and answer their partner's questions with the extra information provided. They should be encouraged to check and clarify the information to ensure that they have understood each other correctly.

Students A should then find out what mistakes De Lorean made with market design and finance issues.

Students B should use their prompts and the *should, shouldn't have* and *could have* structures to explain how the De Lorean car plant failed and make suggestions as to how they could have managed it better.

Students B should then ask students A about failures in the production and dealership area. Students A should use their prompts and the target language to give their opinions about the reasons for failure of the investment.

Finally, both students should read the final outcome of the manufacturing venture together.

Extension activity. You might like to ask one pair to present the scenario jointly to the class, offering suggestions and opinions on how the company *should have/could have* acted, etc. You could also invite comment and discussion from the class. As this text is a rich source of relevant key vocabulary, a class review of the key vocabulary could be very beneficial for your students. The text source is *Wikipedia, the free encyclopedia*.

4.2 aims to get students to use the second conditional and vocabulary from each of the module's four units, to talk about issues raised throughout Module 4. (Investment and environmental issues relating to the automotive industry, cross cultural issues, the newspaper industry and presentation skills.)

Students A and B use the information given on their sheets to form the opening half of the second conditional sentence in the past simple, which their partner should finish, using *would (not)* + infinitive. Students complete the sentences on their sheets.

After the pair work exercise has been completed, a class review of the ideas expressed in the second half of the conditional sentences could be done.

MODEL ANSWERS

A1. If we all 'drove' smaller, more manoeuvrable cars, parking in cities would/might be easier.

A2. If we all 'went over' to using electric cars, there 'would be' no need for petrol stations.

A3. If the Metro newspaper 'was not' free, its readership 'would not be' so high.

A4. If I 'didn't want' the audience to ask questions during my presentation, I 'could ask' them to hold questions until the end.

A5. If we 'made' our own film, we 'would/could shoot' it in the Czech Republic.

A6. If you 'were' CEO of a large multinational company, you 'could give' everybody a pay rise.

B1. If there 'was' massive investment in hybrid car technology, we 'would see' far more hybrid cars on the road.

B2. If congestion charges 'were introduced' in every city, demand for cars 'would/could slump'.

B3. If your Chinese colleague 'tipped' his head back and 'sucked' air in, you 'would know' he was finding it difficult.

B4. If you 'didn't state' your presentation objectives, your audience 'would have' difficulty following your presentation.

B5. If the Metro newspaper editors 'did not have' such a scientific approach to distribution, the Metro 'would not be' so successful.

B6. If Bollywood 'didn't make' films in English, they 'would not be' so successful in Europe.

1.1 Student A

Activity 1

Information exchange
Ask your partner questions to complete the information about the different teambuilding events.

Paintball **Location:** Forest (1 hour from office) **Accommodation:** Not necessary **Length of event:** _____ **Day(s):** Friday **Cost:** _____ **Average number of participants:** 20-30 **Additional details:** Formal dinner after the event. **Popularity rating:** 8/10	**Outdoor Activities** **Location:** In the mountains (____ hours from office) **Accommodation:** _____ **Length of event:** 3days **Day(s):** Friday–Sunday **Cost:** $21,000 **Average number of participants:** 25 maximum **Additional details:** Participants will take part in rock climbing, canoeing, and mountaineering. There will be a barbecue every evening. **Popularity rating:** 7/10
Theatre Workshop **Location:** _____ (1 hour from the office) **Accommodation:** Hotel **Length of event:** 2 days **Day(s):** Over the weekend **Cost:** $18,000 **Average number of participants:** _____ **Additional details:** Participants will write and produce their own theatrical production. **Popularity rating:** 7/10	**Team Building Bay** **Location:** At the office **Accommodation:** Not necessary **Length of event:** 1 day **Day(s):** _____ **Cost:** $6,000 **Average number of participants:** _____ maximum **Additional details:** Participants will perform a variety of problem solving exercises and take part in business simulations. **Popularity rating:** _____

Activity 2

Compare the events using the following adjectives:
popular
expensive
serious
convenient
long
far
interesting
fun

1.1 Student B

Activity 1

Information exchange
Ask your partner questions to complete the information about the different teambuilding events.

Paintball **Location:** Forest (1 hour from office) **Accommodation:** Not necessary **Length of event:** 1 day **Day(s):** Friday **Cost:** $12,000 **Average number of participants:** _____ **Additional details:** Formal dinner after the event. **Popularity rating:** _____	**Outdoor Activities** **Location:** _____ (3 hours from office) **Accommodation:** In a tent **Length of event:** 3 days **Day(s):** Friday–Sunday **Cost:** _____ **Average number of participants:** 25 maximum **Additional details:** Participants will take part in rock climbing, canoeing, and mountaineering. There will be a barbecue every evening. **Popularity rating:** 7/10
Theatre Workshop **Location:** In a theatre in the city (1 hour from the office) **Accommodation:** _____ **Length of event:** 2 days **Day(s):** _____ **Cost:** $18,000 **Average number of participants:** 18–20 **Additional details:** Participants will write and produce their own theatrical production. **Popularity rating:** 7/10	**Team Building Bay** **Location:** At the office **Accommodation:** Not necessary **Length of event:** 1 day **Day(s):** Wednesday **Cost:** _____ **Average number of participants:** _____ **Additional details:** Participants will perform a variety of problem solving exercises and take part in business simulations. **Popularity rating:** 6/10

Activity 2

Compare the events using the following adjectives:
popular
expensive
serious
convenient
long
far
interesting
fun

1.2 Student A

Employee

You are a sales manager at a large IT company. Last year, you received the benefits package below. You are going to meet your boss to discuss this year's package. You are aware that the company's profits have been low recently so you may not be offered any new benefits.

- You don't mind losing the evening course, but you would expect to be sent on an English language course in the UK instead.
- You feel strongly that your performance targets are unrealistic so the performance bonus should be much higher.
- You would like to have use of the company crèche.

Benefits Package
• membership to local gym • private healthcare • company contributions to pension • subsidised lunches • free evening course at local college (choice of courses range from art, to languages, to yoga) • performance bonus (100 per cent target – $2,000) • company car

---

1.2 Student B

Boss

Last year, your employee received the benefits package below. You are going to hold a meeting with him/her to discuss this year's package. You are keen to offer him/her a good package because he/she is a highly motivated and productive employee. However, due to poor profits, some of the benefits will have to be cut.

You want to cut:
- company car (not often needed for company business)
- private healthcare
- pension contributions
- free evening courses

You can:
- increase the performance bonus a little (provided that your employee agrees to lose other benefits)
- offer free financial advice
- offer the opportunity to occasionally work from home

Benefits Package
• membership to local gym • private healthcare • company contributions to pension • subsidised lunches • free evening course at local college (choice of courses range from art, to languages, to yoga) • performance bonus (100 per cent target – $2,000) • company car

2.1 Student A

First, the company name _____ (chose). The appropriate forms _____ (complete) and _____ (witness) by the partners and directors.

↓

During this period, the legal requirements for setting up a company must _____ (fulfil).

↓

This number is essential. It _____ (require) _____ (display) on all company documents. It _____ (use) to deduct VAT by the tax authorities.

→

↑

The contracts then _____ (send) to the tax office from which the tax ID number _____ (obtain).

↑

Various internal company procedures _____ (govern) by the rules stated in these documents, once the company _____ (form).

↑

© Copyright Thomson Heinle 2007, a part of the Thomson Corporation

2.1 Student B

Next, they _____ (send) to the commercial registry. The company name _____ (record) in the commercial register where it _____ (reserve) for three months.

For non-Spanish company partners and directors, a Spanish tax identification number must _____ (obtain) from the tax office.

Once the company _____ (establish), any member of the public _____ (allow) to view these documents in order to verify the legality of the company.

So these _____ (draw up) by a lawyer and _____ (sign) by the partners and board of directors.

In order to get this ID number, a package of legal documents, known in the UK as an Incorporation Package, needs _____ (submit) to the tax authorities.

2.2 Student A

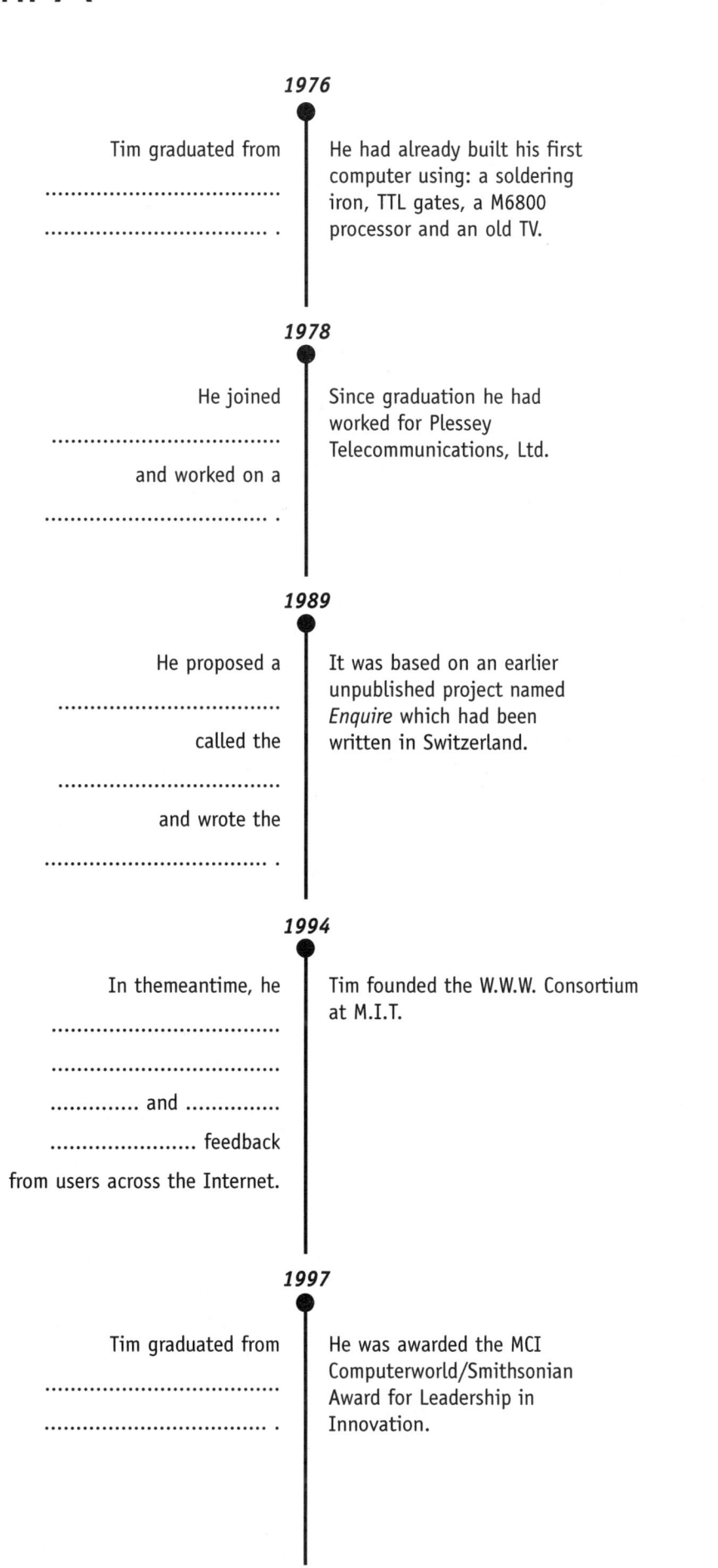

1976

Tim graduated from ....

He had already built his first computer using: a soldering iron, TTL gates, a M6800 processor and an old TV.

1978

He joined .... and worked on a ....

Since graduation he had worked for Plessey Telecommunications, Ltd.

1989

He proposed a .... called the .... and wrote the ....

It was based on an earlier unpublished project named *Enquire* which had been written in Switzerland.

1994

In themeantime, he .... and .... feedback from users across the Internet.

Tim founded the W.W.W. Consortium at M.I.T.

1997

Tim graduated from ....

He was awarded the MCI Computerworld/Smithsonian Award for Leadership in Innovation.

2.2 Student B

1976

He .... already .... using: ...., TTL gates, a M6800 processor and ....

He graduated from Queens College, Oxford University.

1978

Since graduation he .... for ....

He joined D.G Nash, Ltd and worked on a multi-exercising operating system.

1989

It was based on an earlier unpublished project named *Enquire* which .... in ....

He proposed a global hypernet project called the World Wide Web and wrote the first W.W.W. Server 'httpd'.

1994

Tim founded the .... at ....

In the meantime he had continned working on the design of the Weband had coordinated feedback from users accross the Internet.

1997

He was awarded the .... Award for Leadership in Innovation.

He had already received the Kilby's Foundation's 'Young Innovator of the Year' award.

116

© Copyright Thomson Heinle 2007, a part of the Thomson Corporation

3.1

COMMITTED	FLEXIBLE	PATIENT	LOGICAL
PLEASANT	NUMERATE	MATURE	LITERATE
CREATIVE	CAPABLE	POLITE	REPLACEABLE
COOPERATIVE	FORMAL	PERFECT	RESPONSIBLE
INTERESTED	ACTIVE	MODEST	REGULAR
POPULAR	EFFICIENT	PRECISE	RATIONAL

3.2

Call your service provider to say that you haven't received a document that he/she promised to send.	Call your colleague to ask if you can arrange a meeting sometime next week.
Call your friend to tell him/her that you can't attend his/her party on Saturday.	Call a job candidate to say that, following a successful interview, you would like to offer him/her a job.
You are a training manager. Call an employee to tell him/her that you have managed to arrange an intensive English language course for him/her in the USA.	Call a well-known business person to ask if you can interview him/her for an article which will feature in a national newspaper.
Call your supplier and complain about a delivery you received this morning. You asked for 40 units not 14!	You are aware that Mr Alexander is on holiday at the moment. However, leave a message with his assistant. You need to know the details of his trip to Sydney as soon as possible.
Call a corporate event organiser and book a teambuilding day for your company next month.	Call a colleague to invite him/her for lunch at the weekend.

4.1 Student A

The De Lorean Motor Company (DMC) was a short-lived car manufacturer established by automobile industry executive John De Lorean in 1975. It produced only one model – the stainless steel De Lorean DMC 12 sports car – which later shot to worldwide fame as the time machine car in the *Back to the Future* movie trilogy, but which sadly ended in receivership and bankruptcy in 1982.

Who was John De Lorean?

Most of the investment capital came from the Bank of America, as well as some private investment. Capital was also raised through a dealer investment programme which made dealerships selling De Lorean cars shareholders in the De Lorean company.

What additional financial incentives did De Lorean look for?

Believing that the British government would provide his company with Export Credit financing, in the form of a loan of 80 per cent of the wholesale cost of the vehicles ($20,000) upon completion and delivery for shipping, De Lorean took up a last-minute offer from the UK's Northern Ireland Development Board to begin construction of the DMCL manufacturing plant in a suburb of Belfast. In October 1978, construction of the manufacturing plant began. Unfortunately, in 1982 the De Lorean Motor Company went bust, taking with it 2,500 jobs and over $100 million in investments.

What had gone wrong?

Production
- the first cars only rolled off assembly lines in early 1981, two years after the scheduled date
- engineering delays
- budget overruns
- generally inexperienced factory workers
- early production quality issues

Dealership issues
- only a 12 month, 12,000 mile car warranty
- dealers not reimbursed for early warranty work and therefore refusing to do more warranty work
- dealership–customer disputes

The Final Downfall
In January 1982, due to SEC questions about the company's viability, the company was forced to cancel the stock issue for the holding company that De Lorean had hoped would raise about $27 million. As a result, the British government refused financial aid, unless De Lorean was able to find a matching amount from other investors. Unfortunately, the De Lorean Motor Company went bankrupt.

4.1 Student B

The De Lorean Motor Company (DMC) was a short-lived car manufacturer established by automobile industry executive John De Lorean in 1975. It produced only one model, the stainless steel De Lorean DMC 12 sports car, which later shot to worldwide fame as the time machine car in the *Back to the Future* movie trilogy, but which sadly ended in receivership and bankruptcy in 1982.

John De Lorean founded the De Lorean Motor Company in Detroit, Michigan in 1975. He was already well-known as a first rate engineer, maverick business innovator, jetsetter and youngest person to become a General Motors executive.

Where did his investment capital come from?

To fund construction of the company's automobile manufacturing facilities, De Lorean looked to build his first factory in a country or area where unemployment was particularly high, and where government and economic organisations were offering lucrative financial incentives.

Where did De Lorean chose to build his manufacturing plant and why?

What had gone wrong?

Market Reaction
- sales price of $25,000 cost-prohibitive for the majority of the market
- a 0–60 mph time of 10.5 seconds considered too slow for a sports/GT car in this price category

Design Issues
- car surface tended to show fingerprints
- car could not easily be painted
- every factory original De Lorean looked virtually identical
- only factory option initially available was an automatic transmission

Finance Issues
- estimated breakeven point between 10,000 and 12,000 units
- actual sales figures around 6,000

The Final Downfall
In January 1982, due to SEC questions about the company's viability, the company was forced to cancel the stock issue for the holding company that De Lorean had hoped would raise about $27 million. As a result, the British government refused financial aid, unless De Lorean was able to find a matching amount from other investors. Unfortunately, the De Lorean Motor Company went bankrupt.

4.2 Student A

If we all **drive** smaller, more manoeuvrable cars, …

If we all **go over** to using electric cars, …

If the Metro newspaper **not be** free, …

If I **not want** the audience to ask questions during my presentation, …

If we **make** our own film, …

If you **are** the CEO of a multinational company, …

4.2 Student B

If there **be** a massive investment in hybrid car technology, …

If congestion charges **be** introduced in every city, …

If your Chinese colleague **tip** his head back and **suck** air in, …

If you **not** state your presentation objectives, …

If the Metro newspaper editors not **have** such a scientific approach to distribution, …

If Bollywood **not make** films in English, …

FEEDBACK FRAMEWORKS

ACCURACY FEEDBACK FRAMEWORK

Activity: **Date:**

Good examples *(to be completed by the teacher):*

Points to improve:

	You said: *(to be completed by the teacher)*	**You should have said:** *(to be completed by the student)*
Grammar		
Vocabulary		
Pronunciation		
Useful phrases		

Checklist
(to be completed by the student)
Taking the above corrections into consideration, identify three areas that you should work on when speaking:
1.
2.
3.

FEEDBACK FRAMEWORKS

SOCIAL ENGLISH FEEDBACK FRAMEWORK

Activity: **Date:**

Appropriacy
Topics

Questions

Active listening
Showing interest/understanding

Positive responses/encouraging comments

Checking and clarifying

Questions
Open questions/comments
Closed questions
Probing questions
Reflecting questions
Encouraging questions
Intonation

Interrupting
Tone of voice

Wording

Body language

Cultural awareness

© Copyright Thomson Heinle 2007, a part of the Thomson Corporation

FEEDBACK FRAMEWORKS

TELEPHONING FEEDBACK FRAMEWORK

Activity: **Date:**

Preparation
Aim
Organisation
Structure

Opening
Greeting
Identifying self
Giving reason for call
Responding
Making requests and offers

Appropriacy
Level of formality

Providing information
Clarity and conciseness

Active listening
Showing understanding/interest
Checking details
Reformulating/summarising new information
Dealing with numbers and spelling

Closing
Final check/confirming action
Thanking
Signalling the end

Voice
Speed, intonation and volume

Overall impression
(friendly, helpful, polite, efficient, etc.)

Additional comments

WRITING FEEDBACK FRAMEWORK

Activity: **Date:**

Aim
Does the communication achieve its aim?

Will the audience understand what action needs to be taken?

Structure
Clear and logical paragraphing (*Is related information together?*)

Length of paragraphs

Length of sentences

Coherence
Are thoughts connected?

Use of linking words (*however, so, therefore, etc.*)

Language
Formality/tone (*if formal, avoidance of slang and contractions - I'll, I've, etc.*)
Clarity (*avoidance of ambiguous language*)
Conciseness (*avoidance of redundant language*)
Appropriacy for audience (*avoidance of technical terms for a non-technical audience*)
Directness

Style
Appropriate opening and closing salutation

Accuracy
Punctuation

Spelling

Grammar

Additional comments

FEEDBACK FRAMEWORKS

LEADING MEETINGS FEEDBACK FRAMEWORK

Student: **Date:**

How you managed:

Purpose
Stated objectives

Items on the agenda

Summarised outcomes

Process
Time limit

Item introduction

Management of turn taking

Management of time

Assigned action points

People
Introduction of participants

Assignment of minutes taker

Request of opinions/ideas

Fair inclusion of participants

FEEDBACK FRAMEWORKS

PARTICIPATING IN MEETINGS FEEDBACK FRAMEWORK

Student: **Date:**

Active listening
Checked understanding of task

Clarified ideas

Participation
Gave opinions
Agreed
Disagreed
Offered alternatives
Interrupting

General accuracy

Pronunciation

Grammar

Vocabulary

PRESENTATION FEEDBACK FRAMEWORK

Student: **Date:**

Topic of presentation

Content
Objectives

Audience interest

Appropriacy

Introduction
Introduced yourself

Topic

Stated your objectives

Role of audience

Timing

Structure
Organisation

Signposting

Linking

Grammar
Accuracy

Vocabulary
Appropriacy

Delivery
Pronunciation

Sentence stress

Pitch

Pausing

Speed

Non-verbal communication
Posture

Eye contact

FEEDBACK FRAMEWORKS

PRESENTATION PREPARATION FRAMEWORK

Student: **Date:**

Topic of presentation
Who is my audience?
What is its role?
What are my presentation objectives?
How long is my presentation?

Stage
Key language

Key points

Introduction

Main points of delivering the objectives
1.
2.
3.

Closing

Signposting and linking phrases

Referring to visuals

128   © Copyright Thomson Heinle 2007, a part of the Thomson Corporation